# DEVIANCE AND SOCIAL CONTROL

Ronald A. Farrell

*State University of New York
at Albany*

Victoria L. Swigert

*Holy Cross College
Worcester, Massachusetts*

Scott, Foresman and Company    Glenview, Illinois

*Dallas, Tex.    Oakland, N.J.    Palo Alto, Cal.    Tucker, Ga.    London, England*

*To our parents*

*Anthony and Margaret Farrell*

*George and Eleanor Swigert*

**Library of Congress Cataloging in Publication Data**
Farrell, Ronald A.
  Deviance and social control.

  Bibliography.
  Includes index.
  1. Deviant behavior. 2. Social control.
I. Swigert, Victoria Lynn.          II. Title.
HM291.F26        302.5                 81-5791
                                       AACR2

ISBN 0-673-15268-5

## ACKNOWLEDGMENTS

From new introduction by Leonard D. Savitz to *Criminal Man* by Gina Lombroso-Ferrero. Copyright © 1972 by Patterson Smith Publishing Corporation. Reprinted by permission.

From "Aggressive Behavior and the XYY Male" by Patricia Jacobs, Muriel Brunton, and Marie Melville, *Nature*, Vol. 208, No. 5017, December 25, 1965, pp. 1351–1352. Copyright © 1965 Macmillan Journals Limited. Reprinted by permission.

From "The Professional Ideology of Social Pathologists," by C. Wright Mills from *American Journal of Sociology*, Vol. 49, No. 2, September 1943. Copyright © 1943 by The University of Chicago Press. Reprinted by permission of The University of Chicago Press.

Excerpts from "The Functions of Deviance in Groups" by Robert Dentler and Kai T. Erikson, *Social Problems*, Vol. 7, No. 2, Fall 1959. Copyright © 1959 by The Society for the Study of Social Problems. Reprinted by permission.

From "Deviance and Moral Boundaries" by Pat Lauderdale, *American Sociological Review*, Vol. 41, No. 4, August 1976. Copyright © 1976 American Sociological Association. Reprinted with permission.

# Preface

No other area of sociology has spawned as many different perspectives as has the study of deviant behavior. This profusion of theoretical orientations has been accompanied by ideological commitments to particular perspectives and to the purity of interpretation by scholars whose works comprise the foundations of those perspectives. Together, these commitments reinforce the fragmentation of the discipline and hinder additional research into the causes and nature of deviant behavior. Thus, current research is most typically oriented to single theoretical approaches, and entire scholarly careers become identified with advocacy of or opposition to selected theoretical traditions. This singular approach can be seen in deviance textbooks, which are usually organized around single perspectives, and in college courses, which become arenas for recruiting new devotees and opponents of the various theories. While this adversarial approach to the discipline can generate considerable enthusiasm, serious questions arise regarding its effectiveness in teaching about deviant behavior. Ultimately, commitments to singular points of view illuminate only those perspectives and obscure the more comprehensive explanations of deviant behavior.

In recent years, several deviance textbooks have attempted to include numerous theoretical perspectives by describing the central concepts and arguments, highlighting points at which the approaches differ, and summarizing the supporting and refuting evidence. While these textbooks encourage a breadth of familiarity with the discipline, they remain oriented to the perspectives themselves and continue to deflect attention from the study of deviant behavior.

*Deviance and Social Control* is an attempt to redirect the focus of the sociology of deviant behavior from the study of deviance theories to the study of deviance itself. At the same time, we preserve the integrity of the theoretical traditions that have yielded the wealth of concepts and empirical findings that comprise the discipline. Accomplishing both ends has meant making a number of procedural and organizational decisions. To ensure a comprehensive coverage of the sociology of deviant behavior, the chapters are organized according to the six paradigms that have helped shape the contemporary discipline: *functionalism, definitional theory, the labeling perspective, anomie theory, the theory of social and cultural support,* and *the conflict perspective.* We present each theory in terms of its contribution to a more general understanding of deviant behavior. Thus, the perspectives and their central concepts are not treated as inviolable but as subject to revision in light of what has been observed. Empirical patterns must be acknowledged, and falsified hypotheses or contradictory evidence demand explanation; we present and reformulate the theoretical generalizations accordingly.

While we de-emphasize the perspectives' adversarial qualities, we do demonstrate the need to qualify critical arguments and to identify the context within which deviance definitions arise. Furthermore, rather than emphasizing distinctions among perspectives, we attend primarily to the compatibility of the perspectives. Throughout the work, we examine theoretical approaches for their *utility* in exploring different aspects of deviance, and as *complementary* rather than competing paradigms.

The final chapter of the book seeks to maximize the theoretical and empirical contributions of the individual perspectives by drawing them together in a *general theory* of deviance and social control. Because the perspectives address deviance at different levels of analysis, no one of them is comprehensive enough to explain the several dimensions of the phenomenon generally. For this, we formulate a theory that provides for the simultaneous and mutually reinforcing influences—structural, interactional, and social psychological—that operate at several levels of analysis. In *Deviance and Social Control*, we link the various perspectives and encourage an integrative approach to a discipline characterized by fragmentation and conflict.

Several people have offered important comments and suggestions throughout the development of this work. We are especially grateful to Edwin M. Lemert of the University of California at Davis and Albert J. Reiss, Jr. of Yale University for their reactions to the original draft of the manuscript. Their criticisms were rigorous and served as invaluable contributions in subsequent revisions of the work. We also owe a special gratitude to Anthony R. Harris of the University of Massachusetts at Amherst for his thoughtful input into latter stages of the book, to Peter M. Blau of the State University of New York at Albany and Columbia University whose own work has helped us conceptualize the rationale for the development of the general theory presented in Chapter 8, and to Walter Dinteman for his encouragement and guidance. The editorial group at Scott, Foresman, and in particular Andrea Berg, Isobel Hoffman, and Marjorie Williams, has also provided consistent support and the highest quality technical assistance at various stages in the production of *Deviance and Social Control*.

*Ronald A. Farrell*

*Victoria L. Swigert*

# Contents

# 1

# Introduction

There are in all societies individuals whose behavior, attitudes, or physical attributes elicit negative responses from the collectivity. The objects of this condemnation have been referred to as devils, witches, pariahs, nonconformists, criminals, and deviants. All, however, occupy a common status in their communities. They are the dispossesed—people who are cut off from common discourse, shamed, deprived of their freedom or even of their lives.

An essential element shared by society's outcasts is that they have violated, or are believed to have violated, its *norms*. The disfigured and disabled breach norms of physical beauty, well-being, and mobility. The mentally ill violate the societal expectation for rationality in thought and behavior. The robber fails to conform to proscriptions against the illegal taking of other people's property.

Although norm violation may be necessary for becoming disvalued, it is not sufficient. There are many rules whose infraction elicits little, if any, public condemnation. Traffic violations, many corporate crimes, illegal gambling, and income tax fraud may earn the offender official sanctions. Some of the penalties may even be severe. Yet, for the most part, the perpetrators are not ostracized from their communities. Rather, their claims to respectability and membership in good standing continue to be honored.

What distinguishes the rule violator from the disvalued? Why is deviance a persistent feature of human society? Why are some people selected for condemnation and others not? What are the consequences of the disvalued status for those who occupy it? These are the questions to be addressed in the chapters that follow.

## DEVIANCE EXPLANATIONS IN HISTORICAL PERSPECTIVE

Deviant behavior has long been a focus of scholarly attention. Efforts to understand it have resulted in a proliferation of theoretical explanations. Until the middle of the twentieth century, these theories were consistent in their underlying thesis: Deviance was seen as the pathological consequence of pathological events and conditions acting on the individual.

### Deviance as Personal Pathology

Perhaps the oldest and most persistent explanation of deviance was that it was caused by diabolical forces. Witches, devils, and evil spirits were said to produce a wide range of aberrant behaviors by taking possession of the minds and bodies of human hosts. Crime, sexual perversion, insanity, and even physical disease and disability were either the products of collusion with the forces of evil or punishments for offenses against supernatural powers. Popular notions of sin and satanic intervention continue to reflect this thesis.

The first systematic approach to deviance began with the assumption that nonconformity was the product of an individual's will to deviate. According to what has come to be known as the classical school of criminology (for example, Beccaria, 1764; Bentham, 1838), individuals choose behaviors that allow them to maximize pleasure and minimize pain. This approach assumes that individuals rationally calculate the consequences of various lines of action before deciding on any particular one. People violate societal rules when they perceive that the rewards of misbehavior exceed the possible punishments. This principle of free will is the basis of the U.S. system of criminal justice. Imprisonment, physical and emotional degradation, and death become reasonable punishments only when it is assumed that the offender chooses to violate the law. Punishment is intended to remind both the offender and those who would contemplate similar activities that the wages of wrongdoing are painful. Although treatment and rehabilitation have come to play an increasingly important role in official policies regarding deviance, the use of force remains a fundamental correctional strategy.

**Biological Factors of Deviance.** A more deterministic approach to human behavior challenged the philosophy of free will in the late nineteenth century. In addition to proposing an explanation of nonconformity that was diametrically opposed to that of the classical school, the new positivists (for example, Lombroso, 1876; Ferri, 1884; Garofalo, 1885) based their arguments on an empirical analysis of criminality. Thus, the positivist school of criminology constituted the first attempt to scientifically study nonconformity.

Borrowing heavily from Charles Darwin's (1859, 1871) research on biological evolution, these early criminologists proposed that organic anomalies within individual offenders predisposed them to antisocial behavior. The shape of the skull, the thickness of the brow, the density of body hair, and other anatomical features were thought to be indicators of organic problems. A major proponent of this approach was Cesare Lombroso (1876), who argued that certain forms of these indicators reflected evolutionary regression to a more primitive stage of human development. People who had them were atavistic throwbacks with dulled moral sensibilities and uninhibited predatory urges. Given opportunities and environmental conditions conducive to crime, these constitutionally inferior persons were expected to demonstrate a tendency for chronic law violation.

# Criminal Man

*Cesare Lombroso*

It will, perhaps, be of interest to American readers . . . to learn how the first outlines of [the Criminal Man] arose in my mind and gradually took shape in a definite work. . . .

On consulting my memory and the documents relating to my studies on this subject, I find that its two fundamental ideas—that, for instance, which claims as an essential point the study not of crime in the abstract, but of the criminal himself, in order adequately to deal with the evil effects of his wrongdoing, and that which classifies the congenital criminal as an anomaly, partly pathological and partly atavistic, a revival of the primitive savage—did not suggest themselves to me instantaneously under the spell of a single deep impression, but were the offspring of a series of impressions. The slow and almost unconscious association of these first vague ideas resulted in a new system which, influenced by its origin, has preserved in all its subsequent developments the traces of doubt and indecision, the marks of the travail which attended its birth.

The first idea came to me in 1864, when, as an army doctor, I beguiled my ample leisure with a series of studies on the Italian soldier. From the very beginning I was struck by a characteristic that distinguished the honest soldier from his vicious comrade: the extent to which the latter was tattooed and the indecency of the designs that covered his body. This idea, however, bore no fruit.

The second inspiration came to me when on one occasion, amid the laughter of my colleagues, I sought to base the study of psychiatry on experimental methods. When in [18]66, fresh from the atmosphere of clinical experiment, I had begun to study psychiatry, I realised how inadequate were the methods hitherto held in esteem, and how necessary it was, in studying the insane, to make the patient, not the disease, the object of attention. In homage to these ideas, I applied to the clinical examination of cases of mental alienation the study of the skull, with measurements and weights, by means of the esthesiometer and craniometer. Reassured by the result of these first steps, I sought to apply this method to the study of criminals—that is, to the differentiation of criminals and lunatics. . . . But as at that time I had neither criminals nor moral imbeciles available for observation, . . . and as I was skeptical as to the existence of those "moral lunatics" so much insisted on by both French and English authors . . . I was anxious to apply the experimental method to the study of the diversity, rather than the analogy, between lunatics, criminals, and normal individuals. Like him, however, whose lantern lights the road for others, while he himself stumbles in the darkness, this method proved useless for determining the differences between criminals and lunatics, but served instead to indicate a new method for the study of penal jurisprudence, a matter to which I had never given serious thought. I began dimly to realise that the *a priori* studies on crime in the abstract, hitherto pursued by jurists, especially in Italy, with singular acumen, should be superseded by the direct analytical study of the criminal, compared with normal individuals and the insane.

I, therefore, began to study criminals in the Italian prisons, and, amongst others, I made the acquaintance of the famous brigand Vilella. This man possessed such extraordinary agility, that he had been known to scale steep mountain heights bearing a sheep on his shoulders. His cynical effrontery was such that he openly boasted of his crimes. On his death one cold grey November morning, I was deputed to make the *post-mortem,* and on laying open the skull I found on the occipital part, exactly on the spot where a spine is found in the normal skull, a distinct depression which I named *median occipital fossa,* because of its situation precisely in the middle of the occiput as in inferior animals, especially rodents. This depression, as in the case of animals, was correlated with the hypertrophy of the *vermis,* known in birds as the middle cerebellum.

This was not merely an idea, but a revelation. At the sight of that skull, I seemed to see all of a sudden, lighted up as a vast plain under a flaming sky, the problem of the nature of the criminal—an atavistic being who reproduces in his person the ferocious instincts of primitive humanity and the inferior animals. Thus were explained anatomically the enormous jaws, high cheek bones, prominent superciliary arches, solitary lines in the palms, extreme size of the orbits, handle-shaped or sessile ears found in criminals, savages, and apes, insensibility to pain, extremely acute sight, tattooing, excessive idleness, love of orgies, and the irresistible craving for evil for its own sake, the desire not only to extinguish life in the victim, but to mutilate the corpse, tear its flesh, and drink its blood.

I was further encouraged in this bold hypothesis by the results of my studies on Verzeni, a criminal convicted of sadism and rape, who showed the cannibalistic instincts of primitive anthropophagists and the ferocity of beasts of prey.

The various parts of the extremely complex problem of criminality were, however, not all solved hereby. The final key was given by another case, that of Misdea, a young soldier of about twenty-one, unintelligent but not vicious. Although subject to epileptic fits, he had served for some years in the army when suddenly, for some trivial cause, he attacked and killed eight of his superior officers and comrades. His horrible work accomplished, he fell into a deep slumber, which lasted twelve hours and on awaking appeared to have no recollection of what had happened. Misdea, while representing the most ferocious type of animal, manifested, in addition, all the phenomena of epilepsy, which appeared to be hereditary in all the members of his family. It flashed across my mind that many criminal characteristics not attributable to atavism, such as facial asymmetry, cerebral sclerosis, impulsiveness, instantaneousness, the periodicity of criminal acts, the desire of evil for evil's sake, were morbid characteristics common to epilepsy, mingled with others due to atavism.

Source: Cesare Lombroso, "Introduction," in Gina Lombroso–Ferrero, *Criminal Man: According to the Classification of Cesare Lombroso* (Montclair, N.J.: Patterson Smith, 1972), pp. xxi–xxvi.

The research of Lombroso and his students relied exclusively on small numbers of incarcerated offenders. When similar measurements were made on the general population, the "indicators" were found to occur with the same frequency among conformers as among deviants (Goring, 1913). Nevertheless, this research has left a lasting imprint on the study of nonconformity. Variations of the physiological approach have continued into the twentieth century. Investigations of the criminality of identical and fraternal twins (Lange, 1931), genealogical traces of particularly notorious nonconformers (Dugdale, 1910; Goddard, 1925), and examinations of the body types of delinquents (Hooton, 1939; Sheldon, 1949; Glueck and Glueck, 1956) have persistently located the causes of deviance in the inheritance of criminal impulses or predispositions.

# The Kallikaks

*Henry Herbert Goddard*

[Deborah Kallikak] is a child who has been most carefully guarded. She has been persistently trained since she was eight years old, and yet nothing has been accomplished in the direction of higher intelligence or general education. To-day if this young woman were to leave the Institution, she would at once become a prey to the designs of evil men or evil women and would lead a life that would be vicious, immoral, and criminal, though because of her mentality she herself would not be responsible. There is nothing that she might not be led into, because she has no power of control, and all her instincts and appetites are in the direction that would lead to vice. . . .

"How do we account for this kind of individual? The answer is in a word "Heredity,"—bad stock. We must recognize that the human family shows varying stocks or strains that are as marked and that breed as true as anything in plant or animal life.

Formerly such a statement would have been a guess, an hypothesis. We submit in the following pages what seems to us conclusive evidence of its truth. . . .

When Martin [Kallikak] Sr., of [a] good family, was a boy of fifteen, his father died, leaving him without parental care or oversight. Just before attaining his majority, the young man joined one of the numerous military companies that were formed to protect the country at the beginning of the Revolution. At one of the taverns frequented by the militia he met a feeble-minded girl by whom he became the father of a feeble-minded son. This child was given, by its mother, the name of the father in full, and thus has been handed down to posterity the father's name and the mother's mental capacity. This illegitimate boy was Martin Kallikak Jr., the great-great-grandfather of our Deborah, and from him have come four hundred and eighty descendants. One hundred and forty-three of these, we have conclusive proof, were or are feeble-minded, while only forty-six have been found normal. The rest are unknown or doubtful.

Among these four hundred and eighty descendants, thirty-six have been illegitimate.

There have been thirty-three sexually immoral persons, mostly prostitutes.

There have been twenty-four confirmed alcoholics.

There have been three epileptics.

Eighty-two died in infancy.

Three were criminal.

Eight kept houses of ill fame.

These people have married into other families, generally of about the same type, so that we now have on record and charted eleven hundred and forty-six individuals.

Of this large group, we have discovered that two hundred and sixty-two were feeble-minded, while one hundred and ninety-seven are considered normal, the remaining five hundred and eighty-one being still undetermined. . . .

Martin Sr., on leaving the Revolutionary Army, straightened up and married a respectable girl of good family, and through that union has come another line of descendants of radically different character. These now number four hundred and ninety-six in direct descent. All of them are normal people. Three men only have been found among them who were somewhat degenerate, but they were not defective. Two of these were alcoholic, and the other sexually loose.

## Kallikak Family Lineage

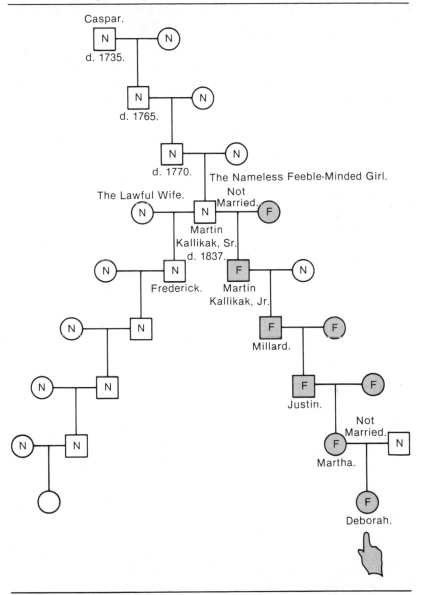

Individuals are represented by squares and circles, the squares being males, the circles, females. Block squares and circles (with a white F) mean feeble-minded individuals; N means normal persons.
Source: Henry Herbert Goddard, *The Kallikak Family: A Study in the Heredity of Feeble-Mindedness* (New York: Macmillan, 1927), p. 36.

All of the legitimate children of Martin Sr. married into the best families in their state, the descendants of colonial governors, signers of the Declaration of Independence, soldiers and even the founders of a great university. Indeed, in this family and its collateral branches, we find nothing but good representative citizenship. There are doctors, lawyers, judges, educators, traders, landholders, in short, respectable citizens, men and women prominent in every phase of social life. They have scattered over the United States and are prominent in their communities wherever they have gone. Half a dozen towns in New Jersey are named from the families into which Martin's descendants have married. There have been no feeble-minded among them; no illegitimate children; no immoral women; only one man was sexually loose. There has been no epilepsy, no criminals, no keepers of houses of prostitution. Only fifteen children have died in infancy. There has been one "insane," a case of religious mania, perhaps inherited, but not from the Kallikak side. The appetite for strong drink has been present here and there in this family from the beginning. It was in Martin Sr., and was cultivated at a time when such practices were common everywhere. But while the other branch of the family has had twenty-four victims of habitual drunkenness, this side scores only two. [See accompanying chart, which shows Kallikak family lineage.]

Source: Henry Herbert Goddard, *The Kallikak Family: A Study in the Heredity of Feeble-Mindedness* (New York: Macmillan, 1927), pp. 12, 18–19, 29–30.

# The Jukes

*Richard L. Dugdale*

[A calculation of the social costs of inherited deviation provided additional justification for the control of "constitutional inferiors." While this early heredity tradition can be easily discredited, the search for biological causes of deviance persists. Implicit in these recent contributions is a similar call for greater control of biological inferiority.]

Between the years 1720 and 1740 was born a man who shall herein be called Max. He was a descendant of the early Dutch settlers, and lived much as the backwoodsmen upon our frontiers now do. He is described as "a hunter and fisher, a hard drinker, jolly and companionable, averse to steady toil," working hard by spurts and idling by turns, becoming blind in his old age, and entailing his blindness upon his children and grandchildren. He had a numerous progeny, some of them almost certainly illegitimate. Two of his sons married two out of six sisters [the Jukes] who were born between the year 1740 and 1770. . . . Five of these women . . . were married; the sixth one it has been impossible to trace, for she moved out of the county. Of the five that are known, three have had illegitimate children before marriage. One who is called . . . Ada Juke, but who is better known to the public as "Margaret, the mother of criminals," had one bastard son, who is the progenitor of the distinctively criminal line. Another sister had two illegitimate sons, who appear to have had no children. A third sister had four, three boys and one girl, the three oldest children being mulattoes, and the youngest—a boy, white. The fourth sister is reputed chaste, while no information could be gathered respecting the fifth in this respect, but she was the mother of one of the distinctively pauperized lines and married one of the sons of Max. The progeny of these five has been traced with more or less exactness through five generations, thus making the total heredity which has been enrolled stretch over seven generations, if we count Max as the first. The number of descendants registered incluces 540 individuals who are related by blood to the Jukes, and 169 by marriage or cohabitation; in all, 709 persons of all ages, alive and dead. The aggregate of this lineage reaches probably 1,200 persons. . . .

I submit an estimate of the damage of the family, based on what is known of those whose lives have been learned. . . . [The] financial estimate may be summed up as follows:

| | | Cost |
|---|---|---|
| Total number of persons | 1,200 | |
| Number of pauperized adults | 280 | |
| Cost of alms-house relief | | $15,000.00 |
| Cost of out-door relief | | 32,250.00 |
| Number of criminals and offenders | 140 | |
| Years of imprisonment | 140 | |
| Cost of maintenance, at $200 a year | | 28,000.00 |
| Number of arrests and trials | 250 | |
| Cost of arrests and trials, $100 each | | 25,000.00 |
| Number of habitual thieves, convicted and unconvicted | 60 | |
| Number of years of depredation, at 12 years each | 720 | |
| Cost of depredation, $120 a year | | 86,400.00 |
| Number of lives sacrificed by murder | 7 | |
| Value, at $1,200 each | | 8,400.00 |
| Number of common prostitutes | 50 | |
| Average number of years of debauch | 15 | |
| Total number of years of debauch | 750 | |
| Cost of maintaining each per year | $300.00 | |
| Cost of maintenance | | 225,000.00 |
| Number of women specifically diseased | 40 | |
| Average number of men each woman contaminates with permanent disease | 10 | |
| Total number of men contaminated | 400 | |
| Number of wives contaminated by above men | 40 | |
| Total number of persons contaminated | 440 | |
| Cost of drugs and medical treatment during rest of life, at $200 each | | 88,000.00 |
| Average loss of wages caused by disease during rest of life, in years | 3 | |
| Total years of wages lost by 400 men | 1,200 | |
| Loss, at $500 a year | | 600,000.00 |
| Average number of years withdrawn from productive industry by each courtesan | 10 | |

|  |  | Cost |
|---|---|---|
| Total number of years lost by 50 courtesans | 500 | |
| Value estimated at $125 a year | | 62,500.00 |
| Aggregate curtailment of life of 490 adults, equivalent to 50 mature individuals | 50 | |
| Cash cost, each life at $1,200 | | 60,000.00 |
| Aggregate of children who died prematurely | 300 | |
| Average years of life each child | 2 | |
| Cash cost, each child at $50 | | 15,000.00 |
| Number of prosecutions in bastardy | 30 | |
| Average cost of each case, $100 | | 3,000.00 |
| Cost of property destroyed, blackmail, brawls* | | 20,000.00 |
| Average capital employed in houses, stock, furniture, etc., for brothels | | 6,000.00 |
| Compound interest for 26 years at 6 per cent | | 18,000.00 |
| Charity distributed by church | | 10,000.00 |
| Charity obtained by begging | | 5,450.00 |
| Total | | $1,308,000.00 |

*One house, with furniture worth $1,100, was burned by a mob.

Over a million and a quarter dollars of loss in 75 years, caused by a single family 1,200 strong, without reckoning the cash paid for whiskey, or taking into account the entailment of pauperism and crime of the survivors in succeeding generations, and the incurable disease, idiocy and insanity growing out of this debauchery, and reaching further than we can calculate. It is getting to be time to ask, do our courts, our laws, our alms-houses and our jails deal with the question presented?

Source: Robert L. Dugdale, *The Jukes: A Study in Crime, Pauperism, Disease, and Heredity* (New York: G. P. Putnam's Sons, 1910), pp. 14–15, 67–68, 70.

The most recent physiological investigations have focused on the functions and malfunctions of the endocrine glands. Findings that the behavioral traits of dominance, aggression, and hostility are related to production of the male hormone testosterone, that exclusively homosexual males show lower levels of this hormone and reduced sperm counts, and that female deviance seems to be related to menstrual cycles have been cited as evidence of the importance of the glandular system in determining behavior (Shah and Roth, 1974).

Similar conclusions have been reached regarding abnormalities in the chromosome structure. Male chromosomes are indicated by XY; female chromosomes, by XX. In 1961, an XYY configuration was isolated. Subsequent analysis revealed that a significant proportion of incarcerated males possessed such a trait, which has suggested to some researchers that the extra Y may constitute a factor that predisposes its bearer to acts of crime (Jacobs, et al., 1965; Hook, 1973).

# Aggressive Behavior and
# the XYY Male

*Patricia A. Jacobs, Muriel Brunton, and Marie Melville*

[The question of this research is]—whether an extra *Y* chromosome predisposes its carriers to unusually aggressive behavior. We decided that if this were the case, then we might expect an increased frequency of *XYY* males among those of a violent nature. The purpose of this communication is to report our findings in a survey of mentally sub-normal male patients with dangerous, violent or criminal propensities in an institution where they are treated under conditions of special security.

In the course of routine physical and haematological examination a blood sample was obtained for chromosome studies. Of the total of 203 patients available, six declined to give a blood sample so that chromosome observations were made on the remaining 197. . .

The most important finding in this group is that eight individuals have an additional *Y* chromosome. Very little is known about the *XYY* male, as only a few cases have so far been described, and these refer to a heterogeneous group of children and adults from whose description no clear picture of the *XYY* male has emerged. However, the finding that 3.5 per cent of the population we studied were *XYY* males must represent a marked increase in frequency by comparison with the frequency of such males at birth. On theoretical grounds *XYY* males at birth must be less common than *XXY* males, who form approximately 0.2 per cent of the new-born male population. We have examined 266 randomly selected new-born male babies without finding an *XYY* individual, and we have also examined 209 randomly selected adult males, again without finding one with an *XYY* constitution. In addition, we have examined the chromosomes of approximately 1,500 males for a variety of reasons and only one of these was found to have an *XYY* sex chromosome constitution.

Source: Patricia A. Jacobs, Muriel Bronton, and Marie Melville, "Aggressive Behavior, Mental Subnormality, and the XYY Male," *Nature* 208 (December 1965): 1351–1352.

**Psychological Factors of Deviance.**  In the early decades of the twentieth century, a number of scholars turned their attention from the physiology of individual offenders to their psychologies (for example, Healy, 1915; Abrahamsen, 1952; Aichorn, 1953). The developing science of psychiatry, made popular by the work of Sigmund Freud, was readily adaptable to the study of crime and deviance. According to this approach, all persons tend toward deviance.

The *id*, that level of the mind possessed of primitive, animal-like passions for both survival and death, renders humans potentially bestial in their interpersonal relationships. Through effective socialization, however, individuals acquire the norms, values, and standards that allow them to inhibit the antisocial impulses of the *id*. The mental repository for the rules of sociability is the *superego*. The conscious, acting self, or *ego*, mediates the id and the superego to become what we think of as personality. If childhood experiences interfere with the effective integration of the personality, pathologies in later life may result. Frustrated needs for security, new experiences, recognition, and freedom from supervision eventually manifest themselves in deviant, delinquent, or criminal behavior (Healy, 1915; Healy and Bronner, 1936).

Explorations of the organic and psychological causes of nonconformity, however, have been characterized by a number of validity problems. Primary among them is that much of the work has been conducted on institutionalized populations or persons under treatment. The implicit assumption is that such individuals are not only representative of nonconformers generally, but that they are distinct from law-abiding and nondeviant groups. This assumption is not valid. Referral to a correctional or treatment facility alone is not an adequate measure of deviation. Only a very small portion of all nonconformers are ever officially dealt with as such. Studies that have relied on this population are more likely addressing the causes of formal intervention than the causes of deviance.

A second problem has been that physiologically and psychologically based explanations have approached nonconformity as if it were an absolute and objective phenomenon. Deviance, however, is not a fixed property of human behavior or attributes. Rather, it involves highly subjective and relativistic social definitions that are both culturally and temporally specific. Many actions presently defined as criminal were only recently proscribed. For example, the criminalization of marijuana was first initiated by the Marijuana Tax Act of 1937. Before passage of the Harrison Tax Act of 1914, the use of opium-based substances, such as heroin, was not only legal but, in some cases, recommended (Brecher, 1972). Physicians often prescribed heroin to their alcohol-addicted patients; since regulated amounts of the drug had no toxic side effects, it was preferred to alcohol, whose deteriorating potential was undisputed. Opium products were readily available in local groceries, pharmacies, and mail-order houses; and their typical user was the middle-aged, middle-class, white suburban housewife. When heroin was made illegal a new criminal class emerged. The contemporary drug addict, an object of popular fear and vigorous condemnation, is not a universally recognizable pathology but is the product of the application of a legal definition at a finite period in U.S. history.

Conversely, some behaviors once thought malignant are treated more leniently today. A ruling of the Supreme Court in 1973 declared the previously heinous offense of abortion legal, literally overnight. Similarly, changing attitudes toward nonmarital sex, formal religious observance, and divorce have rendered traditional norms in these areas ineffective. Arguments that individuals inherit or are predisposed to nonconformity fail to take into consideration the fact that definitions of deviance are socially constructed and subject to change.

Homosexuality is particularly interesting in this regard. Societal reactions to homosexuality vary considerably across cultures. In some societies, it is of little concern; in others, it is a required part of designated ritual performances (West, 1967). In Western civilization, however, it has long been actively condemned. Guided by traditional Judeo-Christian proscriptions, Western societies have included ostracism, mutilation, and even death among the sanctions they accorded homosexuals (West, 1967). Persons accused of homosexuality were slated for the ovens in Nazi Germany and were mercilessly persecuted by U.S. Senate investigations during the McCarthy era. In the United States, the radicalizing influence of the Vietnam War era resulted in a far more tolerant approach to homosexuality. The creation of the Gay Liberation Front in 1969 was both reflective of changing popular attitudes and instrumental in securing additional legal and social reforms. Antidiscrimination legislation in areas of housing and employment, abolition of sodomy statutes in many states, and the open admission of homosexuality by thousands of adults were indicative of the success of the group as a social and political lobby.

Recently, however, some evidence suggests a return to the punitive norms of the prewar period. Legal reversals of hard-won civil rights in several states, the use of solicitation statutes in police harassment, and media coverage of spectacular cases of homosexual child molestation and murder may foreshadow renewed efforts at stigmatizing homosexual conduct. Within a very short period of time, homosexuality has elicited reactions that fluctuated between vigorous condemnation and relative tolerance. To argue that homosexuality is a manifestation of pathology is to ignore this variability.

Finally, organic and psychological approaches to nonconformity, given their almost exclusive reliance on institutionalized populations, have tended to focus on conventional deviations and predominantly lower-class deviants. The resultant theories provide very little explanation of higher-status rule violation. White-collar criminality, corporate and political crime, and the innumerable acts of nonconformity committed by the middle and upper classes are not easily explained in terms of inherited imbecility, faulty genetic and glandular structures, or inadequate ego integration. A satisfactory causal theory must be able to address the many variations of nonconformity found within all segments of society.

The assumptions generated by nonsociological approaches, however, have influenced both the law and treatment strategies. For example, starting with Indiana in 1907, many states passed laws calling for the sterilization of institutionalized imbeciles. At present, twenty-six states have involuntary sterilization statutes—laws that have withstood several challenges in the Supreme Court (Kittrie, 1973). Similarly, legislation appeared in the mid-1930s which called for the indefinite confinement of sexual psychopaths—persons suspected of having irresistible sexual impulses (Sutherland, 1950; Szasz, 1963). In many jurisdictions, court-attached psychiatric clinics were established to screen defendants for evidence of this disease. Persons diagnosed as sexually psychopathic, by order of the judge and without a hearing, may be committed to a mental facility until they are judged cured. Since the disease bears a poor prognosis and state hospitals are more custodial than treatment oriented, confinement may be for life.

The role of psychiatry generally has expanded to such an extent that it affects virtually every level of the legal process (Szasz, 1963). Persons may be detained by the police for evidence of mental disease, they may be examined while awaiting trial, and testimony regarding their mental health may be introduced into the trial itself. If determined to be insane at the time of the offense, the defendant, although technically acquitted, may be ordered to a psychiatric facility for an indeterminate period. If found to be sane at the time of the crime but presently incompetent to stand trial, the accused may be subject to involuntary treatment until such time as he or she is considered capable of assisting the defense. Finally, should the defendant be convicted and imprisoned, he or she is subject to psychiatric intervention at any time during the period of confinement and may have to accept it as a condition of parole. The expanding domain of psychiatry in the twentieth century has resulted in an institution for the control of deviance that is both parallel to and protected by the law.

Physiological and psychological studies of deviance have produced widely different causal explanations; furthermore, within each approach is considerable variation with regard to the particular locus of nonconformity and the conditions and processes that underlie its eventual manifestation. All these theories, however, attribute nonconformity to conditions operating within individual offenders. Defective genes, intelligence, glands, morals, physical development, and minds are the human pathologies that have been said to produce the social evils of crime and deviance.

## Social Disorganization and Nonconformity

In the twentieth century, the study of nonconformity has increasingly become the province of the social sciences. The rapidly growing sociology of deviant behavior distinguished itself by insisting that the individualistic approach of the early criminologists and psychologists be abandoned. Arguing that nonconformity was more than the product of idiosyncratic pathologies, this emerging perspective focused its energies on processes and conditions operating in the social environment.

The first major attempt to replace the psycho-biogenic models of deviance causation with a sociogenic explanation came with the development of social disorganization theory during the early 1900s. A central concept of the theory is *socialization,* the process by which societal norms, values, and beliefs are transmitted from one generation to another. The most important agent in the communication of this information is the *primary group.* Primary groups are small and intimate associations distinguished by a thorough familiarity among the members and by an intrinsic valuation of the relationship. By contrast, *secondary groups* are characterized by instrumental, or goal-oriented, relationships. Since the interaction is based upon predefined goals, secondary relations tend to be impersonal and tend not to include complete information about the other participants. It is through association with people in the primary group, and especially the family, that individuals acquire the normative patterns prescribed by society. If this socialization process is disrupted, individuals may not develop behaviors that are consistent with cultural expectations.

**Societal Development and Change.**  In all societies situations arise wherein particular primary groups fail to socialize their members. Group-specific events such as divorce, death, illness, poverty, and the like may disrupt the learning environments necessary for conformity. When this occurs, deviance is a likely outcome; it is a product of isolated instances of disorganization. A far more serious problem arises when the socialization process itself becomes disorganized. Social disorganization theorists argued that the increasing incidence of deviance in modern society was indicative of such a trend. Responsibility was attributed to the forces of modernization, industrialization, and especially urbanization.

As the modern, industrial city became a temporary residence for a highly mobile and heterogeneous population, the community ties necessary for behavioral control were disrupted. The permanence and local history required for the growth of primary relationships were absent (Faris, 1948). The result was social disorganization, a condition marked by a "decline in the number of activities in which the members of the group collaborate, by a decrease in the frequency of interaction between these members, and by a weakening of the control exercised by the group over the behavior of individuals" (Homans, 1950: 369). The breakdown of neighborhood and family ultimately produced behavioral disorganization, or deviance.

Disorganization was also attributed to the rapidly changing nature of modern society. Advocates of the approach suggested that social systems are composed of two components: the technological, or material, culture and the nonmaterial culture, which consists of norms and values (Ogburn, 1922). Changes in technology occur very rapidly because of the expanding pool of resources to which each innovation contributes as well as the accelerated demand for such advances by the population. The nonmaterial culture, on the other hand, changes much more slowly, since internalized norms and values are not easily forsaken. This *culture lag,* then, involves the simultaneous existence of a rapidly changing technological order and a normative structure that may have supported an earlier technological era but is no longer functional. In the absence of norms relevant to the new situation, society cannot provide its members with the guidelines necessary for conformity.

**Cultural Heterogeneity.** One of the more useful concepts generated by social disorganization theory is that of *cultural heterogeneity.* Although its origins and effects were viewed as essentially pathological, heterogeneity, or cultural diversity, has come to occupy a central place in contemporary sociological explanations of deviance. The development of the concept received its greatest impetus from the study of immigrants during the late nineteenth and early twentieth centuries.

According to Louis Wirth (1931), the problem of delinquency that arose among the children of the foreign born was attributable to a conflict of diverse cultural codes. Many first-generation immigrants settled in the ethnic enclaves that developed in major U.S. cities. The people within these communities were generally exposed to the same values and norms they had known in the Old World. Since many adult immigrants had little reason to venture beyond the protective and self-sufficient confines of Little Italy, Little Poland, or Chinatown, their contacts with conflicting codes were minimal. Children of the foreign born, on the other hand, had to go to school; and many acquired peer play groups from outside their communities. Therefore, they were more frequently exposed to norms, values, and expectations that differed considerably from those of their parents. Wirth contended that this simultaneous participation in different cultural systems resulted in conflicting role demands that often led to personal ambivalence, or confusion. Children who were unable to resolve this state of internal culture conflict were cut off both from their families and from the larger society. Not fully belonging to either culture, the immigrant child might resort to flagrant violation of the law as an expression of stress and isolation, especially if the child became part of a group that positively sanctioned or actively promoted such behavior.

Immigration was also said to be responsible for a weakening of traditional social controls (Thomas and Znaniecki, 1920). Pressures that ensured conforming behavior in the Old World were incompatible with the new social structure and no longer functioned effectively. Evidence suggested that parents who applied old-world child-rearing practices regarding, for example, chastity, respect for elders, or the use of leisure time were frequently unsuccessful in producing the desired effects. The social meaning these practices had in the old country was lost (Thomas and Znaniecki, 1920).

From this early perspective, deviance was a product of the existence of two cultures in conflict within the same family (Tannenbaum, 1938: 44–45). Children and parents had two different ways of life, consisting of different languages, attitudes, and values. The home was weakened by these differences and often failed to transmit to the children either the older cultural forms or those consistent with the new ways. "The family ceased to be an effective agency for education and control because it was not culturally in tune with the environment" (Tannenbaum, 1938: 44–45). Since other community agencies could not absorb the responsibility of socialization imposed by the failure of the family, individuals were left isolated and socially disorganized. A person caught between two cultures and marginal to both might suffer maladjustments ranging from malaise to insanity or crime (Stonequist, 1937: Chapter 10).

The *internal culture conflict* theorists did not restrict their analyses to immigrants. Contemporary society generally was viewed as promoting increased isolation and alienation (Wirth, 1931). In the complexity and mobility of modern urban life, "contacts are extended, heterogeneous groups mingle, neighborhoods disappear, and people, deprived of local and family ties, are forced to live under the loose, transient, and impersonal relations that are characteristic of cities" (Wirth, 1931: 488). Innovations in technology, expanded interpersonal relations, increasing excitement, and changing social values have, it is argued, produced problems of adaptation and adjustment:

> Immigration, internal migration, and improved communication have brought into intimate contact groups with varying outlooks on life and varied patterns of behavior. The Southern Negro has migrated to the unac-

customed Northern metropolis. The Kentuckian has changed residence and brought his individualistic traditions with him and into conflict with groups where self-reliance is not carried to such extremes. Conservative and radical, the religiously orthodox and religious liberal or agnostic, rural farm hand and urbanite, advocates of the old and of the new morality—all have been brought into contact. Newspapers, magazines, radio, motion pictures, and television have exposed to our willing or unwilling attention a medley of conflicting ideals and patterns of behavior. Myriad ways to be good or to be bad, to manage a home "properly," to worship a god "piously," to make love "decently," have attracted but also confused the people. Such confusion breeds unadjustment and, for some, crime. [Taft and England, 1964: 28]

# The Professional Ideology
# of Social Pathologists

*C. Wright Mills*

[Social disorganization theory was shaped by the predominantly small-town, unindustrialized society from which the social pathologists emerged. Indicators of disorganization, therefore,] are typically rural in orientation. . . . Most of the "problems" considered arise because of the urban deterioration of certain values which can live genuinely only in a relatively homogeneous and primarily rural milieu. The "problems" discussed typically concern urban behavior. When "rural problems" are discussed, they are conceived as due to encroaching urbanization. The notion of disorganization is quite often merely the absence of that *type* of organization associated with the stuff of primary-group communities having Christian and Jeffersonian legitimations. . . .

The aim to preserve rurally oriented values and stabilities is indicated by the implicit model which operates to detect urban disorganization; it is also shown by the stress upon *community* welfare. The community is taken as a major unit, and often it sets the scope of concern and problematization. It is also within the framework of ideally democratic communities that proposed solutions are to be worked out. It should be noted that sometimes, although not typically or exclusively, solutions are conceived as dependent upon abstract moral traits or democratic surrogates of them, such as a "unanimous public will."

"Cultural lag" is considered by many pathologists to be the concept with which many scattered problems may be detected and systematized. Whereas the approach by deviation from norms is oriented "ideologically" toward a rural type of order and stability, the cultural-lag model is tacitly oriented in a "utopian" and progressive manner toward changing some areas of the culture or certain institutions so as to "integrate" them with the state of progressive technology. . . . Cultural lag is an assertion of unequal "progress." It tells us what changes are "called for," what changes "ought" to have come about and didn't. In terms of various spheres of society it says what progress is, tells us how much we have had, ought to have had, didn't have, and when and where we didn't have it. . . .

Another model in terms of which disorganizations are instituted is that of "social change" itself. This model is not handled in any one typical way, but usually it carries the implicit assumption that human beings are "adjusted" satisfactorily to any social condition that has existed for a long time and that, when some aspect of social life changes, it may lead to a social problem. . . . [The] slow, "evolutionary" pace of change is taken explicitly as normal and organized, whereas "discontinuity" is taken as problematic. . . . A conception of "balance" is usual and sometimes is explicitly sanctioned. The question, "Changes in what spheres induce disorganization?" is left open; the position taken is usually somewhere between extremes, both of which are held to be bad. This comes out in the obvious fact that what a conservative calls *dis*organization, a radical might well call *re*organization. . . .

Besides deviation from norms, orientation to rural principles of stability, cultural lag, and social change, another conception in terms of which "problems" are typically discussed is that of adaptation or "adjustment" and their opposites. The pathological or disorganized is the maladjusted. This concept, as well as that of the "normal," is usually left empty of concrete, social content; or its content is, in effect, a propaganda for conformity to those norms and traits ideally associated with small-town, middle-class milieux. . . . Use of "adjustment" accepts the goals and the means of [the] smaller community. . . . They do not typically consider whether or not certain groups or individuals caught in economically underprivileged situations can possibly obtain the current goals without drastic shifts in the basic institutions which channel and promote them. . . .

The ideally adjusted man of the social pathologists is "socialized." This term seems to operate ethically as the opposite of "selfish"; it implies that the adjusted man conforms to middle-class morality and motives and "participates" in the general progress of respectable institutions. If he is not a "joiner," he certainly gets around and into many community organizations. If he is socialized, the individual thinks of others and is kindly toward them. He does not brood or mope about but is somewhat extravert, eagerly participating in his community's institutions. His mother and father were not divorced, nor was his home ever broken. He is "successful"—at least in a modest way—since he is ambitious; but he does not speculate about matters too far above his means, lest he become "a fantasy thinker," and the little men don't scramble after the big money. The less abstract the traits and fulfilled "needs" of "the adjusted man" are, the more they gravitate toward the norms of independent middle-class persons verbally living out Protestant ideals in the small towns of America.

Source: C. Wright Mills, "The Professional Ideology of Social Pathologists," *American Journal of Sociology*, 49 (September 1943): 165–180.

The theme running through social disorganization theory has been that industrialization, modernization, and urbanization are inimical to a well-adjusted society. The rapid social change associated with these forces was believed to disrupt a well-integrated normative system. Uncertainty regarding appropriate behavior and conflicting moral standards ultimately resulted in deviant behavior. This perspective dominated the sociological study of nonconformity for more than half a century and closely parallels popular explanations of deviance as well. Its longevity is reflected in the fact that it has only been within recent years that college courses in "social disorganization" and "social pathology" have been replaced by those in the "sociology of deviant behavior." Although disorganization theory successfully shifted the focus of attention from the individual actor to the social environment, it maintained the traditional belief that deviance is pathological. Whereas physiological and psychological theories located the causes of the pathology in the offender, however, disorganization theory found it operating in society generally.

## THE SOCIOLOGY OF DEVIANT BEHAVIOR: CONTEMPORARY PERSPECTIVES

The persistence of deviance across cultures and over time challenges the assertions of social disorganization theory. That is, deviance may be not evidence of the lack of organization or the failure of social control but a product of the same social processes that shape conforming behavior. This perspective originated around the turn of the twentieth century, achieved prominence in the mid-1960s, and continues to influence contemporary sociological explanations of deviance. Attempts to develop a conceptual framework that explains both deviance and conformity may be seen in such diverse theoretical orientations as *functionalism, definitional theory,* the *labeling perspective, anomie theory, social and cultural support theory,* and *theories of social and cultural conflict.* These explanations of the causes and nature of deviance are rich in theoretical elaboration and empirical support and comprise the focus of this work. A comprehensive treatment of these theories in subsequent chapters provides the basis for a systematic understanding of deviance and its control.

The first perspective to apply general sociological principles to the study of deviant behavior was *functionalism,* which argued that nonconformity is a property of all societies created in much the same manner as conformity and essential to the very maintenance of social systems. The theory was introduced in 1904 in *The Rules of Sociological Method* by Émile Durkheim, who defined deviance not as an intrinsic quality of behavior but as a definition accorded that behavior by the collective conscience. The participants of a social system, in recognition of their unity, seek to delimit those normative boundaries that distinguish their collectivity from all others. Durkheim suggested that this is accomplished through the creation of deviance, which, by standing in marked contrast to conformity, emphasizes the preferred standards and values of the community.

At the heart of the *definitional theory* of social deviance is the proposition that defining behavior and individuals as deviant is self-fulfilling (Thomas, 1923; Merton, 1957). The approach is predicated on W. I. Thomas's assertion that "if men define situations as real, they are real in their consequences"—once a meaning has been assigned to particular behavior or events, subsequent action will be guided by that meaning. The public designation of individuals as deviant, therefore, may lead to the withholding of opportunities for conformity as well as the refusal to recognize any claims to legitimate identity.

The social-psychological effects of self-fulfilling definitions have been elaborated by the *labeling school* of deviance, which draws heavily from the symbolic interactionist approach to the development of the self (see especially Cooley, 1902; Mead, 1934). According to this approach, individuals base their identities on the reactions they perceive from people who are important to them. By internalizing these reactions, individuals develop their definitions of self. This dependence on others for identity is the basis of labeling theory's concern with the impact of societal reactions to nonconformity. Individuals who perceive that they are being responded to as deviant will adopt deviant self-definitions and roles.

*Anomie theory* has been one of the most popular explanations of deviance. The concept of anomie was first developed by Émile Durkheim (1897) to explain suicide during periods of rapid social change. Durkheim observed that some people took their own lives when they experienced a sudden loss of the normative guidelines that regulate social aspirations. Such a disruption may occur through war, unexpected prosperity or economic depression, or any similar shock to the social order. The resultant state of deregulation, or normlessness, was termed *anomie.*

Contemporary developments within this perspective have focused on inadequate integration of the components of social structure as the source of anomie (Merton, 1938). All social systems include normatively defined goals and positively evaluated means for their attainment. These structures may vary independently of one another in such a way that goals and means receive unequal emphasis. In the United States, for example, more emphasis is placed on material success than on the legitimate avenues for becoming successful. This structural disequilibrium is a primary cause of normlessness. If achievement is frustrated, some persons may try to adapt through illegitimate means.

Certain groups in the population will be especially susceptible to the effects of anomie. Class societies, such as that of the United States, are characterized by the systematic exclusion of lower-status persons from the educational and occupational opportunities that facilitate achievement. Since wealth is a valued goal among all strata of society, those who experience discrimination will more frequently engage in deviance to relieve the stress that accompanies blocked achievement.

According to *social and cultural support theory*, all behavior is acquired through association with significant others (Sutherland, 1947). Individuals become deviant if they are isolated from membership in legitimate groups and participate in associational networks oriented to nonconformity. The normative definitions of deviant groups are transmitted to the individual through a process of socialization involving the basic learning mechanisms of imitation, instruction, identification, and reinforcement. The learning includes the techniques, motives, drives, rationalizations, and attitudes conducive to norm violation.

*Conflict theory* proposes by far the most relativistic view of crime and deviance. One variation of this perspective, which developed out of the social disorganization approach, focused on increased rates of deviant behavior among immigrants to the United States (Wirth, 1931; Sellin, 1938). The contact between disparate cultures resulted in a clash of sometimes mutually exclusive behavioral expectations. This culture conflict ultimately resulted in nonconformity.

Expanding upon this idea, some theoreticians have noted that complex societies contain a variety of groups with diverse normative structures. Deviance occurs when membership in any one of these groups requires behavior that is disapproved by the larger society. Nonconformity, then, is the product of attempts to adhere to the socially disvalued standards of one's significant associations (Miller, 1958; Vold, 1958).

A second and more recent trend in conflict theory addresses the political implications of social pluralism. This perspective finds the origins of nonconformity in the economic and political structures that comprise society (Chambliss and Seidman, 1971; Spitzer, 1975; Quinney, 1977). The law, family, religion, education, and government are institutions that support the existing hierarchies of status and power and protect those groups whose interests lie in the economic foundations of society. Labels of crime and deviance are applied to control populations that would otherwise threaten the dominant order. The activities or attributes of persons unable to participate in the economy and the actions of those who seek to alter the present system are defined as needing treatment or sanction insofar as they call into question relationships of domination and subordination.

## ORGANIZATION OF THE BOOK

Functionalism, definitional theory, the labeling perspective, anomie theory, social and cultural support theory, and theories of social and cultural conflict are the perspectives that dominate the contemporary study of deviant behavior. Each approach proposes an alternative explanation of nonconformity. No one of these theories, however, is comprehensive enough to explain either the several dimensions of deviance or its many forms. On the one hand, the exclusive focus of functionalism and conflict theory on social structure fails to attend to the interpersonal and social psychological processes that comprise the everyday reality of deviance. On the other hand, the concern of labeling theory with the meaning of deviance designation for individuals does not address the reasons why certain behaviors become disvalued or the implications of deviant identities for the social order.

Because these perspectives address different levels of analysis, however, we may utilize elements of each to construct a more comprehensive theory of social deviance. This cannot be a haphazard process of selecting only those concepts and propositions that most easily fit together. The individual approaches must first be carefully scrutinized, elaborated, and reformulated in terms of the voluminous research conducted within each. Out of those theoretical generalizations that are empirically supported, a new theory can be induced.

The remainder of this book represents such a process. Chapters 2 through 7, which deal with the major sociological perspectives on deviance, include comprehensive coverage and integration of the theoretical and empirical contributions to each approach. Concepts are inspected and reformulated in terms of their consistency with both classical and contemporary theoretical statements as well as extant research. Each chapter is intended to provide not only an intensive focus on a single approach to deviant behavior but a systematic treatment of a particular aspect of the overall process of deviance creation. As such, these chapters are the foundation for the general theory of deviance and social control presented in Chapter 8.

## REFERENCES

Abrahamsen, David
  1952  Who are the Guilty: A Study of Education and Crime. New York: Holt, Rinehart and Winston.
Aichorn, August
  1953  Wayward Youth. New York: Viking Press.
Beccaria, Cesare
  1764  On Crime and Punishments. Henry Paolucci, trans. New York: Bobbs-Merrill, 1963.

Bentham, Jeremy
  1838   Principles of Penal Law. Edinburgh: W. Tait.
Brecher, Edward M.
  1972   Licit and Illicit Drugs. Mount Vernon, New York: Consumer Union.
Chambliss, William J., and Robert S. Seidman
  1971   Law, Order, and Power. Reading, Massachusetts: Addison-Wesley.
Cooley, Charles Horton
  1902   Human Nature and the Social Order. New York: Charles Scribner's Sons.
Darwin, Charles
  1859   Origin of Species. New York: New American Library, Mentor, 1958.
  1871   The Descent of Man and Selection in Relation to Sex. New York: D. Appleton.
Dugdale, Richard Louis
  1910   The Jukes: A Study in Crime, Pauperism, Disease, and Heredity. New York: Putnam.
Durkheim, Émile
  1897   Suicide. John A. Spaulding and George Simpson, trans. New York: Free Press, 1951.
  1904   The Rules of Sociological Method. Sarah A. Solovay and John H. Mueller, trans. George E. G. Catlin, ed. New York: Macmillan, 1938.
Faris, Robert E. L.
  1948   Social Disorganization. New York: Ronald Press.
Ferri, Enrico
  1884   Criminal Sociology. Joseph Killey and John Lisle, trans. Boston: Little, Brown, 1917.
Garofalo, Raffaele
  1885   Criminology. Robert Wyness, trans. Boston: Little, Brown, 1914.
Glueck, Sheldon, and Eleanor T. Glueck
  1956   Physique and Delinquency. New York: Harper and Row.
Goddard, Henry H.
  1927   The Kallikak Family: A Study in Heredity of Feeble-mindedness. New York: Macmillan.
Goring, Charles
  1913   The English Convict. London: His Majesty's Stationery Office.
Heally, William
  1915   The Individual Delinquent. Boston: Little, Brown.
Heally, William and Augusta Bronner
  1936   New Light on Delinquency and Its Treatment. New Haven: Yale University Press.
Homans, George C.
  1950   The Human Group. New York: Harcourt, Brace.
Hook, Ernest B.
  1973   Behavioral Implications of the Human XYY Genotype. Science 179 (January): 139–150.
Hooton, E. A.
  1939   The American Criminal. Cambridge, Massachusetts: Harvard University Press.

Jacobs, Patricia A., Muriel Brunton, Marie M. Melville
 1965   Aggressive Behavior, Mental Subnormality, and the XYY Male. Nature 208 (December): 1351–1352.
Kittrie, Nicholas N.
 1973   The Right to be Different: Deviance and Enforced Therapy. Baltimore: Penguin Books.
Lange, Johannes
 1931   Crime as Destiny: A Study of Criminal Twins. Charlotte Haldane, trans. London: George Allen and Unwin.
Lombroso, Cesare
 1076   Crime: Its Causes and Remedies. H. P. Horton, trans. Boston: Little, Brown, 1911.
Lombroso–Ferrero, Gina
 1972   Criminal Man: According to the Classification of Cesare Lombroso. Montclair, New Jersey: Patterson Smith.
Mead, George Herbert
 1934   Mind, Self and Society. Chicago: University of Chicago Press.
Merton, Robert K.
 1938   Social Structure and Anomie. American Sociological Review 3 (October): 672–682.
 1957   Social Theory and Social Structure. New York: Free Press.
Miller, Walter B.
 1958   Lower Class Culture as a Generating Milieu for Gang Delinquency. Journal of Social Issues 14: 5–19.
Mills, C. Wright
 1943   The Professional Ideology of Social Pathologists. American Journal of Sociology 49 (September): 165–180.
Ogburn, William F.
 1922   Social Change. New York: Viking Press.
Quinney, Richard
 1977   Class, State, and Crime. New York: David McKay.
Sellin, Thorsten
 1938   Culture Conflict and Crime. New York: Social Science Research Council Bulletin 41.
Shah, Saleem A., and Loren H. Roth
 1974   Biological and Psychophysiological Factors in Criminality. In Handbook of Criminology. Daniel Glaser, ed. Chicago: Rand McNally, 101–173.
Sheldon, W. H.
 1949   The Varieties of Human Physique: An Introduction to Constitutional Psychiatry. New York: Harper & Row.
Spitzer, Steven
 1975   Toward a Marxian Theory of Deviance. Social Problems 22 (June): 638–651.
Stonequist, Everett
 1937   The Marginal Man. New York: Charles Scribner's Sons.
Sutherland, Edwin H.
 1947   Principles of Criminology. Philadelphia: J. B. Lippincott.

1950   The Diffusion of Sexual Psychopath Laws. American Journal of Sociology 56 (September): 142–148.

Szasz, Thomas S.
1963   Law, Liberty, and Psychiatry: An Inquiry into the Social Uses of Mental Health Practices. New York: Macmillan.

Taft, Donald, and Ralph England
1964   Criminology. New York: Macmillan.

Tannenbaum, Frank
1938   Crime and the Community. New York: Columbia University Press.

Thomas, William I.
1923   The Unadjusted Girl. Boston: Little, Brown.

Thomas, W. I., and Florian Znaniecki
1920   The Polish Peasant in Europe and America. Chicago: University of Chicago Press.

Vold, George B.
1958   Theoretical Criminology. New York: Oxford University Press.

West, Donald J.
1967   Homosexuality. Chicago: Aldine.

Wirth, Louis
1931   Culture Conflict and Misconduct. Social Forces 9 (June): 484–492.

# 2

---

# Deviance and Social Organization: The Maintenance of Behavioral Boundaries

Since the beginning of human history, deviance has been a source of both concern and fascination. The prehistoric practice of skull drilling, or trephining, to expel evil spirits; the Greek literary portrayals of evil and its consequences; and the biblical condemnation of such behaviors as homosexuality, adultery, and even blindness reflect this concern. The systematic investigation of deviant behavior, however, is a relatively recent phenomenon. Only since the nineteenth century have scientific methods been applied to the study of nonconformity. The earliest of these efforts focused primarily on the individual offender. Sources of aberrant behavior were variously attributed to biological regression, low intelligence, endocrine gland transformation, and psychological maladjustment. While sociological developments within social disorganization theory shifted the focus from the individual to the social environment, the essential theme remained the same. Conformity was assumed to be an obvious manifestation of health and well-being; deviance was the product of pathological conditions residing within the individual or the social structure.

## THE SOCIAL FUNCTIONS OF DEVIANCE

The major premise of the theoretical perspective to be discussed in this chapter, the *functionalist approach,* is that neither personal nor social disorganization underlies deviant behavior. Rather, deviance is seen as essential to the very organization of society. Its function is to establish and maintain behavioral boundaries and to affirm the value of conformity.

According to functionalism, society is composed of interrelated parts that work together to maintain the system as a whole. An important aspect of such maintenance is the diffusion of common values, which occurs in part through the designation of certain behaviors as deviant. In this manner, society calls attention to the standards upon which it is based. Property is valued, for example, not only because respect for it is engendered by institutional efforts at socialization but also because the propertyless are shamed and the thief imprisoned. In much the same way as the moral leader exemplifies the cultural ideal, the deviant stands for that to which the culture stands opposed. The group derives vitality from repulsion, indignation, and official reaction to deviant conduct. By calling attention to the sins, pathologies, and crimes of the outcast, the group reinforces its cohesivenss and reaffirms its norms. Since social systems depend upon this process for their very existence, functionalists have argued that they are organized in such a way as to produce required levels of nonconformity.

In small groups, as well as in societies characterized by minimal stratification and complexity, behavioral boundaries are likely to be consensually derived. Within modern society, on the other hand, a plurality of social and cultural systems impose expectations for conformity on their members. Through competition among groups for access to the institutions of social control, the victors acquire the right to designate their standards and values as the official morality. In this instance, behavioral boundaries represent politically established limits. These standards are communicated through the boundary maintenance function of deviance and societal reaction to it.

## The Development of Moral Boundaries

The pathological approach to deviance received its first serious challenge in the early years of the twentieth century when Émile Durkheim (1904) argued that nonconformity was a normal part of organized society. We have simply to observe that such behavior has been present in all societies, in all ages, to appreciate the validity of this observation. Deviance is normal, therefore, because there has been no society without it.

Underlying the inevitability of nonconformity is the virtually limitless range of possible human behavior. There are no natural behavioral standards, no immutable patterns universally applicable across generations and cultures. Behavioral boundaries are constructed by societies as they attempt to distinguish themselves from all others by designating certain behaviors as their own (Erikson, 1966). That is the purpose of constitutions and statutes as well as tribal taboos. By defining what is socially acceptable, these codes establish behavioral boundaries that limit the range of activities in which group members may engage.

Yet the communication of many of these behavioral standards to the members of social systems involves little direct tutelage. The young are not frequently instructed in the laws of incest and robbery by their parents or teachers. Rather, the limits of what is socially acceptable become visible insofar as their violation produces the indignation of the conformist and the official sanction of the state. Thus, although few people have read the relevant legal statutes concering murder and theft, even fewer are unaware that these behaviors are against the law. Whether through gossip, media accounts, or official sanction, public denunciations of those who have violated social standards communicate to the society at large the nature of social transgressions and the boundaries beyond which they may not go without jeopardizing their continued membership in the group. In this manner, the persistence of society is ensured.

Although deviance is present in all social systems and is a product of the attempt to establish behavioral limits, its importance becomes most evident as societies approach the urban, industrial ideal. According to Durkheim, human society has seen a progressive movement from *mechanical* to *organic solidarity*. Mechanical systems are characterized by the relatively small population and rudimentary division of labor frequently found in preliterate and rural-agrarian societies. Individuals do not perform specialized functions, but each is responsible for providing for personal and familial needs and services. Since the variety of experiences in these societies is limited, the norms, values, and standards of behavior are likely to be shared by all. Nonconformity is restricted to instances where those differentiations that do occur (on the basis of sex, strength, or leadership, for example) produce alternative norms and behaviors.

The possibility of disparate standards developing increases as societies move toward organic solidarity. The organic society is characterized by an expanding population, by a highly complex division of labor, and by the many distinctions in status, power, and wealth that typify urban industrialized systems. As systems differentiate and populations grow, individuals increasingly lose the homogeneity of experiences conducive to shared norms. The result is an increasing tendency for persons to deviate from the collective type, that is, from the total representation of social norms and values. In the process of social differentiation, therefore, lie the origins of crime and deviance.

> Since there cannot be a society in which the individuals do not differ more or less from the collective type, it is also inevitable that, among these divergences, there are some with a criminal character. What confers this

character upon them is not the intrinsic quality of a given act but that definition which the collective conscience lends them. [Durkheim, 1904: 70]

## Nonconformity and Social Change

Nonconformity is not only a universal aspect of human organization, but it is also an important source of social change. Deviations from the collective type are indicators of the flexibility of a given system. A society so rigid as to preclude behavioral variation precludes deviant and innovator alike. Nonconformity may even provide the direction in which social change may occur. Thus, Durkheim observed:

> Where crime exists, collective sentiments are sufficiently flexible to take on a new form, and crime sometimes helps to determine the form they will take. How many times, indeed, it is only an anticipation of future morality—a step toward what will be! According to Athenian law, Socrates was a criminal and his condemnation was no more than just. However, his crime, namely the independence of his thought, rendered a service not only to humanity but to his country. It served to prepare a new morality and faith which the Athenians needed, since the traditions by which they had lived until then were no longer in harmony with the current conditions of life. [1904: 71]

## Solidarity and Value Consensus

Deviance, then, is not only a *normal* outcome of social differentiation but may in fact perform valuable functions in society. For Durkheim, deviance serves to mark *behavioral boundaries* and to facilitate social change. Subsequent theorists have expanded that position. In particular, George Herbert Mead (1918) argued that nonconformity is essential to the internal cohesiveness of society. Divergent and competing individual interests are a constant source of potential fragmentation. The cry of "thief" or "murderer" provides a common focus that allows the collectivity to minimize internal differences. Rule violators, then, are responsible for feelings of solidarity among members of the social system. By reacting to the offense and expelling the offender from the community at large, conforming citizens are both reaffirmed in their moral superiority and reminded of the awful power of the state. In this manner the nonconformist not only acts to renew those inhibitions and restraints necessary for the common order but also to strengthen the sentiments appropriate to communal living.

At the same time, the deviant lends value to the resources and relationships that characterize the social order. In people's efforts to protect themselves from the thief and the murderer, the value of property and life is affirmed.

> In all this we have our backs toward that which we protect and our faces toward the actual or potential enemy. These goods are regarded as valuable because we are willing to fight and even die for them in certain exigencies. . . . The values thus obtained are not their values in use but sacrificial values. [Mead, 1918: 587]

If, therefore, marriage and virginity are sacred, it is because there exist adulterers and rapists. Likewise, diamonds and gold are more precious than tin not only because of their rarity but also because of our willingness to erect fortresses for their security. This negative approach to valuation supports the view that deviance is not only inevitable but indispensable. If the value of social relationships is a product of the effort we expend to protect them from the transgressor, then nonconformity must be present in quantities sufficient to ensure maintenance of the present standards of value.

## THE ROLE OF NONCONFORMITY IN SMALL GROUPS

The most systematic evidence of the boundary maintenance function of deviance has been obtained from studies of small groups. Whether in their natural settings or under highly controlled experimental conditions, groups do appear to establish boundaries regarding the range of permissible behaviors.

### Individual and Collective Awareness

Anthropologists have long acknowledged the importance of nonconformity for the organization of social systems. Particular attention has been given to the functions of deviant gender identity and performance (Benedict, 1934: 263–265; Devereux, 1937). An example is the role of the *mahu* in the Tahitian village system (Levy, 1971). The mahu is a male who, at a very early age, is selected to spend his life as a woman. Every village cultivates a mahu, and each has only one at any given time. Although the mahu engages in sexual exchanges with other village males, he is most generally described as one "who does woman's work" (Levy, 1971: 15).

The role of the mahu in Tahitian society has a major "message function to the community as audience, particularly to the male members" (Levy, 1971: 17). In these villages, sex-role differentiations are minimal. No gender indications may be found in the language, there are no feminine and masculine first names, and many of the activities of villagers, if differentiated, are not exclusively so. Child rearing is a project whose responsibility is diffused among older female siblings and cousins and is controlled by the mother. The father is only a marginal figure. In the absence of clearly defined sex differentiations and male role models,

> there have been developed various external marks or signs which function to clarify that definition. . . . The mahu role, with its clear cut rules, its high visibility, its strictly limited incumbency, and its pre-empting of homosexual behavior . . . has a message function. It says there clearly, out in the open, is the mahu, the one man who has taken the female role. I am a non-mahu. What ever feelings I have about men are no threat to me and to my eventual role as family head. I can see exactly what *he* is, and I am clear about myself in that I am not he. [Levy, 1971: 18–19]

Through the boundary maintenance role of the mahu, sex-role identifications become crystallized for members of the community.

The visibility of the deviant also ensures that members of a social group acquire the information necessary for collective awareness. That is, deviant categories communicate the standards of behavior that give the collectivity a sense of its shape and substance. The processes by which groups establish definitions of deviance and the functions these designations serve were observed in an experimental study of telephone equipment workers (Homans, 1950).

Fourteen men, previously unacquainted with one another, were taken from their regular departments and placed in a special work room for seven months. Hourly wages were replaced by a complicated system of piecework pay. In effect, output of the group as a whole as well as output of each individual was rewarded. The expectation was that everyone would work as hard as he could and encourage all other workers to do the same in order to maximize group and personal rewards. Instead, the group developed a shared notion of a proper day's work. Two completed telephone banks constituted the output norm, and individuals behaved according to these expectations. Thus, the employees completed most of the work during morning hours. As soon as the men were sure they could complete their quota, effort slowed considerably. The output graph for the experimental group from week to week was a straight line.

Output restrictions represented part of the normative expectations of the group, and around these norms definitions of deviance emerged. Group members who exceeded the production norm were "rate busters"; those who turned out too little work were "chiselers." Finally, the men were expected to say nothing that would injure their co-workers. Violators of this norm were "squealers."

The group also developed an informal system of sanctioning. Pressure was brought to bear on individuals whose output was exceeding group norms through the use of "binging"—delivering a stiff blow to the upper arm—and through the application of epithets such as "speed king" or "slave." These pressures were designed not so much to injure the offending party as to indicate that co-workers were displeased with the boundary transgressions.

Additional evidence of the functions of deviance in the regulation of group boundaries comes from a study of employees in an airplane factory (Bensman and Gerver, 1963). Much of the organization of the plant revolved around the illegal use of the "tap." A tap is an extremely hard steel screw used to cut new threads. In airplane construction, part of the assembly involves matching bolts with previously inset nuts. When the nut and bolt are not in true alignment, the tap can be used to recut the bolt threads so that the parts fit. Anything less than a true alignment of parts, however, jeopardizes maximum strength of the aircraft. The use of the tap, therefore, was the most serious crime conceivable in the factory. Workers could be summarily fired for even possessing one. In fact, however, most employees either owned or had ready access to the tool, and it was around this device that much of the informal plant organization emerged. In particular, definitions of deviance and conformity were established to regulate collective expectations regarding the appropriate use of the device.

People new to the factory became acquainted with the use of the tap through on-the-job socialization. Typically, a new worker who faced an alignment problem would mention it to a partner. The veteran employee would first try every method possible to align the appropriate nut and bolt but, if none worked, would then use the tap while explaining to the novice the dangers of being caught.

For several weeks the new employee was not allowed to use the tap and was forced to rely on others for assistance. Later, the employee was allowed to use the tool under close supervision. The last step in integration into the group was the purchase of a tap.

The appropriate use of the device is indicated by the terms to identify various users. One who relies on the tap over-frequently is a "botcher," and one who seldom uses it is a "mechanic." Employees who refuse to use it at all simply do not get their share of the work done.

All this occurs within the more formal context of the factory. The foreman, plant quality control, and Air Force quality control are all supposed to prohibit the use of the tap. Once again, however, informal norms shape the actual behavior of group members.

Air Force quality control represents the most serious threat to the work group. When these inspectors make their rounds, word passes quickly along the line that the "gestapo" is coming and that all taps should be hidden. The plant inspectors have developed more of an exchange relationship with the workers. They acknowledge that taps exist but encourage employees not to use them in their presence. Finally, plant foremen are most concerned that the etiquette of tap use be upheld. Taps should be used only when necessary, and they should be used discreetly. Thus, an employee who is caught by an inspector and turned over to the foreman is invariably chastised for carelessness in being caught and not for illegal use of the tap.

Both of the preceding studies point to a fundamental principle of social interaction. Groups tend to establish norms and expectations concerning the behavior of their members. These norms and expectations define the nature of the interaction that characterizes the membership and signify the range of behaviors tolerated by the group. To demarcate these limits, informal group sanctions are applied when behavioral boundaries are breached. The use of epithets, cues meaningful to group members, and expulsion become vivid symbols of collective definitions.

## Sustaining Deviants as Boundary Maintainers

An interesting question concerns the role of groups in creating and sustaining portions of their memberships as boundary maintainers. Dentler and Erikson illustrate this point in their studies of Quaker work projects and of schizophrenia among basic trainees in the U.S. Army (1959).

Quaker work projects were established to encourage tolerance, democracy, and pacifism among program participants. Their effectiveness in this regard was found to be associated with the proportion of deviant individuals in the various groups. The greater the number of deviant members, the more successful was the work group in bringing about the desired characteristics. Deviants appeared to play such an important role in these camps that conforming members spent a great deal of energy trying to prevent their full alienation. Deviants who threatened to leave were persuaded to stay, and other participants made personal sacrifices to ensure their continued membership.

A Quaker work-project leader discusses the dynamics of the interaction between the group and the deviant:

X left our group after the first four weeks of the eight-week program. He had never been away from home before although he was about 21 years old. He couldn't seem to adjust to his job at the day camp, and he just couldn't stand doing his share of the housework and cooking. This lack of doing his share was especially hard on us, and we often discussed private-ly whether it would be good for him to relieve him of any household chores. We decided that wouldn't be right, but we still couldn't get him to work. Funny, but this sort of made housework the center of our group life. We are proud that no one else has shirked his chores; there is no quib-bling now. . . . Anyway, X kept being pressured by his mother and brother to come home, but we gave him tremendous support. We talked it all out with him. We let him know we really wanted him to stay. This seemed to unify our group. It was working out the problem of X that seemed to unify our group. It was working out the problem of X that seemed to help us build some group standards. He began to follow some of our standards but he also stayed free to dissent. His mother finally forced him to come home. [Dentler and Erikson, 1959: 103]

Erikson's study of military boot camp revealed a similar pattern. On the basis of interview and questionnaire surveys of U.S. Army trainees, he reconstructed the group lives of eleven schizophrenics prior to their hospitalization. A major finding of this research was that the decision to hospitalize was made by external authorities and not by the members of the squad itself. In fact, the training unit worked diligently to retain the deviant within its ranks. It appears that the pre-psychotic played an important role in the very organization of the squad. Even though he is a low producer, a behavior that jeopardizes the performance of the entire unit,

> the group neither exerts strong pressures on him to conform nor attempts to expel him from the squad. Instead, he is typically given a wide license to deviate from both the performance and behavior norms of the group, and the group in turn forms a hard protective shell around him which hides him from exposure to outside authorities. [Dentler and Erikson, 1959: 105]

The squad performs his duties for him while seemingly asking on-ly that the pre-psychotic be consistent in his helplessness and dependen-cy. He becomes the object of much attention and affection, often refer-red to as " 'our teddy bear,' 'our pet,' 'mascot,' 'little brother,' 'toy,' and so on" [Dentler and Erikson, 1959: 105].

As both the Quaker and Army illustrations suggest, deviant members are important targets toward which group concerns become focused. Not on-ly do they symbolize the group's activities, but they help give other members a sense of group size, its range and extent, by marking where the group begins and ends in space. In general, the deviant seems to help give the group structure a visible "shape." The deviant is someone about whom something should be done, and the group, in expressing this concern, is able to reaffirm its essential cohesion and indicate what the group is and what it can do. [Dentler and Erikson, 1959: 106]

On the basis of such analyses, Dentler and Erikson suggested a series of propositions that have come to constitute the heart of the functionalist approach to nonconformity. First, "groups tend to induce, sustain, and permit deviant behavior" (Dentler and Erikson, 1959: 98). That is, a group will define the range of its behaviors by designating the performance of certain of its members as deviant. Such activity is sustained and permitted to the extent that it is absorbed rather than eliminated by the group.

The second proposition asserts that "deviant behavior functions in enduring groups to help maintain group equilibrium" (Dentler and Erikson, 1959: 100). All groups require that the end points of their ability to perform be clearly marked. Both high producer (leader) and low producer (deviant) constitute important referents for the group membership. "Both are outside links in the communication system which feeds back information about the range of group performance and the limits of the differentiated structure" (Dentler and Erikson, 1959: 100). In a similar manner, deviance contributes to the internal reward system of the collectivity. "The rewards of conformity . . . are seen as 'rewarding' in comparison to other possible outcomes, and obviously the presence of a deviant in the group would provide the continual contrast without which the reward structure would have little meaning" (Dentler and Erikson, 1959: 101). As indicators of the range of expected performance and internal rewards, then, deviants serve a boundary maintenance function.

Finally, Dentler and Erikson (1959: 102) propose that "groups will resist any trend toward alienation of a member whose behavior is deviant." Because the deviant provides a continual test of the limits of group tolerance, the group will try to maintain the membership of the nonconformist until such time as his or her behavior becomes a threat to group survival. Thus, deviance will be tolerated or even rewarded as long as it continues to serve its boundary maintenance function.

## External Threat and the Definition of Deviance

The amount of behavior defined and accepted as deviant depends on the organizational needs of the system. As these needs change, so do definitions of what constitutes deviance. Persons do not simply move back and forth across fixed behavioral limits. Rather, the "moral boundaries of a social system move independently of the actual behavior of individuals defined as 'deviant' by the system" (Lauderdale, 1976: 660). These definitions vary as internal changes or external pressures make new demands on the system's structure and performance. An examination of group adjustment to external threat was conducted by Pat Lauderdale (1976), who explored the process by which boundaries are utilized to maintain the group's integrity in the face of threats to its existence.

Lauderdale randomly assigned experimental subjects to two groups, ostensibly for the purpose of reviewing the case histories of juvenile delinquents. The stated goal was to determine the most appropriate legal dispostion for each case. A confederate assigned to each group was instructed to take a position clearly opposite to the collective recommendations of the members. In both groups, therefore, the behavior of the confederate deviant was identical. In one group, the experimenter commented, following thirty minutes of debate, that perhaps the group should be discontinued. This was the "threat" condition. In the second group, the experimenter introduced a nonthreatening comment into the discussion.

The groups' responses to the experimental conditions were then compared. The extent of socio-emotional communications among group members was measured in order to determine the effects of the threat condition on social solidarity. The findings indicated that an external threat to corporate identity resulted in an immediate, momentary loss of solidarity. That is, there was a significant decrease in positive expressions of attachment. The threatened group became much more rejecting of the behavior of the deviant. In addition, more behaviors were defined as falling beyond the limits of toleration. As boundaries became more restrictive, the cohesiveness of the group was reestablished (see Figure 2–1).

Definitions of deviance, the seriousness with which it was viewed, and the appropriate reactions to it could be attributed to the nature of behavioral boundaries in the two groups. In the threatened group the boundaries were "tightened," and the deviant was propelled away from the group. Internal solidarity and feelings of self-righteousness were thereby increased significantly. Consequently, a solid front could be presented to the threatening authority.

The deviant in the nonthreat group was not alienated by the membership. With its corporate identity unchallenged, this group appeared to be "prepared to keep the deviant in the group . . . 'on the fringe' . . . as a means of reaffirming their righteousness by continually uniting in action against the traitor" (Lauderdale, 1976: 674). In this instance, the deviant, as the object of controlled hostility, became the scapegoat for the group's failure to achieve unanimity. When the very existence of the group was threatened, however, members became unwilling to tolerate the internal disruptions of deviant behavior.

**FIGURE 2-1** **Distribution of the Mean Number of Group Solidarity Communications by Conditions of Threat and Non-Threat**

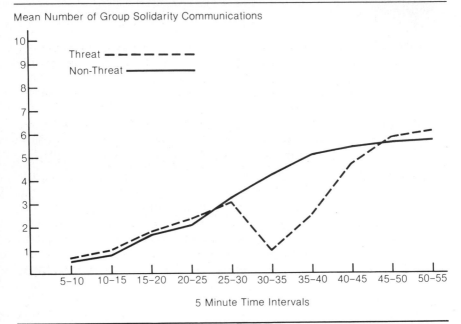

Source: Pat Lauderdale, "Deviance and Moral Boundaries," *American Sociological Review* 41 (August 1976): 670.

The question of the generality of the findings from this study should be raised. Do other natural . . . groups operate in the same manner as this experimental corporate system . . . ? Can the reaction to racial and ethnic minority groups by any society be considered analytically analogous to the scapegoating . . . in the non-threat condition, or can people segregated from their larger social system in mental and penal institutions be considered analogous to the deviant . . . in the threat condition? . . . [Did] stigmatization and separation of . . . Japanese-Americans into concentration camps . . . following the invasion of Pearl Harbor indicate processes similar to those identified in this study? [Lauderdale, 1976: 674]

## CONFLICT AND BOUNDARY MAINTENANCE

The question of the generalizability of findings from functionalist research is a controversial one. The difficulty arises when the approach is used to explain deviance at the societal level. Kai T. Erikson's (1966) classic study of Puritan New England is illustrative.

# Wayward Puritans

*Kai T. Erikson*

When the New England Puritans put an entire ocean between themselves and the rest of the world, they were declaring in effect that issues of the most profound gravity divided them from their contemporaries at home. They had voyaged many miles to establish a new model of Christian fellowship, an ethic they could call the "New England Way," and it was naturally important to them that this ethic have a clear enough character to stand out from other ideologies and other programs in the world of the time. . . . [Within this transitional context,] deviant persons . . . [came to] supply an important service to [the] society by patrolling the outer edges of group space and by providing a contrast which [gave] the rest of the community some sense of their own territorial identity. . . .

Every society handles [its boundary maintenance needs] . . . differently: each has its own mechanisms for naming people to deviant positions and its own mechanisms for regulating the human traffic moving back and forth from its boundaries. . . . [Furthermore,] the way in which this option is exercised has a profound effect both on the forms of deviancy a society experiences and on the kinds of people who come to exhibit it. . . . The Puritans developed a deployment pattern which was uniquely suited to the theological climate in which they lived. . . . The main outlines of that pattern are still reflected in many of our modern attitudes toward deviation.

To characterize the New England deployment pattern . . . we may say (1) that the Puritans saw deviant behavior as the special property of a particular class of people who were more or less frozen into deviant attitudes; and (2) that they generally thought it best to handle the problem by locking these people into fairly permanent deviant roles. Puritan theories of human development began with the assumption that men do not change a great deal as they mature or are exposed to different life experiences, and in this sense the settlers of the Bay had little faith in the promise that men might "reform" or overcome any pronounced deviant leanings. . . . When the Puritans . . . branded [the deviant] on the forehead or otherwise mutilated his face they were marking him with the permanent emblem of his station in life and making it extremely difficult for him to resume a normal social role in the community. To banish him meant almost the same thing; he might earn a better reputation elsewhere, but in local records and in local memories he would remain a deviant forever. . . .

The Puritan deployment pattern was based on the almost permanent exclusion of a deviant class—a category of misfits who would normally be expected to engage in unacceptable activities and to oppose the rest of the social order. . . . [The] system acted to stabilize the volume of deviation appearing in community life . . . [and] made very little allowance for people to move back and forth from the community's boundaries. Once a person had been branded with the mark of disreputability, either figuratively or literally, his status in society had been fairly well stabilized, and it was exceedingly difficult for him to impress others (not to mention himself) that he was suited for another social position. . . .

The theological views which sustained this deployment pattern have largely disappeared from the religious life of the society, but the attitudes toward deviation which were implied in the pattern are still retained in many of the institutions we have built to process and confine deviant offenders. We are still apt to visualize deviant behavior as the product of a deep-seated characterological strain in the person who enacts it, rather than as the product of the situation in which it took place, and we are still apt to treat that person as if his whole being was somehow implicated in what is often no more than a passing deviant episode. . . . Whether these confrontations take the form of criminal trials, excommunication hearings, court-marshals, or even psychiatric case conferences, they act as boundary maintaining devices in the sense that they demonstrate to whatever audience is concerned where the line is drawn between behavior that belongs in the special universe of the group and behavior that does not.

Source: Kai T. Erikson, *Wayward Puritans: A Study in the Sociology of Deviance* (New York: John Wiley and Sons, 1966), pp. 11, 67–68, 196–198.

Within sixty years, Puritan colonists experienced three major threats to established boundaries. In 1636 a crisis known as the Antinomian controversy developed between the magistrates and ministers on the one hand and the colonists on the other. At issue was the right of the leadership to enforce its interpretations of the Bible. Some colonists demanded that the more ambiguous biblical passages be codified, but the ministers wished to protect their divine authority to freely interpret the word of God. The crisis had been precipitated by a group of individuals who spent many evenings reading and discussing various passages from scripture. When the discussions differed from official interpretation, the magistrates charged the group with heresy. By labeling the discussions as heretical and persecuting and banishing the participants, the governors of the colony reaffirmed the religious boundaries of the community.

Twenty years later the Quaker persecutions occurred. Again, the issue around which the crisis developed concerned the right of the religious leadership to determine the nature of the relationship between God and the Puritan colonists. In response to the Quakers' claim that only individuals could engineer their relationships with God, the established leadership defined Quakerism as criminal.

Finally, the year 1692 saw an intense pursuit of persons thought to be witches. The crisis was initiated by a group of young girls, regular visitors of a slave woman, Tituba, from Barbados, who was known for her skills in magic. As this sorority continued, a change seemed to come over the participants, who became very secretive and exhibited a high degree of tension. Some developed bizarre behavior, such as screaming, convulsing, or crawling on the ground and barking like dogs. The malady was feared to be contagious as young women throughout the community began to manifest similar symptoms. Having exhausted all medical explanations and remedies, the town's physician concluded that the colony was beseiged by agents of Satan. Pressed to identify the witches who were tormenting them, the girls identified three women who lived on the margins of the community.

> Three better candidates could not have been found if all the gossips in New England had met to make the nominations. The first, understandably, was Tituba herself, . . . who was probably acquainted with some form of voodoo. The second, Sarah Good, was a proper hag of a witch if Salem Village had ever seen one. With a pipe clenched in her leathery face she wandered around the countryside neglecting her children and begging from others, and on more than one occasion the old crone had been overheard muttering threats against her neighbors when she was in an unusually sour humor. Sarah Osburne, the third suspect, had a higher social standing than either of her alleged accomplices, but she had been involved in a local scandal a year or two earlier when a man moved into her house some months before becoming her husband. [Erikson, 1966: 143]

Not only were the three found guilty, but their confessions launched a wave of recruits that filled the jails and resulted in twenty-two deaths. Not one suspect brought to court was acquitted.

The crisis followed a number of incidents that had undermined the solidarity of governing officials. Land disputes had fractured the leadership, an unpopular and costly war with the Indian confederacy had alienated the population, and Charles II of England withdrew first support for and then the charter of the Puritan colonies. Witches provided a convenient source of materials for the construction of moral boundaries in a situation that threatened group cohesiveness.

Erikson's major hypothesis was that:

> crime (and by extension other forms of deviation) may actually perform a needed service to society by drawing people together in a common posture of anger and indignation. The deviant individual violates rules of conduct which the rest of the community holds in high respect; and when these people come together to express their outrage over the offense and to bear witness against the offender, they develop a tighter bond of solidarity than existed earlier. [Erikson, 1966: 4]

In support of this hypothesis, he proposes that the Antinomian controversy, the Quaker persecutions, and the witch-hunt hysteria were created by the community in order to establish the moral boundaries of the settlement.

William Chambliss (1976) disagrees with Erikson's conclusion. That there were three major waves of deviance in a sixty-year period suggests to Chambliss that they could not have been sources of internal solidarity. Moreover, as Erikson himself makes clear, the outbreaks of deviance were not the product of crises in morality but of power struggles between the rulers and the ruled. Thus, the Antinomian controversy concerned the demand of a growing segment of society to limit the powers of the magistrates and ministers. "Faced with such a threat to their authority, the established Church responded in a time honored fashion. They proceeded to seek and apply a label to the source of the threat that would undermine her influence—heretic" (Chambliss, 1976: 12).

The Quaker persecutions posed a similar challenge. Claiming that religious authorities had no right to impose the conditions of an individual's relationship with God, the Quakers constituted a threat to the established leadership. As the Quaker movement accumulated converts, the authorities defined being a Quaker as a crime.

The witch hunts in 1692 were also motivated by an internal crisis in governance rather than an external threat to authority. Fragmented by property disputes and negative reactions from England, the leadership attempted to regain its legitimacy by recruiting and persecuting scapegoats. "The diversion of witchcraft served at least to give the appearance of a reaffirmed authority in the hands of those who ruled" (Chambliss, 1976: 14).

It appears, in light of Erikson's own evidence, that whatever solidarity emerged from the crises of Puritan New England was not the result of the community rising in angry indignation against a moral threat as Erikson contended (1966: 4). Rather, it seems to have been a product of the "elimination of alternative centers of authority or power" (Chambliss, 1976: 15). In each case, the behaviors were proscribed in order to assert the validity of the traditional order.

This pattern raises a serious question regarding the functionalist assumption of normative consensus. Functionalism, as we have seen it thus far, views society as consisting of a single set of norms and values. As shown in Figure 2–2, this monolithic standard is the ideal, or collective type. Behavior that strays beyond tolerable limits is sanctioned, and

**FIGURE 2–2  Normative Monolithism**

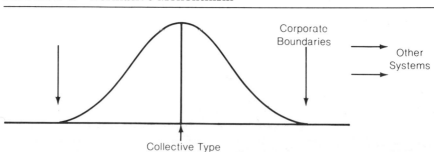

Collective Type

continued membership of the straying individual in the group is jeopardized. In this manner, deviance communicates the nature of communal rules and reaffirms the value of conformity.

It appears that for small groups the assumption of normative consensus is tenable. When status, power, and wealth differentiations are limited and people share a common pursuit of articulated goals, the result tends to be shared definitions of deviance and conformity. The success with which research dealing with small groups has been able to demonstrate functionalist ideas may reflect the consensual nature of these associations.

The larger society, however, is characterized by social and cultural diversity. As differentiations have developed according to sex, race, age, ethnicity, geographical location, and, most importantly, social class, corresponding differences have developed in the standards and values that shape behavior patterns within the various groups. A more accurate depiction of the modern, complex society, then, may resemble Figure 2–3. The larger society includes many subgroups or collectivities whose values sometimes share in, and sometimes differ radically from, the values and beliefs of other subgroups. At the same time, society is organized politically. Constitutions, treaties, federal statutes, and local ordinances establish for all groups the limits of acceptable behavior as officially defined. These official standards reflect the interests of those best able to institutionalize their morality as the dominant one. According to this idea, the designation of behavior as deviant is more an effort on the part of dominant groups to protect their positions of superiority than an effort to maintain consensually derived boundaries.

## Deviance as Functional Type-Scripts

The notion that deviance designations preserve dominant interests is elaborated by Anthony Harris (1977) in his theory of social type-scripts. *Type-scripts* are the fixed role expectations that accompany particular

**FIGURE 2–3   Normative Pluralism**

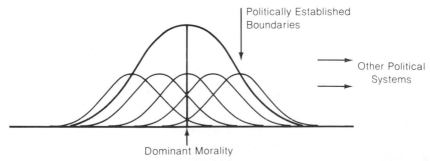

positions. According to Harris, the assignment of individuals to these roles is designed to preserve existing hierarchies of social dominance. White, male, middle-class dominance is protected if blacks are found in the ghettos, women in the home, and the poor in the factories. Through legal, educational, and occupational structures, such assignments become accepted as appropriate both for those who occupy the positions and those who benefit from them. That is, they constitute type-scripts regarding the kinds of behavior it is "likely, possible, unlikely, and impossible for particular types of actors to perform" (Harris, 1977: 11).

Among the dominant order-maintaining type-scripts are those that define deviant behavior. Certain types of actors are scripted for specified types of nonconformity; others are defined as incapable of rule violation. These distinctions are intimately related to the interests and needs of the more powerful groups. Removing black males and blue-collar workers from legitimate positions to serve as boundary maintainers does not threaten the sociopolitical order—these individuals are easily replaced. Their functional dispensability is reflected in the abundance of deviant type-scripts with which they are defined.

On the other hand, male superiority depends on assigning females to the care of the home. Their filling deviant roles would threaten the ability of males to continue in their positions of institutional control, since removal of women from the home would require that males assume the responsibilities traditionally prescribed for the roles of mother and wife. Since women are functionally indispensable to male dominance, there is a noticeable absence of deviant type-scripts for them. According to this theory, females are not expected to be involved in illegitimate activities.

## Moral Crusades and Enemy Deviation

The reformulation of the functionalist approach to include an awareness of the political nature of behavioral boundaries adds much to the theory's explanatory power. There is abundant evidence that deviance categories are important sources of dominant group legitimation. Thus, Joseph Gusfield's (1967) examination of Prohibition reveals that the ban on the manufacture of alcoholic beverages in 1920 was enacted in response to the development of ambiguity with regard to moral leadership. In particular, the social pressure for prohibitionary legislation was inspired by those whose position of social and moral superiority was being eroded by the rapid social changes associated with the rising tide of immigration. The issue was not the alcohol-consuming habits of certain portions of the population, but rather the symbolic aspect of legislated morality.

Gusfield points out that throughout the nineteenth century, growing concern over the manufacture of alcohol paralleled the growing number of Irish Catholics and German Lutherans immigrating to the United States. The new arrivals' attitude toward alcohol consumption was more accepting than the one that prevailed generally in this country. A flagrant disregard for the temperance tradition among those immigrants, who also comprised a large portion of the urban poor, represented by the 1850s a "general clash over cultural values" (Gusfield, 1967: 184). On the one side were the Protestant, rural, native-born middle classes; on the other, the Catholic and Lutheran, urban, foreign-born lower classes. Efforts to turn the morality of the former into legal standards "polarized the opposing forces and accentuated the symbolic impact of the movement. . . . Defeat or victory was [now] a clear-cut statement of public dominance" (Gusfield, 1967: 184).

With the immigration wave of 1890–1915, the possibility that a new morality would jeopardize the old order constituted an even greater incentive for legislative reinforcement of traditional boundaries. Images of a "foreign invasion" and of the imposition of a foreign morality culminated in the ratification of the Eighteenth Amendment, which prohibited the manufacture and sale of alcoholic beverages. Enforcement of the law was limited and irregular. Producing changes in the alcohol consumption patterns of the urban immigrant, however, was not the thrust of the legislation. Rather, it was an attempt on the part of the Protestant middle classes to establish their way of life as morally superior. A legal victory would be symbolic of righteousness and would affirm the group's position of power. This law, then, was far more important in what it symbolized than in what it controlled. "Even if the law was broken, it was clear whose law it was" (Gusfield, 1967: 178).

The use of law to assert a particular morality represented an effort on the part of one group to confirm the superiority of its standards and values and the inferiority of the standards and values of a competing culture. The prohibitionary crusade, therefore, did not represent the generalized will of American society; it symbolized a growing competition between different cultural groups. In making this point, Gusfield distinguishes between *repentant deviation* and *enemy deviation.*

The *repentant deviant* is one whose misbehavior can best be described as a temporary lapse from morality. For example, the speeding driver who admits that speeding is dangerous, the homosexual who visits a psychiatrist in search of a cure of the "disease," and the murderer whose confession of guilt is filled with remorse are all repentant deviants. By displaying guilt and shame for the transgression, the deviant affirms the right of society to attempt to control the behavior in question. Repentance, then, is a product of agreement between the nonconformist and the society concerning established norms.

Society's major institutions are responsible for socializing its members to established boundaries so that people from varying subgroups will come to share common standards. Definitions of acceptable moral conduct are diffused through the family, religion, education, law, economy, and government. As persons participate in these institutions, they acquire the values and motives necessary for the maintenance of politically engineered boundaries. As the Marxists have pointed out, institutions are relatively successful in generating a common, though often false, consciousness among group members independent of their objective positions in society. Thus, the staunchest advocates of the present social order can be found among groups sharing least in the reward system. Workers may defend a production system that exploits their labor; blacks may defer to whites, thus supporting the claim of whites to racial superiority; and women may be found among the most vociferous opponents to equality of the sexes. When social institutions are successful in diffusing a common morality, people who deviate from the established standards feel repentant about their behavior.

In pluralistic societies, however, there may also be groups which maintain values and standards opposed to legislated morality. Gusfield calls this *enemy deviation,* which is characterized by a refusal to recognize the legitimacy of the law or society's enforcement of it. In this instance, the deviant's behavior is guided by an alternate normative order. Thus, members of "street-corner society" (Whyte, 1943) view gambling at cards or shooting dice as respectable, just as, for example, many corporate executives view antitrust law violations as respectable. Since gambling has become part of the culture of the lower classes, the validity of public standards regarding gambling is called into question (Gusfield, 1967).

> The publicly defined deviant is [not] . . . repentant . . . but is instead an upholder of an opposite norm. He accepts his behavior as proper and derogates the public norm as illegitimate. . . . The threat to the middle class in the increased political power of Cornerville is not that the Cornerville resident will gamble more; he already does gamble with great frequency. The threat is that the law will come to accept the morality of gambling and treat it as a legitimate business. If this happens, Boston is no longer a city dominated by middle-class Yankees but becomes one dominated by lower-class immigrants. [Gusfield, 1967: 181–182]

When there is no repentance, boundaries are called into question rather than confirmed. The state must act swiftly and punitively to indicate its intolerance of the behavior in question. Moral campaigns and criminalization of unacceptable activities (Erikson, 1966; Gusfield, 1967) are among the means used by powerful interests to assert their moral integrity in the face of enemy deviation.

The more recent antipornography campaign (Zurcher, et al., 1971) parallels closely the findings reported in Gusfield's study. The members of Interdenominational Citizens' Council for Decency, Inc., and Uprising for Decency, two antipornography movements, perceived pornography as a widespread threat to the traditional norms to which they stood committed.

> The mass media, especially television and movies, reminded them that the "now generation" or the "counter-culture" was becoming more widespread, more prestigeful. Traditional attitudes toward sexual behavior, religion, patriotism, war and so on were felt to be threatened—as were those whose life style incorporated the attitudes. [Zurcher et al., 1971: 222]

Antipornography supporters saw society and themselves in the midst of a moral crisis. The erosion of their values was perceived to be a product of such sinister forces as communism and organized crime operating in concert with the weak-willed liberals.

The legislative changes produced by antipornography campaigns were again more symbolic than enforced. As one member of the movement observed, "Maybe that bookstore will stay open, but the decent people in this town have gone on record about how they feel, and what they can do if they want to, and everybody knows it" (Zurcher et al., 1971: 231). The antipornography campaign, like the American Temperance Movement, was a symbolic crusade.

> By their mobilization for action, citizens concerned with threats to their accustomed life style, to the "basic values" which they cherished, were able to express status discontent, to impel community action, to attract the status-enhancing attention of "important" local and national leaders, and in general by status politics to demonstrate publicly and at least symbolically that their style of life was dominant, prestigeful and not at all powerless. [Zurcher et al., 1971: 233]

This point becomes even more visible in analyses of the role of political leadership in establishing governance standards. In an effort to assert sociopolitical boundaries, systems may demarcate their limits by defining portions of the population as criminal. An instance of the political manufacture of deviance is the Stalinist purge of 1936–1938 (Connor, 1972). In an attempt to secure what he perceived to be a faltering leadership, Stalin launched a series of persecutions that turned millions of Soviet citizens into criminals. The victims, who were defined as political saboteurs, were recruited from the entire spectrum of social classes and occupations.

It is arguable that the purge in fact resulted in a redefinition of Soviet society's behavioral boundaries . . . by making clear to those who remained the degree of political dissent that would be regarded as tolerable (nil), and the degree of personal security one might expect (relatively little) even if one were performing a responsible job to the best of one's abilities. The purge defined boundaries which held to the end of the Stalin era. [Connor, 1972: 412]

Stalin's use of the population as the raw material for boundary maintenance appears to have been deliberate and calculated. Perhaps less conscious, though not less damaging, instances of this phenomenon have occurred in U.S. history. Extralegal executions of alleged black offenders by Southern white vigilantes following the Civil War is a case in point (Inverarity, 1976).

United by a common hatred of blacks and a distrust of the North, the South emerged from the Reconstruction Period with a solidarity that cut across class lines. During the 1870s and 1880s, however, declining agricultural prices and restricted credit caused many members of the Southern white lower classes to join with farmers throughout the United States in a series of political movements intended to remedy their situation. Among the organizations that developed in this period was the Populist Party, which became a distinct political force that directly confronted the myth of the Solid South and thereby seriously jeopardized Southern white cohesiveness. As Populist activities increasingly threatened to disrupt the traditions of the South, the frequency of black lynchings increased (see Figure 2–4). Populism reached its peak in Louisiana, for example, between the years of 1892 and 1896. During this period, Louisiana had an average of thirteen lynchings every year. In the election years of 1892, 1894, and 1896, when the Populist threat to white solidarity was most apparent, the average number climbed to seventeen per year. By comparison, as Populism declined from 1897 to 1918 there was a yearly average of five lynchings (Inverarity, 1976: 268). Furthermore, violence against blacks was successful as a source of cohesiveness, as measured by local voting patterns—Louisiana parishes with higher lynching rates showed a greater percent of anti-Populist vote (Inverarity, 1976: 275).

## CONCLUSION

The research discussed in this chapter has shown the importance of nonconformity in maintaining social boundaries. However, it has also suggested that these boundaries are not always consensually derived. Unlike small groups, large social systems are not only characterized by

**FIGURE 2–4   Frequency of Lynching in Louisiana, 1889–1900**

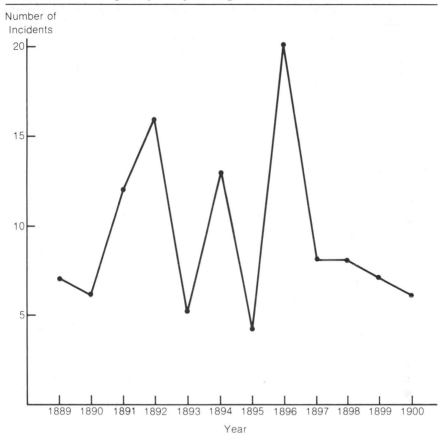

Source: James M. Inverarity, "Populism and Lynching in Louisiana," *ASR,* Vol. 41, 1976, Figure 1 on p. 267 *only.*

cultural diversity but also by political organization. The norms and values of groups that have access to legislative and law enforcement agencies constitute the official morality of the social system. It is these standards that are represented in the various institutions of social control and for which the boundary maintenance functions of deviance are employed.

Nonconformity, whether politically or consensually defined, calls attention to the range of behavior that will be tolerated. Through repeated tests of these boundaries, norms and values are reaffirmed and internal cohesion strengthened. In a crisis, when established standards are called into question, the system may respond by increased recruitment of individuals into deviant roles. Heretics, witches, alcoholics, traitors, blacks, and others come to represent the strength of the system in its attack against the enemy while, at the same time, they validate the virtue of religiousness, abstinence, loyalty, or white supremist beliefs.

## REFERENCES

Benedict, Ruth
  1934   Patterns of Culture. Boston: Houghton Mifflin.
Bensman, Joseph, and Israel Gerver
  1963   Crime and Punishment in the Factory: The Functions of Deviancy in Maintaining the Social System. American Sociological Review 28 (August): 588–598.
Chambliss, William J.
  1976   Functional and Conflict Theories of Crime: The Heritage of Émile Durkheim and Karl Marx. In Whose Law, What Order? William J. Chambliss and Milton Mankoff, eds. New York: John Wiley and Sons.
Connor, Walter D.
  1972   The Manufacture of Deviance: The Case of the Soviet Purge, 1936–1938. American Sociological Review 37 (August): 403–413.
Dentler, Robert A., and Kai T. Erikson
  1959   The Functions of Deviance in Groups. Social Problems 7 (Fall): 98–107.
Devereux, George
  1937   Institutionalized Homosexuality of the Mohave Indians. Human Biology 9 (December): 498–527.
Durkheim, Émile
  1904   The Rules of Sociological Method. Sarah A. Solovay and John H. Mueller, trans. George E. G. Catlin, ed. New York: Macmillan, 1938.
Erikson, Kai T.
  1966   Wayward Puritans: A Study in the Sociology of Deviance. New York: John Wiley and Sons.
Gusfield, Joseph
  1967   Moral Passage: The Symbolic Process in Public Designations of Deviance. Social Problems 15 (Fall): 175–188.
Harris, Anthony R.
  1977   Sex and Theories of Deviance: Toward a Functional Theory of Deviant Type-Scripts. American Sociological Review 42 (February): 3–16.
Homans, George C.
  1950   The Human Group. New York: Harcourt, Brace and World.
Inverarity, James
  1976   Populism and Lynching in Louisiana, 1889–1896: A Test of Erikson's Theory of the Relationship between Boundary Crises and Repressive Justice. American Sociological Review 41 (April): 262–280.
Lauderdale, Pat
  1976   Deviance and Moral Boundaries. American Sociological Review 41 (August): 660–676.

Levy, Robert I.
    1971   The Community Function of Tahitian Male Transvestism: A Hypothesis. Anthropological Quarterly 44 (January): 12–21.
Mead, George Herbert
    1918   The Psychology of Punitive Justice. American Journal of Sociology 23 (March): 577–602.
Whyte, William F.
    1943   Street Corner Society. Chicago: University of Chicago Press.
Zurcher, Louis A., Jr., R. George Kirkpatrick, Robert G. Cushing, and Charles K. Bowman
    1971   The Anti-Pornography Campaign: A Symbolic Crusade. Social Problems 19 (Fall): 217–238.

# 3

# Definitional Processes in the Creation of Deviance

We have seen that from a functionalist perspective deviant behavior is necessary to a social system. By identifying offenders and emphasizing the threat they pose for society, the system both unites group members and reaffirms established norms and values. It has been argued, therefore, that societies organize in such a way as to promote and maintain certain amounts of nonconformity. In this chapter, we expand this argument by focusing on the nature of the social processes by which deviance is created.

Since human behavior has no intrinsic valuation, the distinction between deviance and conformity must be constructed. This is accomplished through a definitional process that makes certain activities recognizable instances of deviance. Gossip, ridicule, social ostracism, and official sanction are the means by which these definitions are assigned. Once behavior is said to fall beyond the limits of social acceptability, the strategies invoked to deal with the transgression may actually ensure its persistence. That is, if individuals are defined as deviant, they may be excluded from opportunities for adopting legitimate roles. Thus, the very organizations given official responsibility to control deviance—the police, the courts, and the various treatment and correctional agencies—perpetuate disvalued behavior.

## SOCIAL DEFINITIONS AND THE CONSTRUCTION OF REALITY

Individuals occupy a socially constructed environment as well as a physical one. That is, unlike other animals, human beings attach meaning to the world around them. This meaning is assigned through the social definition. For example, a house, as a physical entity, is a place of residence. Beyond this, houses have a symbolic, or definitional, meaning that is conveyed in the word *home*. The *social reality* of a home, with its connotations of familial ties, acceptance, and security, far transcends whatever physical properties it may have. Similarly classrooms, desks, and textbooks, as objects, have shape and substance. As social constructs, they symbolize the relationship between student and teacher, the behaviors expected of each, and the general cultural value placed on education. Through sustained interaction, individuals come to share common definitions, which are communicated intergenerationally.

## The Social Reality of Deviance

The definitional, symbolic nature of social reality has important implications for deviance and social control. The history of mental illness and the development of mental hospitals in the United States is a case in point (Rothman, 1971). Before the Civil War, mental illness was said to be an organic disease. Its cause, however, was thought to be found in the very organization of society. It was believed that excessive mobility and ambition resulted in overstriving and stress, which led ultimately to mental disorder. U.S. society

> lacked all points of stability. Americans frenetically pursued wealth and power and knowledge without concern for their effects. Imagine a film of a steeplechase race presented at several times its normal speed. Almost simultaneously one rider jumps over a barrier while another skirts a creek, a third topples on a row of hedges and a fourth dashes down the stretch, all moving at breakneck speed. Such was the critic's perspective on Jacksonian society. [Rothman, 1971: 119]

The diffusion of this view was accompanied by a considerable expanson of the medical definition of mental illness. Any behavior could be interpreted as symptomatic of disease given the context of the patient's life. As concern over the disorganizing effect of society mounted, so did the ranks of the mentally ill.

Large-scale social reorganization was impossible; but, although the frantic pace of life could not be remedied, a model environment could be made available to the disturbed. Institutions, characterized by an "orderly, regular, and disciplined routine" would allow physicians to remove their patients from the corrupting influence of the community. Such an environment would also promote reform by demonstrating to society the benefits of order and routine. "Thus, medical superintendents and laymen supporters moved to create a new world for the insane, one that would not only alleviate their distress but also educate the citizens of the republic. The product of this effort was the insane asylum" (Rothman, 1971: 129).

This account of Jacksonian society illustrates the role played by the definition of the situation in the construction of social reality. In response to a popular conception that mental illness was a product of the social disorganization of the period, a most powerful institution of social control—the mental hospital—emerged.

## Parameters of Deviance Categories

Since definitions of deviance are socially constructed, they vary from culture to culture and time to time. No behaviors are universally condemned. Although proscriptions against incest, theft, and murder may be found throughout the world, what is considered to fall within the definitional limits, or parameters, of these proscriptions is highly variable. In some societies, for example, personal insult may be a legitimate reason to take another's life. Further, whether euthanasia and abortion are recognized as homicide depends upon the particular social system and the particular time.

Many of these normative distinctions are written into law. Thus, in the United States, bloodletting in war, in self-defense, or during psychotic episodes is *officially* excused from criminal sanction. In addition, definitions of deviance include implicit parameters that may affect their application. Chambliss and Seidman (1971: 82) illustrate this point in their discussion of the statute that forbids sleeping in public transportation facilities. The behavior proscribed is clearly discernable, and the statute creates no distinction among kinds of offenders. In practice, however, certain types of sleeping and sleepers may be considered more reprehensible than others. The sleep of a homeless, poorly dressed, unshaved, middle-aged male more clearly violates the implicit meaning of the law than that of the neatly attired business executive awaiting a commuter train. That the behaviors of each are identical may be less relevant than their relationships to the *implicit* parameters of the statute. These parameters are taken for granted among legal representatives and laypersons alike.

The definitional processes that lead to the creation of deviance categories, as well as their explicit and implicit parameters, are ongoing. Boundaries are expanded or contracted in such a way that formerly deviant behaviors are redefined as acceptable and previously acceptable activities are proscribed. Cigarette smoking, for example, was once the exclusive perogative of men. The use of tobacco by women was disvalued, and women who smoked were viewed as immoral. It was not until World War II that smoking became acceptable for both sexes. In more recent years, the use of tobacco has once again been disvalued, this time for both sexes, because of the health hazards it presents. As alternative social realities emerge and norms and values are altered, definitions of deviance change accordingly.

## The Cultural Parameters of Homicide: A Case Study

The United States Penal Code specifies that "a person is guilty of criminal homicide if he purposely, knowingly, recklessly or negligently causes the death of another human being. Criminal homicide is murder, manslaughter or negligent homicide." A fatal argument between friends following a Saturday evening of drinking would leave little doubt as to the applicability of this statute. Fatal bodily harm, however, may just as easily be a product of dangerous factory conditions, polluted air, or unsafe motor vehicles as of bullet wounds, knifings, or beatings. The latter fall clearly within the cultural meaning of criminal homicide; the former do not. The distinction is not legal but definitional. There are no statutory exemptions from criminal responsibility accorded those whose damages to human life occur within the context of the manufacture and sale of consumables. Rather, they have enjoyed *de facto* exemption. A definitional bias has existed that distinguishes among behaviors whose consequences are essentially the same.

Occasionally, cultural definitions of crime change. Parameters are expanded or contracted, and behaviors are realigned relative to the new limits. Criminal homicide is undergoing such a reevaluation. Activities once defined as solely within the purview of administrative enforcement have been identified as falling with the jurisdiction of criminal procedure. On September 13, 1978, a county grand jury in Elkhart, Indiana, indicted Ford Motor Company for three counts of reckless homicide and one count of criminal recklessness.[1] The charges stemmed from the death of three teen-age girls who suffered fatal burns when their Ford Pinto burst into flames following a low-speed, rear-end collision. This action, unique in the history of U.S. jurisprudence,[2] was the culmination of a series of definitional changes that occurred in the eight-year period following the car's introduction to the automotive market.

**Corporate Homicide: The Emergence of the Criminal Definition.**  Until the Highway Safety Act of 1966, automobile defects fell largely within the purview of manufacturer and implied warranties. The *manufacturer's warranty* is an agreement designed to protect consumers against defects of specified parts of the automobile. *Implied warranties* are additional protections provided the purchaser by the courts: if it is determined that a product has caused injuries because it is not reasonably suited for its intended use and purpose, then an implied warranty has been breached and damages may be recovered from the manufacturer. With the growing popularity of this doctrine of strict liability, injured persons have been able in recent years to collect damages by demonstrating that the product was defective at the time it left the manufacturer. They have not had to prove that the manufacturer was negligent or indicate when the defect became a problem. The reasoning behind the theory of strict liability is that the manufacturer who profits from the sale of the product should also be liable for any defects that result in injury to others.

Both types of warranty require that the purchaser identify product defects. The 1966 Highway Safety Act, however, shifted the focus of responsibility by stating that, upon discovering flaws either in design or production, a manufacturer was bound to notify individual owners and to recall the automobile for correction. All attending costs were to be borne by the manufacturer. The National Traffic Highway Safety Administration was created to oversee enforcement of the act.

The debut of the Ford Pinto occurred within this stricter context of regulatory liability. Within a month of its appearace, the 26,000 early production models were recalled for an accelerator linkage problem. Before the end of its first year, all 220,000 cars were recalled, this time to correct a defect in a pollution control device that had resulted in engine compartment fires. It was not until December 30, 1976, however, that the automobile's fuel tank was brought to public attention in a *Washington Post* syndicated column. Columnists Jack Anderson and Les Whitten alleged that:

> Buried in secret files of the Ford Motor Company lies evidence that big auto makers have put profits ahead of lives. Their lack of concern has caused thousands of people to die or be horribly disfigured in fiery car crashes. Undisclosed Ford tests have demonstrated that the big auto makers could have made safer automobiles by spending a few dollars more on each car. [*Washington Post*, December 30, 1976: 137]

The newspaper's accounts of the Pinto from the appearance of this commentary until the 1978 indictment reflect an emerging definition of criminality. The increased attention accorded the automobile and an escalated concern with issues of danger, intent, and civil and criminal liability demonstrate the definitional transition.

The cells in Table 3–1 show the number of article lines devoted to Pinto's problem fuel system over time and the corresponding frequency

**TABLE 3–1   Newsworthiness of the Pinto and the Vocabulary of Deviance**

| Newsworthiness | | | Content Categories | | | | | | | |
|---|---|---|---|---|---|---|---|---|---|---|
| Trimester | Article Lines | | Danger | | Intent | | Civil Liability | | Criminal Liability | |
| | n | % | n | % | n | % | n | % | n | % |
| I (12–30–76 to 7–25–77) | 68 | (6) | 6 | (8) | 3 | (9) | 0 | — | 0 | — |
| II (7–26–77 to 2–18–78) | 338 | (30) | 16 | (22) | 12 | (38) | 2 | (12) | 13 | (39) |
| III (2–19–78 to 9–14–78) | 708 | (64) | 51 | (70) | 17 | (53) | 15 | (88) | 20 | (61) |
| Total | 1,114 | | 73 | | 32 | | 17 | | 33 | |

with which a vocabulary of deviance appears in those lines. During the first trimester of the period December 30, 1976, through September 14, 1978, a total of sixty-eight lines were devoted to the Pinto fuel tank. The vocabulary of these reports is one implying danger and intent. Consumers are warned of potential impact explosions, and incidences of burn deaths and injuries are recounted. Allegations are made that the manufacturer had been fully aware of the hazards of the vehicle and had willfully failed to make corrections in order to protect profits.

The second trimester saw a dramatic 500 percent increase in the newsworthiness of the Pinto, with 338 column lines focused on the issue. It was during this period that the manufacturer was first described in terms of civil and criminal liability. Two events appear to have been particularly important in shaping the emergent vocabulary: publication of an expose charging Ford Motor Company with deliberately endangering the public and a spectacular punitive award to a Pinto burn victim.

The expose, allegedly based on documents obtained from Ford, appeared in the Fall 1977 issue of *Mother Jones*, a West Coast publication. Summarized by the *Post* in several consecutive news releases, the article charged that Ford Motor Company had, for a period of six years, sold cars whose fuel tanks company officials knew to be designed in such a way that they ruptured on impact. The author, Mark Dowie, claimed that between 500 and 900 burn deaths had resulted from explosions caused by such ruptured fuel tanks. Dowie further alleged that, in order to speed production and save costs, the company had ignored tests indicating that the car was dangerous.

Following publication of this article, the U.S. Transportation Department began an investigation of all subcompact cars for possible vulnerability to gasoline tank fires. An initial survey by this agency revealed that, between 1975 and 1977, twenty-six Pintos were involved in fires that took thirty-five lives. Consumer advocate Ralph Nader brought increasing public attention to the controversy by charging Ford with "corporate callousness" and demanding that the vehicle be recalled immediately. In May 1978, the National Traffic Highway Safety Administration announced it had determined that a safety defect did exist in the fuel systems of the 1.9 million Pintos produced from 1970 through 1976. Ford was ordered to recall the cars for corrective repairs in June.

At the same time that the federal regulatory agency was investigating the possible hazards of the automobile, news reports indicated that civil action was also being brought against its manufacturer. An estimated twenty to fifty civil suits were reportedly pending against Ford for damages suffered by Pinto owners. The largest and most publicized court settlement involved the case of Richard Grimshaw. In 1973, the thirteen-year-old boy suffered burns over 95 percent of his body when the Pinto in which he was a passenger was struck from behind and exploded. The seven-month trial revealed that the explosion was a product of faulty welding, which caused the gas tank to become punctured. Ignited gasoline leaked into the passenger compartment, killing the driver and severely burning the child. In what his attorney described as the "loudest noise that the jury has made in any civil suit in American jurisprudence" (*Washington Post*, February 8, 1978: A22), the court awarded $2.841 million for personal compensation and an unsolicited $125 million in punitive damages to the litigant.[3] In order to award punitive damages, it is necessary to establish intentional injury or negligence so gross as to amount to intetional injury. In the Grimshaw decision, the jury found that Ford should not only be held responsible for the boy's personal suffering, but for "willful disregard for the safety of consumers" (*Washington Post*, February 15, 1978: A2).

The attention accorded the Pinto continued to escalate throughout the third trimester, with column lines increasing by more than 100 percent. In addition, substantial increases may be seen in the frequency with which the vocabulary of deviance enters the news accounts.[4] During this period the court awarded a seven-year-old boy $600,000 in damages after he was burned and his parents killed in the fiery rear-end collision of the Pinto in which they were traveling. Counsel for the child argued before the court that Ford had "deliberately failed to warn consumers of the pontential dangers of the . . . [fuel] tank and had made a decision to accept deaths and injuries rather than correct the defect" (*Washington Post*, August 25, 1978: A3).

Diffusion of the emergent definition of willful harm was also evidenced by events in the public sector. Oregon removed hundreds of Pintos from state service in April 1978. Likewise, the Pacific Northwest Telephone Company sold its fleet. In each case, protection of employees and fear of damage suits were cited as the reasons. The United States General Services Administration, too, saw need to eliminate the potential hazards associated with the Pinto and withdrew 300 of the vehicles from the federal motor pool. In August, the press reported that the American Trial Lawyers Association had issued an appeal to Ford to recall all of the cars, while class-action suits in both Alabama and California sought relief for all owners of Pintos, which had come to be viewed as "negligently designed and engineered so that they [were] dangerously vulnerable" (*New York Times*, April 21, 1978: D13).

The successful application of the vocabulary of criminal liability depends upon the extent to which the harm produced by the corporation is *like* the harm associated with conventional criminality. Traditionally, the harmful activities of corporations and those of conventional criminals have been defined as involving very different consequences. Corporate misbehavior has been viewed as entailing a diffuse, impersonal cost to society. Price fixing, false advertising, and mislabeling, for example, have been perceived to increase financial burdens on the consumer. This kind of injury differs dramatically from the intensely personal harm threatened by the robber, rapist, or murderer. Thus, social definitions of harm provide important distinctions between, for example, air and water pollution on the one hand and assault and battery on the other. Before injurious activities of corporations can be recognized as conventional crime, the social harms produced by those activities must be recognized as conventional harms. In the case of Pinto, this seems to have been accomplished through a *personalization of harm*. Throughout the period preceding the indictment, attention to the in-

**TABLE 3–2  Personalization of Harm Associated
with the Pinto Fuel Tank**

| Trimester | Lines Devoted to Machine Defects | | Lines Devoted to Personal Harm | | Total |
|---|---|---|---|---|---|
| | n | % | n | % | n |
| I (12–30–76 to 7–25–77) | 8 | (57) | 6 | (43) | 14 |
| II (7–26–77 to 2–18–78) | 39 | (46) | 45 | (54) | 84 |
| III (2–19–78 to 9–14–78) | 31 | (38) | 50 | (62) | 81 |

juries and deaths of Pinto burn victims increased and attention to the consumer issue of product defect decreased. Thus, during the first trimester, the fuel system was discussed in eight (57 percent) news lines, while descriptions of human injuries were found in six (43 percent). By the third trimester, 38 percent of the lines (thirty-one lines) were devoted to the automobile's defects, and 62 percent (50 lines) to accounts of personal harm. This public recognition of personal harm, we suggest, was ultimately reflected in the Elkhart grand jury's decision that the Pinto-related deaths of three Indiana teenagers were *like* homicide.

Definitions of deviance are shaped not only by public reaction but also by the responses attributed to the deviant. An important dimension of this response is whether the deviant is perceived to be repentant or nonrepentant. As we have seen in the preceding chapter, the nonrepentant, or enemy, deviant refuses to acknowledge having breached a norm. In this failure to legitimize the norm, the actor intensifies public resentment and opens the way for formal designation as deviant (Gusfield, 1967).

Accounts of Ford Motor Company's response to the problems of the Pinto fuel tank were virtually absent from media reports until the second trimester (see Table 3–3). From this time through the period of indictment, Ford is consistently depicted as refusing to acknowledge the problems or to accept responsibility. Only 18 percent of the references to the corporation's response attributed repentance to the automobile manufacturer. Illustrative of these accounts is a reported assertion of Henry Ford that "the lawyers would shoot me for saying this, but I think there is some cause for concern about the car. I don't even listen to the cost figures—we've got to fix it. . . . The Pinto . . . recall campaign is a matter of great concern to Ford Motor Company and

**TABLE 3–3  Media Accounts of the Corporate Response**

| References to Repentance | | | | References to Nonrepentance | | | | Total |
|---|---|---|---|---|---|---|---|---|
| Trimester | By Self | | By Others | | By Self | | By Others | | |
| | n | % | n | % | n | % | n | % | n |
| I (12–30–76 to 7–25–77) | 0 | — | 0 | — | 0 | — | 1 | (100) | 1 |
| II (7–26–77 to 2–18–78) | 0 | — | 0 | — | 13 | (81) | 3 | (19) | 16 |
| III (2–19–78 to 9–14–78) | 5 | (22) | 2 | (9) | 12 | (52) | 4 | (17) | 23 |

to me personally" (*Washington Post*, August 26, 1978: D8). The great majority of accounts during the second and third trimesters (82 percent), however, depicted Ford as rejecting a definition of harm and liability. For example, in the same news article that reported Ford's claim of "personal and corporate concern," a quotation from Ralph Nader stated that "this is the first expression of concern that Henry Ford has made regarding the Pinto fuel tank problem since 1971" (*Washinton Post*, August 26, 1978: D8).

The corporation's unwillingness to acknowledge the seriousness of the issue is also depicted in accounts of Ford's public statements regarding the punitive damages awarded in the Grimshaw settlement and the Elkhart, Indiana, grand jury's request for the testimony of Henry Ford II and former president Lee Iacocca. In the first instance, a Ford official was quoted as saying that the verdict was so "unreasonable and unwarranted" that it would be appealed (*Washington Post*, February 15, 1978: A2). Regarding the indictment hearings, the corporation reportedly announced that "the needs of the grand jury can be met by the appearance of other company personnel and . . . it will not be necessary for Mr. Ford or Mr. Iacocca to appear" (*Washington Post*, September 8, 1978: F2). In a subsequent report, Ford is described as having "resisted efforts to have high company executives come to Indiana to testify about the company's knowledge of the possible fuel tank problem" (*Washinton Post*, September 14, 1978: C1). In its decision to contest civil suits and resist the grand jury's request for its highest officials to testify, the corporation refused to recognize that it had transgressed moral boundaries. This opened the way for the manufacturer to be defined as a force against whom the power of the law *must* be directed.

The emergent themes of deviance, personalization of harm, and nonrepentance were soon to culminate in a precedent-making action. The Elkhart, Indiana indictment of September 13, 1978, officially recognized a new public harm—homicide by a corporation.[5] After three days of deliberation, the grand jury determined that a crime had been committed and that Ford Motor Company was to be tried as the responsible party. The applicability of the criminal definition was based on evidence that the manufacturer had consciously decided to proceed with production in spite of its awareness of the fuel tank problem. This decision, the jury maintained, was based on a cost-benefit analysis. Officials at Ford predicted the number of severe burn injuries and deaths that would result from the defect and estimated that the cost of repairing the car would exceed anticipated court settlements. This profit strategy was seen as evidence of the willfullness and intentionality of the corporate action, themes that were already central to the emergent public vocabulary. Once the company policy had been defined in these terms, the indictment became possible.

# Pinto Madness

*Mark Dowie*

The next time you drive behind a Pinto (with over two million of them on the road, you shouldn't have much trouble finding one), take a look at the rear end. That long silvery object hanging down under the bumper is the gas tank. The tank begins about six inches forward of the bumper. In late models the bumper is designed to withstand a collision of only about five miles per hour. Earlier bumpers may as well not have been on the car for all the protection they afforded the gas tank.

*Mother Jones* has studied hundreds of reports and documents on rear-end collisions involving Pintos. These reports conclusively reveal that if you ran into that Pinto you were following at over 30 miles per hour, the rear end of the car would buckle like an accordian, right up to the back seat. The tube leading to the gas-tank cap would be ripped away from the tank itself, and gas would immediately begin sloshing onto the road around the car. The buckled gas tank would be jammed up against the differential housing (that big bulge in the middle of your rear axle), which contains four sharp, protruding bolts likely to gash holes in the tank and spill still more gas. Now all you need is a spark from a cigarette, ignition, or scraping metal, and both cars would be engulfed in flames. If you gave that Pinto a really good wack—say, at 40 mph—chances are excellent that its doors would jam and you would have to stand by and watch its trapped passengers burn to death.

This scenario is no news to Ford. Internal company documents in our possession show that Ford has crash-tested the Pinto at a top-secret site more than 40 times and that *every* test made at over 25 mph without special structural alteration of the car has resulted in a ruptured fuel tank.... Eleven of these tests, averaging a 31-mph impact speed, came before Pintos started rolling out of the factories.... Despite this, Ford officials denied under oath having crash-tested the Pinto....

Lee Iacocca [then president of Ford] was fond of saying, "Safety doesn't sell." Heightening the anti-safety pressure on Pinto engineers was an important goal set by Iacocca known as "the limits of 2,000." The Pinto was not to weigh an ounce over 2,000 pounds and not to cost a cent over $2,000. "Iacocca enforced these limits with an iron hand," recalls ... [a Ford] engineer.... So, even when a crash test showed that [a] one-pound, one-dollar piece of plastic stopped the puncture of the gas tank, it was thrown out as extra cost and extra weight....

Stated in its simplest terms, cost-benefit analysis says that if the cost is greater than the benefit, the project is not worth it—no matter what the benefit. Examine the cost of every action, decision, contract part or change, the doctrine says, then carefully evaluate the benefits (in dollars) to be certain that they exceed the cost before you begin a program or—and this is the crucial part for our story—pass a regulation.

As a management tool in a business in which profits matter over everything else, cost-benefit analysis makes a certain amount of sense.

Serious problems come, however, when public officials who ought to have more than corporate profits at heart apply cost-benefit analysis to every conceivable decision. The inevitable result is that they must place a dollar value on human life.

Ever wonder what your life is worth in dollars? Perhaps $10 million? Ford has a better idea: $200,000. . . .

Ford had gotten the federal regulators to agree to talk auto safety in terms of cost-benefit analysis. But in order to be able to argue that various safety costs were greater than their benefits, Ford needed to have a dollar value figure for the "benefit." Rather than be so uncouth as to come up with such a price tag itself, the auto industry pressured the National Highway Traffic Safety Administration to do so. And in a 1972 report the agency decided a human life was worth $200,725. . . .

Furnished with this useful tool, Ford immediately went to work using it to prove why various safety improvements were too expensive to make.

Nowhere did the company argue harder that it should make no changes than in the area of rupture-prone fuel tanks. Not long after the government arrived at the $200,725-per-life figure, it surfaced, rounded off to a cleaner $200,000, in an internal Ford memorandum. This cost-benefit analysis argued that Ford should not make an $11-per-car improvement that would prevent 180 fiery deaths a year. (This minor change would have prevented gas tanks from breaking so easily both in rear-end collisions . . . and in rollover accidents, where the same thing tends to happen).

---

### $11 vs. a Burn Death

Benefits and Costs Relating to Fuel Leakage
Associated with the Static Rollover
Test Portion of FMVSS 208

## Benefits

*Savings:* 180 burn deaths, 180 serious burn injuries, 2,100 burned vehicles.
*Unit Cost:* $200,000 per death, $67,000 per injury, $700 per vehicle.
*Total Benefit:* $180 \times (\$200,000) + 180 \times (\$67,000) + 2,100 \times (\$700) = \$49.5$ million.

## Costs

*Sales:* 11 million cars, 1.5 million light trucks.
*Unit Cost:* $11 per car, $11 per truck.
*Total Cost:* $11,000,000 \times (\$11) + 1,500,000 \times (\$11) = \$137$ million.

From Ford Motor Company internal memorandum: "Fatalities Associated with Crash-Induced Fuel Leakage and Fires."

Ford's cost-benefit table [see figure] is buried in a seven-page company memorandum entitled "Fatalities Associated with Crash-Induced Fuel Leakage and Fires." The memo argues that there is no financial benefit in complying with proposed safety standards that would admittedly result in fewer auto fires, fewer burn deaths and fewer burn injuries. Naturally, memoranda that speak so casually of "burn deaths" and "burn injuries" are not released to the public. They are very effective, however, with Department of Transportation officials. . . .

All Ford had to do was to convince [the Transportation Department] . . . that certain safety standards would add so much to the price of cars that fewer people would buy them. This could damage the auto industry, which was still believed to be the bulwark of the American economy. "Compliance to these standards," Henry Ford II prophesied at more than one press conference, "will shut down the industry.". . .

So when J. C. Echold, Director of Automotive Safety (which means chief anti-safety lobbyist) for Ford, wrote to the Department of Transportation . . . he felt secure attaching a memorandum that in effect says it is acceptable to kill 180 people and burn another 180 every year, *even though we have the technology that could save their lives for $11 a car. . . .*

The original draft of the Automobile Safety Act [of 1966] provided for criminal sanction against a manufacturer who willfully placed an unsafe car on the market. Early in the proceedings the auto industry lobbied the provision out of the bill. Since then, there have been those damage settlements, of course, but the only government punishment meted out to the auto companies for non-compliance to standards has been a minuscule fine, usually $5,000 to $10,000. *One wonders how long the Ford Motor Company would continue to market lethal cars were Henry Ford II and Lee Iacocca serving 20-year terms in Leavenworth for consumer homicide.* [Emphasis added.]

Source: Mark Dowie, "Pinto Madness," *Mother Jones* 2 (September–October 1977): 20, 22, 24, 28, 32.

---

While the State of Indiana saw grounds to indict, the trial jury, after listening to ten weeks of testimony and deliberating three days, returned a verdict of not guilty. Opinions regarding the potential impact of the acquittal are mixed. As reported in the *National Law Journal* (Bodine, 1980: 3), the president of the National District Attorneys Association predicts more criminal prosecutions against corporations: "A psychological barrier has been broken, and the big corporations are now vulnerable." Conversely, P. A. Heinen, vice president and general counsel of the Chrysler Corporation in Detroit asserts in the same report: "I have a feeling we have peaked in the wave of attempts to pound away at the corporations in court."

Continuing legal actions would suggest, however, that the concept of corporate homicide may have become part of an enduring vocabulary of crime. Thus, on February 23, 1979, Norfolk and Western Railway Company was indicted in Delaware County, Indiana, on charges on reckless homicide (Clark, 1979: 920); and a three-count information in Toledo, Ohio, charging Conrail with aggravated vehicular homicide was also filed (Bodine, 1980: 3). In the legislature, Democratic representative George Miller of California and 41 cosponsors introduced a bill (H.R. 4973, July 26, 1979) to the Subcommittee on Crime of the House Judiciary Committee. The bill's sponsor introduced the legislation because of:

> " injuries and deaths allegedly resulting from asbestos production in New Jersey, corporate poisoning of water wells in California, use of the chemicals DBCP, kepone, and benzidene, production of the Firestone 500 tires and 'an alleged eight-year coverup by Ford of a design flaw in the sitting of the gas tank of Pinto automobiles. . . . These case histories describe a pattern of corporate behavior which cannot be tolerated.' " (Bodine, 1980: 17).

Revisions of state and federal penal codes to include corporations as criminal offenders, the indictment against Ford Motor Company and other major corporations, and legislative action intended to control activities perceived as dangerous suggest that the corporation, whose actions have traditionally been excluded from the cultural parameters of criminal homicide, no longer enjoys definitional immunity.

## COMMUNICATING DEFINITIONS OF DEVIANCE

W. I. Thomas explained that a child is born into a situation already bound by social definitions, "where he has not the slightest chance of making his [own] definitions and following his wishes without interference" (Thomas, 1923: 42). Reflecting Durkheim's formulation of the *collective conscience,* he suggested that these definitions are the accumulated norms and values of society. More specifically, they are the practical translations of these norms and values conveyed to the individual through the family and the community.

> As soon as the child has free motion and begins to pull, tear, pry, meddle, and prowl, the parents begin to define the situation through speech and other signs and pressures. "Be quiet," "Sit up straight," "Blow your nose," "Wash your face,", "Mind your mother," "Be kind to sister," etc. This is the real significance of Wordsworth's phrase, "Shades of the prison house begin to close upon the growing child." His wishes and activities begin to

be inhibited, and gradually, by definitions within the family, by playmates, in the school, in the Sunday school, in the community, through reading, by formal instruction, by informal signs of approval and disapproval, the growing member learns the code of his society." [Thomas, 1923: 43]

In the earlier, folk-oriented society, this process was especially effective. Since individuals were almost completely subordinate to the group, they more readily acquired the definitions that restrained their behavior. Thomas believed that the complexity, impersonality, and volatility of the modern world has tended to decrease individuals attachment to society. The cultural transmission of societal definitions, therefore, is never perfect. Thus, the way is open for the individual to act upon spontaneous definitions. If such action conflicts with established codes, it may be designated as deviant.

An informal but nonetheless powerful means of designating deviance is gossip, which fixes the position of the individual by attaching praise or blame. In this regard, the community often disgraces persons by using epithets—thief, whore, queer, crook, swindler, cheat, con artist, hoodlum, and the like—that serve as brief emotional definitions of the situation. If, for example, the word *whore* or *queer* is associated with an individual because of perceived sexual behavior, that individual will be viewed and treated accordingly by a large segment of the community. Thomas pointed out that "winks, shrugs, nudges, laughter, sneers, haughtiness, coldness, 'giving the once over' are also language defining the situation and painfully felt as unfavorable recognition" (Thomas, 1923: 50).

## The Self-Fulfilling Prophecy

Social definitions allow individuals to interpret their environment. They provide the *descriptions* and *evaluations* that lend meaning to situations. In addition, social definitions are *prescriptive*. That is, they serve to guide the way people act toward that which has been defined. It has been proposed, therefore, that if people "define situations as real, they are real in their consequences" (Merton, 1957: 421). This often-quoted statement of William Isaac Thomas has come to be known as the "Thomas theorem" of the *self-fulfilling prophecy.* In its simplest form, it means that predictions, or prophecies, can become true as a result of the individual and collective actions that follow from the definitions involved. If, therefore, an event is recognized as deviant, procedures deemed appropriate for that situation are invoked. These procedures may be ultimately responsible for the event's conforming to the definition of deviance that has been applied to it.

Building on Thomas's original idea, Robert K. Merton asserted that prophecies are such powerful social forces that they can shape reality regardless of whether they are built on a factual base. Merton used a hypothetical example to show how the rumor of financial insolvency led to hundreds of bank failures during the Depression:

> It is the year 1932. The Last National Bank is a flourishing institution. A large part of its resources is liquid without being watered. Cartwright Millingville has ample reason to be proud of the banking institution over which he presides. Until Black Wednesday. As he enters his bank, he notices that business is unusually brisk. A little odd, that, since the men at the A.M.O.K. steel plant and the K.O.M.A. mattress factory are not usually paid until Saturday. Yet here are two dozen men, obviously from the factories, queued up in front of the tellers' cages. As he turns into his private office, the president muses rather compassionately: "Hope they haven't been laid off in midweek. They should be in the shop at this hour."
>
> But speculations of this sort have never made for a thriving bank, and Millingville turns to the pile of documents upon his desk. His precise signature is affixed to fewer than a score of papers when he is disturbed by the absence of something familiar and the intrusion of something alien. The low discreet hum of bank business has given way to a strange and annoying stridency of many voices. A situation has been defined as real. And that is the beginning of what ends as Black Wednesday—the last Wednesday, it might be noted, of the Last National Bank.
>
> Cartwright Millingville had never heard of the Thomas Theorem. But he had no difficulty in recognizing its workings. He knew that, despite the comparative liquidity of the bank's assets, a rumor of insolvency, once believed by enough depositors, would result in the insolvency of the bank. And by the close of Black Wednesday—and Blacker Thursday—when the long lines of anxious depositors, each frantically seeking to salvage his own, grew to longer lines of even more anxious depositors, it turned out that he was right.
>
> The stable financial structure of the bank had depended upon one set of definitions of the situation: belief in the validity of the interlocking system of economic promises men live by. Once depositors had defined the situation otherwise, once they questioned the possibility of having these promises fulfilled, the consequences of this unreal definition were real enough. [Merton, 1957: 422]

Merton pointed out that a number of social phenomena can be similarly attributed to the self-fulfilling effects of a false definition. In particular, many aspects of the racial problem in the United States are predicated on prophecies of black inferiority. Thus, the widely held assumption that blacks are marginally educable has resulted in different educational policies for black schools. Poor facilities, understaffing, and low pay have obvious consequences for the quality of education offered to minority groups. This is ultimately reflected in "objective" measures of performance, and the prophecy is fulfilled. On the basis of such evidence the original policies are reaffirmed.

A similar process characterized black exclusion from the labor union movement. Acting on the stereotypic assumption that blacks could not be organized, the unions excluded them. When strikes did occur, blacks, as nonunion workers, became the logical source of strike-breaking employees. Once again, the prediction that blacks were inimical to unionization became the reality.

# A Prophecy Fulfilled

*Robert Rosenthal and Lenore Jacobson*

[A] patient suffering from advanced cancer . . . was admitted to the hospital virtually dying. He had been exposed to the information that Krebiozen might be a wonder drug, and it was administered to him. The improvement was dramatic and he was discharged to his home for several months. Then came exposure to the information that Krebiozen was probably ineffective. He relapsed and was readmitted to the hospital. There, his faith in Krebiozen was restored though the injections he received were of saline solution rather than of Krebiozen. Once again he was sufficiently improved to be discharged. Finally, he was exposed to the information that the American Medical Association denied completely the value of Krebiozen. The patient then lost all hope and was readmitted to the hospital, this time for the last time; he died within forty-eight hours.

Source: Robert Rosenthal and Lenore Jacobson, *Pygmalion in the Classroom: Teacher Expectation and Pupil Intellectual Development* (New York: Holt, Rinehart and Winston, 1968a), p. 14.

## Dramatization of Deviance Definitions

Once people have assigned meaning to a situation, their behavior and some of the consequences of that behavior are determined by it. Public definitions of a situation are prophecies that become an integral part of the situation and affect subsequent developments as well. An explicit application of these processes to the area of deviance was first offered by

Frank Tannenbaum (1938). According to Tannenbaum, the relationship between the community and the young nonconformer begins as a divergence of behavioral definitions. What to the child is "fun," "adventure," or "mischief" is often from the community's point of view "nuisance," "evil," or "delinquent" (Tannenbaum, 1938: 17). As the conflict increases, designating these specific *acts* as evil gradually shifts to designating the *child* as evil, so that all the acts come to be looked upon with suspicion.

> In the process of identification, his companions, hangouts, play, speech, income, all his conduct, the personality itself, become subject to scrutiny and question. From the community's point of view, the individual who used to do bad and mischievous things has now become a bad and unredeemable human being. From the individual's point of view there has taken place a similar change. He has gone slowly from a sense of grievance and injustice, of being unduly mistreated and punished, to a recognition that the definition of him as a human being is different from that of other boys in his neighborhood, his school, street, community. [Tannenbaum, 1938: 17]

Recognition of the community's definition influences the individual's self-concept and facilitates identification with and integration into a group that shares the disvalued activities. When this occurs—when persons become what they are described as being—the continuation of the deviant behavior is virtually assured. Youngsters become delinquent because they are defined as such.

The community's response to deviance may reflect its need for consistency in the character of its members. People cannot deal with those whom they cannot define. That is the underlying importance of personal reputation; it lets the collectivity position group members in such a way as to ease routine interaction. Once a person's reputation has been established, the various community forces—schools, church, businesses, and the like—combine to maintain that definition. Since the community cannot tolerate unpredictability, it organizes to ensure its predictions and thus increase its understanding and control of its members (Tannenbaum, 1938).

Tannenbaum pointed out that the successful application of a deviance definition is made possible by the dramatic nature of the community's response. "The verbalization of the conflict in terms of evil, delinquency, incorrigibility, badness, arrest, force, punishment, stupidity, lack of intelligence, truancy, criminality, gives the innocent divergence of the child from the straight road a meaning that it did not have in the beginning and makes its continuance in these same terms . . . so much the more inevitable" (Tannenbaum, 1938: 18). This *dramatization of evil* is an important determinant of subsequent behavior.

The transition from simple nonconformity to delinquency may occur through the drama associated with legal intervention. A child caught by the police is exposed to a series of events unshared by most other children. The personnel, procedures, and symbols associated with official intervention define this child as different from the rest of the group. He or she becomes the "center of a major drama" which renders nonconformist behavior sinister. Made conscious of being deviant, the child becomes aware that the world has changed and that in the new world he or she has a place very different from the one once occupied. "The process of making the criminal, therefore, is a process of tagging, defining, identifying, segregating, describing, emphasizing, making conscious and self conscious; it becomes a way of stimulating, suggesting, emphasizing, and evoking the very traits that are complained of" (Tannenbaum, 1938: 19–20).

The dramatization of evil ensures that the line between morality and immorality is clearly drawn (Matza, 1969). The performance of "evil" acts by persons who possess "good" qualities creates uncertainty regarding the appropriateness of negative sanction and, therefore, the firmness of behavioral boundaries. By casting the actor as the embodiment of deviance, that uncertainty is removed.

> To be signified as thief is to lose the blissful identity of one who among other things happens to have committed a theft. It is a movement, however gradual, toward being a thief and representing theft. The two movements are intimately related; without a population selected and cast as thieves, we might have to look elsewhere to comprehend . . . theft. [Matza, 1969: 156]

Dramatizing the evil of the actor and the behavior involves an escalation of deviance definitions. That is, nonconformity does not usually involve an abrupt transition from one state of being to another; it is more likely to result from a graduated process of increasing recognition. For example, in England the public designation of "debt defaulter" is the outcome of a series of definitions which convey graduated levels of deviance. Defining a debtor as deviant is made up of "deliberately staged phases" (Rock, 1968: 178), each designed to put more pressure on defaulters that, if ignored, brings them closer to a highly routinized designation as deviant. In this process, debt collectors have access to a system of courts and prisons to coerce the selected population; "their definitions receive authoritative approval from the state" (Rock, 1968: 177). Thus, "the debtor is serially an applicant, a debtor, a defaulter, a defendant and a prisoner" (Rock, 1968: 185). The critical factor in the sequence is not the behavior of the debtor but the definitions and actions of creditors, collection agencies, and legal officials.

# INSTITUTIONALIZED DEFINITIONS AS SELF-FULFILLING PROPHECIES

The responsibility for dealing with deviant populations has been assigned to the official institutions of social control, which are based on the assumption that people who engage in certain behaviors or possess specified characteristics should be treated, punished, or rehabilitated. To the extent that such definitions preclude alternative approaches to the situation, they are self-fulfilling. Thus, institutions of social control—the police, the courts, and the various treatment and correctional agencies—may actually facilitate the creation of deviance.

## The Spiraling Search for Witches

The processes by which institutional definitions create deviance may be seen in Elliott Currie's (1968) study of legal reaction to witchcraft in Renaissance Europe. The problem of witchcraft on the Continent differed considerably from the same problem in England. These differences were a product of the nature of the efforts to control the behavior in the respective legal systems.

Although statutes that forbade witchcraft existed prior to the fifteenth century, the activity was not regarded as a particularly serious offense. The laws were not often enforced, nor was the punishment severe. Witches were regarded simply as persons who worshipped idols and believed in their own supernatural abilities. During the fifteenth and sixteenth centuries, however, the witch became the object of redefinition. Witches were no longer seen as persons who had delusions of supernatural power but as persons who had indeed made pacts with the devil. These satanic contracts empowered them to employ the forces of evil for antisocial and un-Christian purposes. Thus, in 1484 Pope Innocent IV issued the following Bull affirming the reality and the seriousness of the crime.

> It has recently come to our attention not without bitter sorrow, that many persons of both sexes, unmindful of their own salvation and straying from the Catholic Faith, have abandoned themselves to devils ... and by their . . . accursed charms and crafts, enormities and horrid offenses, have slain unborn infants and the offspring of cattle, have blasted the produce of the earth. . . . These wretches furthermore afflict and torment men and women . . . with terrible and piteous pains. . . . Over and above this they blasphemously renounce the Faith which is theirs by the sacrament of Baptism, and do not shrink from committing and perpetrating the foulest abominations and filthiest excesses. [Currie, 1968: 10]

The theological and legal institutions, through such definitional proc-
lamations, officially created a new form of deviance. Witchcraft came to
be seen as responsible for virtually all social evils and disasters. It
became, in short, a crime to be "hunted down and suppressed" (Currie,
1968: 11).

While concern was universal, control of witchcraft varied dramatically. In continental Europe, an elaborate bureaucracy developed to
deal with the problem. Based on the procedures of the Spanish Inquisition of an earlier period, the new system found ample justification for
suspending procedural safeguards. "In the interest of maintaining the
ideological purity of Christendom," (Currie, 1968: 12) rules of evidence,
criteria for selecting witnesses, and laws on the use of torture ceased to
apply.

Confessions played an important part in the witch hunts of continental Europe. Not only was confessed guilt necessary to invoke the
death penalty, but it was useful in ensuring a steady flow of alleged accomplices to the court. Confessions were extracted through torture,
threats to leave the accused eternally damned through the denial of last
rites, and rarely kept promises of pardon. Guilt was further affirmed by
placing suspected witches in impossible dilemmas:

> If the accused was found to be in good repute among the populace, he or
> she was clearly a witch, since witches invariably sought to be highly
> thought of; if in bad repute, then he or she was clearly a witch, since no
> one approves of witches. If the accused was especially regular in worship
> or morals, it was argued that the worst witches made the greatest show of
> piety. Stubbornness in refusing to confess was considered a sure sign of
> alliance with the Devil, who was known to be taciturn. [Currie, 1968:
> 15–16]

A most important characteristic of the control of witches on the
Continent concerned the right of the court to confiscate their property.
"The chief consequence of this practice was to join to a system of virtually unlimited power a powerful motive for persecution" (Currie,
1968: 16).

In Renaissance England, which had no history of Inquisition, the
control of witchcraft took an entirely different form. Throughout the
period, English witch trials were characterized by restraint. Although
witchcraft was a capital crime punishable by death, the trials continued
to operate according to common-law principles. Most importantly, confiscation of property was not part of the prosecutory process. "As a consequence, unlike the continental authorities, the English officials had no
continuous vested interest in the discovery and conviction of witches"
(Currie, 1968: 20).

These variations affected the character of the problem in the two regions. "On the Continent, the convergence of a repressive control system with a powerful economic motive created something very much like a large-scale industry based on . . . mass stigmatization . . . and the confiscation of property" (Currie, 1968: 21). The control of witches created jobs for a significant portion of the population. In order to sustain the industry a steady income was required. The confiscation of property provided well for this economic need. Like any economic system, that based on the control of witches required an ever-expanding base of recruits. "Through the use of torture to extract names of accomplices from the accused, legitimate new suspects became available" (Currie, 1968: 22). The economy of the continental approach also had implications for the kinds of people selected for prosecution. Because of the material advantage they could provide, men and women of wealth and property were most frequently accused.

> The mass nature of the witchcraft industry, the high number of witches in Europe, and the upper-income character of a sufficient portion of them were all due to the lack of restraints on court procedure—especially, of the systematic use of torture—coupled with the legal authority to confiscate property, which added material interest to unrestrained control. [Currie, 1968: 23]

In Renaissance England, on the other hand, because there were no continuous vested interests in the persecution of witches and because common law restrained the conduct of witch trials, there were fewer witches, weaker attempts to control witchcraft, and fewer executions of persons accused of the crime. The English had neither an interest in nor the power necessary for manufacturing deviance.

Witchcraft in Renaissance Europe became what officials designated it to be. The self-fulfilling effects of its definition and control on the Continent are especially clear. As more witches came to the attention of authorities, more extreme measures became justified. Further relaxation of procedural safeguards with regard to torture, confessions, and evidence of guilt continued, in this spiraling manner, to reveal more and more evidence of their prevalence. The nature and extent of witchcraft in Renaissance Europe, therefore, may be viewed as self-fulfilling effects of the society's attempt to deal with it systematically.

## Criminal Definitions in the Legal Process

The idea that institutionalized procedures to control deviance may produce deviant behavior has a more contemporary manifestation. In particular, prophecies concerning the tendency of certain portions of the population to lives of lawlessness may underlie the crime rates generated in support of such beliefs.

Official statistics on violent crimes, for example, indicate that the majority of individuals arrested for such offenses are male, lower class, and black. Based on this observation, many social scientists and laypersons have concluded that violence is a predictable pattern among these segments of the population. A question should be raised, however, regarding the extent to which official decision-makers rely on such definitions in their determinations of criminality.

On the other hand, women are generally perceived to be less capable of violence than men. Therefore, females arrested for violent crimes are more likely to be acquitted or found guilty of reduced offenses (Swigert and Farrell, 1976, 1977). The leniency with which they are treated gives further support to the original belief. The effects of this definition of women are most evident in the legal reaction to intersexual offenses (Farrell and Swigert, 1978b). Since women do not conform to the stereotype of the violent criminal, their sex is a mitigating factor when they are the accused and an aggravating condition when they are the victims. If a male kills another male, there may be a serious question of provocation on the part of the victim; both are viewed as equally capable of aggression. If a male murders a female, however, she is less likely to be blamed for provoking the attack, since relatively little ideology exists to support such a belief. Conversely, women accused of murdering men have not only the advantage of being viewed as essentially nonviolent but also the advantage of having violence attributed to their male victims (Farrell and Swigert, 1978b). Institutionalized beliefs concerning the criminality of men and women may be self-fulfilling; the prophecy becomes the reality as males come to be overrepresented and women underrepresented in criminal statistics.

The operation of criminal definitions in the legal process most typically occurs at an informal level. U.S. society is characterized by an official commitment to equality before the law. Introduction of overtly discriminatory procedures, which would seriously threaten this collective myth, is illegal. Decisions guided by popularly accepted definitions of criminality, however, are beyond the sanction of legal control and are not believed to jeopardize basic principles of equal justice.

Such definitions may even assume an institutionalized status. An instance of this phenomenon was discovered in a study of the legal treatment of defendants in criminal homicide (Swigert and Farrell, 1976, 1977). In the jurisdiction in which the investigation was conducted, a court-attached psychiatric clinic was charged with evaluating all persons arrested for murder. Analysis of the clinic reports revealed a diagnostic category—the *normal primitive*—that exemplifies the official use of a criminal imagery. This category has become part of the standard diagnostic terminology of the clinic's staff. The characteristics of the normal primitive, as defined by the clinic, are summarized in the following account:

> While treated as a diagnostic category, the designation normal primitive constitutes a *social* description of a group of people whose behavior, *within their own social setting,* is best described as normal. The normal primitive comes largely from the foreign-born and black populations. Their lives are characterized by impoverished economic conditions that, as with their behavior, may be described as primitive. Occupational achievements center around unskilled, menial labor, and these careers are often sporadic. Educational levels are minimal, and testing indicates borderline to low-average intelligence. While the children of the foreign born do acclimate to a less primitive existence, the offspring of the black population seem unaffected by improved educational and social opportunities.
>
> The personality characteristics of the normal primitive are childlike or juvenile, the behavior and attitude being similar to that of an eight- to twelve-year-old boy. At the same time, acceptance as a *man* by his group is very important. In this regard, the normal primitive is sensitive and takes offense to any question of his masculinity.
>
> Interaction among such individuals often occurs in bars where arguments readily result in aggressive encounters. Compelled to fight any challenger of his masculinity or courage, the normal primitive protects himself by carrying a lethal weapon.
>
> While sexual patterns among the foreign born are relatively stable, promiscuity among blacks provides additional grounds for aggression. Sexual prowess is a reflection of the masculinity of males, but is denied to females. Thus, when infidelity occurs, "as it inevitably does," the humiliation perceived by the male will result in threats and physical abuse that may produce the death of any one, or all members, of the sex triangle.
>
> In sum, ". . . the primitive man is comfortable and without mental illness. He has little, if any, education and is of dull intelligence. His goals are sensual and immediate—satisfying his physical and sexual needs without inhibition, postponement or planning. There is little regard for the future—extending hardly beyond the filling of his stomach and the next payday or relief check. His loyalties and identifications are with a group that has little purpose in life, except surviving with a minimum of sweat and a maximum of pleasure. He has the 10-year-old-boy's preoccupation with muscular prowess and 'being a man.' Unfortunately, he lacks the boy's external restraint and supervision so that he is more or less an intermittent community problem and responsibility" (clinic description, cited in Swigert and Farrell, 1977: 19).

The normal primitive classification represents a conception of criminality that combines both class and race characteristics. The imagery suggests a group of people whose style of life and innate attributes predispose them to violence. The tendency toward physical aggression over "trivial" issues, histories of family disorganization, and weak marital ties, combined with the offender's view that violence is appropriate and necessary, are manifestations of the volatile life-style in which the normal primitive is said to exist. The race and class bias of the popular conception of criminality reflects the imagery of the "dangerous classes" that has long characterized popular sentiment in the United States. The prolonged poverty of the unattached and unemployed black and immigrant masses has been a perceived threat to the propertied classes since the industrial developments of the nineteenth century (Silver, 1967).

The primary effect of the label in the adjudicative process was a lack of availability of legal resources to people classified as normal primitives. They were often denied bail and were more frequently adjudicated without benefit of trial by jury. Thus, the presumption of guilt implied by the application of the label was amplified when the court decided that bail should be withheld or when a plea of guilt before the bench was encouraged. In addition, such individuals could not afford to retain a private attorney. Those with public attorneys, no access to bail, and a nonjury trial format were more likely to be found guilty and to be convicted of the more serious charges (see Figure 3-1).

Expecting individuals who conform to a certain description to exhibit criminal behavior constitutes a presumption of guilt. Consequently, the processing of such persons takes on a routine nature; for little justification can be found for providing defendants who are presumed guilty with the tools essential for successful defense of their cases. The lack of legal resources that mediate between initial charge and final outcome is, in turn, instrumental in maintaining an imagery of guilt.

**FIGURE 3–1    The Normal Primitive and the Law**

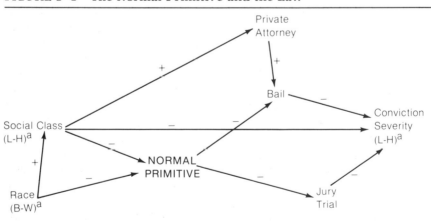

[a]L-H is low to high.
F-M is female to male.
B-W is black to white.

Assignment of public counsel identifies the individual with that class of persons—the indigent class—out of which the criminal stereotype is formulated; denial of bail defines the defendant as a potential danger to society; and waiver of trial implies admission of criminal involvement. The sequence of events from designation as apparently criminal through lack of adequate defense produces the outcome predicted by legal wisdom—criminal conviction.

**The Normal Primitive and the Subculture of Violence.**   The most influential theory of violent behavior is that of the *subculture of violence.* According to this theory, the tendency to use excessive force reflects a subculture in which the normative system "designates that in some types of social interaction a violent and physically aggressive response is either expected or required of all members sharing in that system of values" (Wolfgang and Ferracuti, 1967: 150–163). The over-representation of the lower classes and minorities among people who commit homicide is a product, it is argued, of the more frequent exposure of these groups to the traditions of this subculture.

The theory of the subculture of violence includes an image of the violent offender that bears remarkable resemblance to the definition of the normal primitive. It has been argued, for example, that the majority of homicides occur at

> that level of feeling, thought, and action in which the individual is accustomed to, and perhaps is incapable of adjusting to the criteria of our culture. He has the mental equipment to gauge his situation accurately, but the ethical perception is dulled or remains undeveloped because of his family or community setting, which entered into the formulation of his personality. A person in this subcultural group is perhaps more likely to get into situations where violence may occur, and has less innate equipment for keeping his violent tendencies in check than most of us. [Banay, 1952: 26]

Descriptions of the lower-class or minority offender in terms of disorganization of family and social life and "unsystematic and unregulated chaos in which individual desire, choice and whim govern behavior" (Harlan, 1950: 738–739) also reflect a view similar to the concept of normal primitiveness. But perhaps the closest approximation to this criminal imagery comes from the work of Marvin Wolfgang who wrote:

> There appears to be a sub-culture where the collective *id* dominates social consciousness—i.e., where basic urges, drives, and impulses of the group members are less harmonized with each other or external reality; where basic drives are less inhibited, restricted, or restrained; where reduction of

> tension and satisfaction of needs are characterized by immediacy and
> directness; and where the social regulators of conduct are weak and less
> omnipresent than in the larger culture of which this collectivity is a part.
> [Wolfgang, 1958: 329]

While the theoretical developments associated with the subculture
of violence reflect the social scientists' approach to the problem of
causality, a similar imagery exists more generally in society and, more
importantly, within those institutions officially charged with the control of criminal behavior. Thus, to theorize that blacks and members of
the lower classes are prone to violent behavior is to state a specific
aspect of the popular belief that these individuals are prone to higher
levels of criminality. Terms may vary over time from the "dangerous
classes" to the "criminal element," but the imagery remains the same.
U.S. society defines members of lower-status groups as being criminally
motivated. The scientific "discovery" of a violent subculture testifies to
the success with which this definition has been applied (see Swigert and
Farrell, 1976).

## The Creation of Career Offenders

The contemporary "career offender" is an individual thought to be
chronically involved in law violation. Career offenders are identified by
official records that document prior instances of criminality. Like the
procedures used to detect witches in fifteenth century Continental
Europe, the use of criminal records in judicial decisions may produce
the very population the judicial system seeks to control (Farrell and
Swigert, 1978a). Prior record has become an important source of information at several stages in the legal process. It is a criterion in eligibility
for suspension of sentence or probation and in the standards for award
of bail and is admissible evidence of a defendant's character in courtroom proceedings. Laws also prescribe longer sentences for defendants
previously found guilty of the same or similar crimes.

This reliance on prior record, however, overlooks the possibility
that a criminal history may, in fact, be a product of prior differential
justice. This possibility becomes even more apparent when we consider
that criminal records reflect earlier definitions of situations. They are
the end products of decisions by complainants to report, policemen to
arrest, district attorneys to prosecute, and judges or juries to convict.
Such records, therefore, may not be measures of criminal events but of
subjective decisions within the legal system and the community at
large.

Official decisions, furthermore, may be influenced by a definitional bias against certain portions of the population (Robinson, 1936;

Sutherland, 1949; Goldman, 1963; Stinchcombe, 1963; Cameron, 1964; Sudnow, 1965; Chambliss and Liell, 1966; Gallo et al., 1966; Skolnick, 1966; Chevigny, 1969; Black, 1970; Swigert and Farrell, 1976, 1977). Saturated patrol of slums and lower-class neighborhoods, detention of "suspicious" persons, and routine processing of people who conform to popular conceptions of criminals indicate the extent to which such definitions have become institutionalized. The self-fulfilling effects of these practices appear in the form of high arrest rates and criminal records among the black and the poor (Robinson, 1936: 228; Westley, 1953; Stinchcombe, 1963; Chambliss and Liell, 1966; Reiss, 1968; Chevigny, 1969; Swett, 1969; Black, 1970).

A criminal record, once constructed, becomes an important determinant of subsequent legal involvement. Persons with criminal histories are more likely to be suspected of crime. If arrested, they are more likely to be found guilty. This occurs both through the impediment that prior record poses for access to bail and adequate legal representation and through its direct influence on the court's assessment of guilt. Finally, the additional conviction becomes part of the defendants' records; in future contacts with the law, it too will contribute to the growing presumption of guilt with which they are processed (Farrell and Swigert, 1978a; see also Figure 3–2).

**FIGURE 3–2   Criminal Record as a Self-Fulfilling Prophecy**

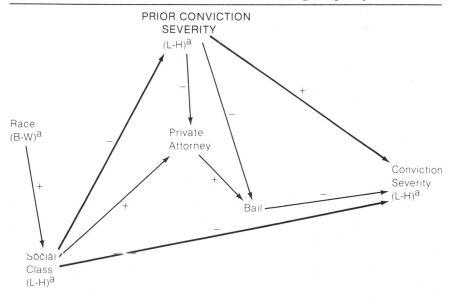

The use of prior record in the criminal justice system, therefore, constitutes an institutionalized self-fulfilling prophecy. Lower-class individuals, by virtue of their reduced status, more often accumulate the more serious convictions. These convictions justify differential treatment in subsequent legal proceedings. This continuous process serves to fulfill the original prediction that the lower classes are prone to lives of crime.

Once deviance becomes the dominant definition, a structured sequence of events is set into motion that precludes outcomes inconsistent with the original presumption. Discovery of persons who make pacts with the devil or of those whose lives are dedicated to crime is made possible by the very means used to detect them. Whether through the impossible dilemma confronting the accused witch or the criminal record and consequent withholding of resources necessary for defense confronting the lower-class offender, the initial definition shapes the eventual outcome—guilty as charged.

## BEHAVIORAL CONSEQUENCES OF INSTITUTIONALIZED EXPECTATIONS

Defining the situation also affects self-concept and individual behavior. This issue has been explored by Robert Rosenthal and Lenore Jacobson (1968a, 1968b) in their work on educational performance and teacher expectations. A serious problem in U.S. education has been its inability to reach the socially and culturally "disadvantaged," blacks, Chicanos, Puerto Ricans, and others living under conditions of extreme poverty. Children from such backgrounds are commonly thought to perform poorly in school because of their disadvantaged status. Rosenthal and Jacobson suggest, however, that their failure may be the effect of this very expectation.

This hypothesis was generated by Rosenthal's experiments with rats. In a laboratory study, twelve psychology students were each given five rats from the same breed. Half of the students were told that their rats were specially bred for an ability to run a maze. The other six students were told that, for genetic reasons, they should not expect their animals to perform well. The students were then assigned the task of teaching the rats to run a maze. In reality, the rats were randomly drawn from the same group, and there was no reason to expect that their learning abilities differed. However, from the very beginning, the rats designated as genetically superior outperformed those said to be dull (Rosenthal and Fode, 1963).

When the subjects were asked to evaluate their rats, the allegedly brighter animals were called brighter, more pleasant, and more likeable than the allegedly duller rats. In dealing with the animals, students with the "bright" rats were friendlier and more enthusiastic. They also reported that they handled their rats more frequently and more gently than did the students who expected their rats to perform poorly (Rosenthal and Jacobson, 1968b).

**Teacher Expectations and School Performance.** In an effort to study similar conditions in human learning, Rosenthal and Jacobson conducted an experiment at an elementary school in a predominantly lower-class neighborhood of San Francisco. Although there were some middle-class youngsters in the group, most of the children were from low-income families, families on social welfare, and families of Mexican-American background.

Near the closing of the school year, teachers were asked to administer a new test, supposedly designed to predict academic blooming in children. This test, allegedly developed at Harvard, was given the impressive title "Test of Inflected Acquisition." The teachers were led to believe that the results of this test indicated that certain of the children were likely to show marked intellectual growth. The students designated as "spurters," however, had actually been randomly selected from the entire list of children who had been tested. The only difference was that they were predicted to show rapid acceleration.

The "spurters" and the control group of undesignated youngsters were tested on separate occasions over a two-year period. Children from whom the teachers expected intellectual improvement actually did show considerably more progress than others. "The control-group children . . . gained well in IQ, 19 percent of them gaining twenty or more total IQ points. The 'special' children, however, showed 47 percent of their number gaining twenty or more total IQ points" (Rosenthal and Jacobson, 1968a: 176).

When asked to describe the gifted pupils at the conclusion of the study, the teachers stated that they were more curious and interesting and were likely to be more successful and happier later in life. They were also said to be more attractive, affectionate, and adjusted. In sum, the children from whom intellectual growth was expected were perceived by their teachers to possess the qualities commonly associated with academic ability.

Speculating on the dynamics of this process, Rosenthal and Jacobson suggested that the greater attentiveness accorded the "special" children may have acted as a rapid reinforcement that stimulated their learning. Teachers may also have been particularly reflective or thoughtful in assessing the academic performance of the "gifted" children, which may have contributed to the students' own reflective abilities. Such an increase in a cognitive quality would have improved the nonverbal skills measured by the IQ test.

By what she said, by how and when she said it, by her facial expressions, postures, and perhaps by her touch, the teacher may have communicated to the children of the experimental group that she expected improved intellectual performance. Such communications together with possible changes in teaching techniques may have helped the child learn by changing his self concept, his expectations of his own behavior, and his motivation, as well as his cognitive style and skills. [Rosenthal and Jacobson, 1968a: 180]

# Clever Hans

*Robert Rosenthal and Lenore Jacobson*

In 1904, there was a case of self-fulfilling prophecies involving the behavior of a horse known as Clever Hans. . . . By means of tapping his hoof Hans could add, subtract, multiply, and divide. He could spell, read, solve problems of musical harmony, and answer personal questions. His owner, Mr. von Osten, a German mathematics teacher, unlike the owners of other clever animals of the time, did not profit financially from his horse's talents, and it seemed unlikely that he had any fraudulent intent. He was quite willing to let others question Hans even in his absence so that cues from the owner could be ruled out as the reason for the horse's abilities. In a brilliant series of experiments [a German scientist] discovered that Hans could answer questions only if the questioner himself knew the answer and was visible to the horse during his foot-tapping of the answer. Finally, it was discovered that whenever people asked Hans a question, they leaned forward very slightly the better to see Hans' hoof. That, it turned out, was the unintentional signal for Hans to begin tapping. Then, as Hans approached the number of hooftaps representing the correct answer, the questioners would typically show a tiny head movement. That almost imperceptible cue was the signal for Hans to stop tapping, and Hans was right again. The questioner, by expecting Hans to stop at the right answer, was actually "telling" Hans the right answer and thereby fulfilling his own prophecy.

Source: Robert Rosenthal and Lenore Jacobson, *Pygmalion in the Classroom: Teacher Expectation and Pupil Intellectual Development* (New York: Holt, Rinehart and Winston, 1968a), p. 36.

**Superior Expectations and Work Performance.** The behavioral consequences of expectations were also investigated in a study of work performance (King, 1971). A random selection of "hard-core" unemployed men participating in a work training program were said to have done exceptionally well on a mechanical aptitude test. Their supervisors were told that they could expect unusually good development from these workers. Subsequent differences in training performance between this group and the undesignated others could only be explained as a result of the supervisors (King, 1971).

At the end of the training period, the supervisors' evaluations of the "high-potential" group were uniformly higher than those of the undesignated workers. The former were "rated as being more knowledgeable about jobs, producing better volume of neat and accurate work, showing greater ability to learn new duties, having more initiative, giving better cooperation, exerting more logic in job tasks, and generally showing best performance" (King, 1971: 373). Peer ratings indicated that trainees preferred to work and socialize with members of the high-performance group, in spite of the fact that none of the workers were apprised of the supposed performance scores. Finally, measures of skill demonstrated that the "high-potential" group not only outperformed the others but thought of themselves as the better workers.

Expectations were communicated to the trainees by the supervisors with cues and symbols so subtle as to be almost undetectable. Their expectations toward the trainees were likewise communicated to other workers, apparently alerting them to hold higher expectations and evaluations of the high-performance designees. "Such collective predictions could serve to reinforce [the high performers'] motivations for achievement and raise their individual expectancy for success" (King, 1971: 377).

For ethical reasons, researchers could not manipulate situations so that school children and disadvantaged workers would receive negative expectations. On the basis of the findings, however, such a possibility can easily be envisioned. The process of communicating expectations for behavior is the same for nonconformity as for conformity.

## Official Control and Deviance Expectations

Agencies of social control are an important source of the communication of deviance expectations. Procedures based on these institutionalized expectations may shape the conduct and self-concepts of people who are the objects of control efforts. An example is the relationship between the enforcement of public drunkenness statutes and the cultural patterns that have developed around urban vagrancy (Spradley, 1970). In the United States, more arrests are made for public intoxication than for any other crime. This policy reflects a popular evaluation of those "whose style of life does not conform to the main stream of American culture" (Spradley, 1970: 252). Yet the punitive approach to this behavior may actually guarantee the persistence of urban nomadism.

For many reasons, among them personal problems and the attractiveness of the nomadic life, people are drawn to Skid Row. "Whatever the initial impetus, once a man moves to the edge of this world he will be thrust to its center by repeated incarceration" (Spradley, 1970: 253). The mobility of Skid Row dwellers, a defining characteristic of urban nomadism, is a product of law enforcement efforts directed against them.

> Repeated arrests mean a growing criminal record which cuts a man off from jobs and friends. With each succeeding arrest, the length of time he must serve in jail is increased. The only sure way to maintain a good record is to leave town.... Whereas most Americans are *drawn to* a destination when they travel, urban nomads are *pushed from* a destination.... In a multitude of ways, then, the practices of the police and courts, which are intended to control and punish, actually perpetuate the core of this culture—a nomadic style of life. [Spradley, 1970: 254]

Similarly, urban nomads are alienated from the rest of society. Beginning with rejection by friends and relatives for excessive drinking or unemployment, alienation has increased dramatically by the time of the first arrest. They are now "drunken bums" to themselves, employers, and remaining friends. In the drunk tank, communication with the outside is cut off. Personal hygiene becomes a problem, confirming the predominant ideas of the vagrants' essential nature to themselves and others around them.

> With each repeated arrest they may have less to lose, less which binds them to the larger society. For most men the stripping process works more deeply each time until finally, the alienation has become permanent and their personal identities are thoroughly spoiled for a meaningful life anywhere except in the tramp world. And thus our institutions perform a rite of passage for these men, moving them out of the larger society and transforming their identities without providing a way for them to move back again or to alleviate the sting of rejection. [Spradley, 1970: 255]

The poverty of urban nomads can also be attributed to law-enforcement procedures. Their forced mobility results in their having sporadic careers as harvesters, pensioners, or on-the-spot employees. Bail, court, and jail costs further contribute to their poverty, while this very poverty makes them increasingly unable to meet such costs.

Without the ability to finance release from jail and with an employment history that does not suggest the feasibility of probation, urban nomads become even more likely to spend time in jail as a result of their contacts with police.

Mobility, alienation, and poverty, the characteristics that define urban nomadism, are a product of official efforts to deal with vagrancy and public drunkenness. These nomads embody the self-fulfilled prophecy of the system that defined them. Their experience in this regard is not unique, however.

> It is by now a thoroughly familiar argument that many of the institutions built to inhibit deviance actually operate in such a way as to perpetuate it. For one thing, prisons, hospitals, and other agencies of control provide aid and protection for large numbers of deviant persons. But beyond this, such institutions gather marginal people into tightly segregated groups, give them an opportunity to teach one another the skills and attitudes of a deviant career, and even drive them into using these skills by reinforcing their sense of alienation from the rest of society. [Erikson, 1962: 311]

The pattern is repeated in the official policies toward certain types of drug abuse (Young, 1971). For example, the popular stereotype has historically pictured the marijuana smoker as an immature, unstable individual who has been corrupted by the pusher. Users have been commonly seen as having substituted a preoccupation with the drug for basic social values and as living out their lives in socially isolated and highly disorganized environments. It has been claimed that marijuana produces extreme sexuality, criminality, and psychosis and that it leads eventually to the use of even more dangerous substances.

The reality of marijuana use in its early stages is very different from the public conception. Yet, enforcement policies tend to reshape many aspects of the phenomenon to conform to the popular image. Police action against marijuana smoking forces users to develop a heightened consciousness of themselves as separate from and antagonistic toward the community at large. Marijuana becomes the symbol both of their exclusion and of their commitment to one another as exclusive sources of social support. This isolation is exacerbated by the need of users to protect themselves from the threat that "straight" friends may act as informers. Prolonged involvement in the world of other users increasingly attenuates the possibility of an eventual return to legitimate society.

The illegalization of the drug results in spiraling price increases. Inflated profits capture the interest of organized crime, which may use the available marijuana network for the distribution of other drugs as well. The social exclusion of marijuana smokers, their exposure to subterranean values regarding drug use generally, and the availability to them of a variety of drugs from a centralized source combine to increase the likelihood that they will experiment with other illegal substances.

As the problem of drug abuse becomes more visible, additional pressure is placed on the police to step up enforcement. The result is the detection of more users, who are driven deeper into subcultural involvement and who increase thereby the visibility of the problem. With each turn of the cycle, the "fantasy is translated into reality" (Young, 1971: 46).

Society's reaction against persons defined as deviant leads to their isolation and alienation from legitimate groups. Separated from the culture of the larger society, deviant populations develop their own subcultural norms and values, which elicit even more rejection. Such amplification of deviance results in the prophecy's being fulfilled, ensuring the persistence of the original cultural definitions (Wilkins, 1965).

## CONCLUSION

Social reality is definitionally constructed; that is, through ongoing communication, meanings are assigned to the properties and events that comprise the social environment. Definitions of the situation not only allow individuals to share a common understanding of the world around them, but they also render that world predictable. That is, once a situation is recognized to occupy a particular category, individuals are able to respond to it in ways prescribed by the original definition. In this sense definitions are self-fulfilling. By precluding alternative courses of action, social definitions shape the very outcomes predicted.

Society's normative boundaries become social reality through the application of definitions of deviance. Gossip, ostracism, imprisonment, and hospitalization make visible the limits of behavior that will be tolerated by the collectivity. At the same time, once deviance becomes the dominant definition of the situation, procedures may be invoked that ensure that prophecy's being fulfilled. By limiting the deviant's opportunities for legitimate claims or performance, the prediction becomes the reality. Thus, as long as the disadvantaged are expected to fail, as long as crime and deviance are said to be the behaviors of certain kinds of people, and as long as society continues to "tag, define, identify, segregate, describe, emphasize, make conscious, and self conscious" it will continue to "stimulate, suggest, emphasize, and evoke the very traits that are complained of" (Tannenbaum, 1938: 19–20).

## NOTES

1. The September 13, 1978, indictment of Ford Motor Company was modified before the trial. At the prosecutor's request, the charge of criminal recklessness was dropped.

2. There have been a number of indictments against corporations for homicide. Consistently, however, the appellate courts have ruled that corporations are not capable of forming intent or malice and, therefore, are not liable for personal injury offenses (*American Jurisprudence* 19, §1436 et seq.; see also Stone, 1975).

3. The $127.8 million award was subsequently reduced by the trial judge to $6.3 million.

4. The increased use of a vocabulary of deviance is not independent of the number of lines the newspaper devotes to the issue. In fact, across trimesters, references to danger, intent, and civil and criminal liability comprise 13.2, 12.7, and 14.5 percent of the lines, respectively. We are not arguing, therefore, that there has been an increase in the relative use of the vocabulary of deviance but rather that there have been absolute increases in both the newsworthiness of the problem and the deviance vocabulary used to describe it.

5. The state of Indiana adopted the definition of corporations as criminally liable in 1976. This statutory revision formed the basis for the 1978 Ford indictment.

## REFERENCES

American Jurisprudence, 2d.
 1965 Corporations. Rochester, New York: Lawyers Cooperative Publishing Company 19: §1436, fn 17.
Banay, Ralph S.
 1952 Study in Murder. Annals of the American Academy of Political and Social Science 284 (November): 26–34.
Black, Donald J.
 1970 Production of Crime Rates. American Sociological Review 35 (August): 733–748.
Bodine, Larry
 1980 Prosecutors Undeterred by Pinto Acquittal: Defense Bar Says It's in Driver's Seat Now. National Law Journal 2 (March): 3, 17.
Cameron, Mary Owen
 1964 The Booster and the Snitch: Department Store Shoplifting. New York: Free Press.
Chambliss, William J., and John T. Liell
 1966 The Legal Process in the Community Setting: A Study of Law Enforcement. Crime and Delinquency 12 (October): 310–317.
Chambliss, William J., and Robert B. Seidman
 1971 Law, Order and Power. Reading, Massachusetts: Addison–Wesley.
Chevigny, Paul
 1969 Police Power: Police Abuses in New York City. New York: Vintage Press.
Clark, Glenn A.
 1979 Corporate Homicide: A New Assault on Corporate Decision-Making. Notre Dame Lawyer 54 (June): 911–924.

Currie, Elliott P.
  1968  Crimes Without Criminals: Witchcraft and Its Control in Renaissance Europe. Law and Society Review 3 (October): 7–32.
Dowie, Mark
  1977  Pinto Madness. Mother Jones 2 (September–October): 18–32.
Erikson, Kai T.
  1962  Notes on the Sociology of Deviance. Social Problems 9 (Spring): 307–314.
Farrell, Ronald A., and Victoria Lynn Swigert
  1978a Prior Record as a Self-Fulfilling Prophecy. Law and Society Review 12 (Spring): 437–453.
  1978b Legal Disposition of Inter-Group and Intra-Group Homicides. Sociological Quarterly 19 (Autumn): 565–576.
Gallo, John J., Justice Stanley Mosk, Lawrence H. Jacobson, and R. Michael Rosenfeld
  1966  The Consenting Adult Homosexual and the Law. UCLA Law Review 13 (March): 686–742.
Goldman, Nathan
  1963  The Differential Selection of Juvenile Offenders for Court Appearance. New York: National Research and Information Center, National Council on Crime and Delinquency.
Gusfield, Joseph R.
  1967  Moral Passage: The Symbolic Process in Public Designations of Deviance. Social Problems 15 (Fall): 175–188.
Harlan, Howard
  1950  Five Hundred Homicides. Journal of Criminal Law, Criminology, and Police Science 40 (March–April): 736–752.
King, Albert Sidney
  1971  Self-Fulfilling Prophecies in Training the Hard Core: Supervisors' Expectations and the Underpriviledged Worker's Performance. Social Science Quarterly 52 (September): 369–378.
Matza, David
  1969  Becoming Deviant. Englewood Cliffs, New Jersey: Prentice–Hall.
Merton, Robert K.
  1957  Social Theory and Social Structure. New York: Free Press.
Reiss, Albert J., Jr.
  1968  Police Brutality—Answers to Key Questions. Transaction 5 (July–August): 10–19.
Robison, Sophia
  1936  Can Delinquency Be Measured? New York: Columbia University Press.
Rock, P. E.
  1968  Observations on Debt Collection. British Journal of Sociology 19 (June): 176–190.
Rosenthal, Robert and Kermit L. Fode
  1963  The Effect of Experimenter Bias on the Performance of the Albino Rat. Behavioral Science 8 (July): 183–189.
Rosenthal, Robert, and Lenore Jacobson
  1968a Pygmalion in the Classroom: Teacher Expectation and Pupil Intellectual Development. New York: Holt, Rinehart and Winston.

1968b Teacher Expectations for the Disadvantaged. Scientific American 218 (April): 19–23.

Rothman, David

1971 The Discovery of the Asylum: Social Order and Disorder in the New Republic. Boston: Little, Brown.

Silver, Allan

1967 The Demand for Order in Civil Society: A Review of Some Themes in the History of Urban Crime, Police, and Riot. *In* The Police: Six Sociological Essays. David J. Bordua, ed. pp. 1–24. New York: John Wiley and Sons.

Skolnick, Jerome H.

1966 Justice Without Trial: Law Enforcement in Democratic Society. New York: John Wiley and Sons.

Spradley, James P.

1970 You Owe Yourself a Drunk: An Ethnography of Urban Nomads. Boston: Little, Brown.

Stinchcombe, Arthur J.

1963 Institutions of Privacy in the Determination of Police Administrative Practice. American Journal of Sociology 69 (September): 150–159.

Stone, Christopher, D.

1975 Where the Law Ends: The Social Control of Corporate Behavior. New York: Harper & Row.

Sudnow, David

1965 Normal Crimes: Sociological Features of the Penal Code in a Public Defender Office. Social Problems 12 (Winter): 255–276.

Sutherland, Edwin H.

1949 White Collar Crime. New York: Holt, Rinehart and Winston.

Swett, Daniel H.

1969 Cultural Bias in the American Legal System. Law and Society Review 4 (August): 79–110.

Swigert, Victoria Lynn, and Ronald A. Farrell

1976 Murder, Inequality, and the Law. Lexington, Massachusetts: D. C. Heath, Lexington.

1977 Normal Homicides and the Law. American Sociological Review 42 (February): 16–32.

1980 Corporate Homicide: Definitional Processes in the Creation of Deviance. Law and Society Review 15 (Fall): 101–122.

Tannenbaum, Frank

1938 Crime and the Community. New York: Columbia University Press.

Thomas, William I.

1923 The Unadjusted Girl. Boston: Little, Brown.

Westley, William A.

1953 Violence and the Police. American Journal of Sociology 59 (July): 34–41.

Wilkins, Leslie, T.

1965 Social Deviance. London, England: Tavistock Publications.

Wolfgang, Marvin E.

1958 Patterns in Criminal Homicide. Philadelphia: University of Pennsylvania Press.

Wolfgang, Marvin E., and Franco Ferracuti
  1967  The Subculture of Violence. London: Methuen.
Young, Jock
  1971  The Role of the Police as Amplifiers of Deviancy, Negotiators of Reality, and Translators of Fantasy. *In* Images of Deviance. Stanley Cohen, ed. Middlesex, England: Penguin Books.

# 4

## The Social Response and Individual Reaction

In Chapter 3, we saw that the self-fulfilling effects of deviance definitions are, in part, a result of the restriction of legitimate opportunities that accompanies disvalued positions. If persons are designated deviant, they may be denied access to the means for demonstrating otherwise. Thus, the very strategies used to control deviant behavior may actually preclude nondeviant alternatives.

Definitions of deviance also have social-psychological consequences. An explanation of the processes involved here is the focus of the interactionist, or labeling, theory of deviance. This perspective addresses the effects of the social response on personal identity and behavior. Developing out of the more general theory of *symbolic interactionism*, the labeling approach posits that self-concept and associated role behavior are shaped in sustained interaction with significant others. Imputations of deviance introduced into this interaction may cause the individual to organize life around the emergent definition.

### INTERACTION AND THE SOCIAL SELF

The fundamental assumption of symbolic interactionism is that social reality is made up of *shared symbols*, verbal and nonverbal signs that interacting individuals understand in more or less the same way. By internalizing these symbols, people become capable of recognizing the world around them and their roles in it. Individuals acquire beliefs and behaviors appropriate to age, sex, class, and other socially important positions through their interaction with significant others. Thus, behavioral categories in a social system are determined by *social defini-tion,* and behavior comes to have personal meaning for group members through the *symbolic communication* of these definitions.

An important outcome of symbolic interaction is the development of self-awareness. Concern with this dimension of social reality has characterized the several contributions to the theory since the early works of Charles Horton Cooley (1902) and George Herbert Mead (1934). Cooley maintained that *awareness of self is made possible by the sym-bolic communication of the individual with significant others.* Thus, " 'society' and 'individual' do not denote separable phenomena, but are simply collective and distributive aspects of the same thing" (Cooley, 1902: 37).

Similarly, Mead (1934) believed that the individual does not ex-perience the self directly but becomes an object to himself or herself by assuming the attitudes of people with whom he or she interacts. The outcome of this process is a self that consists of the *I,* the *me,* and the *generalized other.* The *I* is the response of the organism to the attitudes of others and is the behavioral component of personality. The *me* is the organized set of attitudes that the self assumes as its own; the person's beliefs concerning his or her personality and social and physical characteristics comprise this aspect of self. Such beliefs are acquired from the *generalized other*—people to whom the individual looks for in-formation concerning personal identity. When the individual takes these attitudes as his or her own, self-concept and behavioral patterns emerge.

Cooley's (1902: 179–184) depiction of the "looking-glass self" cap-tures vividly the concept of the social nature of identity. Defining the self as "a system of ideas, drawn from communicative life, that the mind cherishes as its own" (1902: 179), Cooley wrote:

> The social reference takes the form of a somewhat definite imagination of how one's self—that is any idea he appreciates—appears in a particular mind, and the kind of self-feeling one has is determined by the attitude toward this attributed to that other mind. . . . [This] social self . . . might be called the reflected or looking-glass self:
>> Each to each a looking-glass
>> reflects the other that doth pass.
> . . . A self-idea of this sort seems to have three principal elements: the imagination of our appearance to the other person; the imagination of his judgment of that appearance; and some sort of self-feeling, such as pride or mortification. [Cooley, 1902: 183–184]

According to Cooley, persons tend to conform to their interpreta-tions of what others think they are. Perceiving disapproval in the reactions of others may be the source of negative self-evaluation. "If failure or disgrace arrives, if one suddenly finds that the faces of men show coldness or contempt instead of the kindness and deference that he is used to, he will perceive from the shock, the fear, the sense of being outcast and helpless, that he was living in the minds of others without knowing it" (Cooley, 1902: 208). People who possess deviant aims or attributes are particularly subject to negative self-feelings:

> The peculiar relations to other persons attending any marked personal deficiency or peculiarity are likely to aggravate, if not to produce, abnormal manifestations of self-feeling. Any such trait sufficiently noticeable to interrupt easy and familiar intercourse with others, and make people talk and think *about* a person or *to* him rather than *with* him, can hardly fail to have this effect. . . . One who shows signs of mental aberration [for example] is, inevitably perhaps, but cruelly, shut off from familiar, thoughtless intercourse, partly excommunicated; his isolation is unwittingly proclaimed to him on every countenance by curiosity, indifference, aversion, or pity, and insofar as he is human enough to need free and equal communication and feel the lack of it, he suffers pain and loss of a kind and degree which others can only faintly imagine, and for the most part ignore. He finds himself apart, "not in it," and feels chilled, fearful, and suspicious. Thus "queerness" is no sooner perceived than it is multiplied by reflection from other minds. The same is true in some degree of dwarfs, deformed or disfigured persons, even the deaf and those suffering from the infirmities of old age. [Cooley, 1902: 259–260]

Put simply, symbolic interactionists suggest that the responses people perceive in others will affect the way they eventually feel about themselves. They respond to their own behavior in the same way they believe others are responding to them. Both Mead and Cooley thought that the mere anticipation of group definitions and reactions might influence the individual's self-conception and behavior. This ability to anticipate the responses of others and their effects on the self is largely a result of what individuals have learned about their position from earlier socialization and experience. That is, people respond to their own definitions of a given situation, definitions acquired through prior interaction.

From the symbolic interactionist perspective, then, personal identity and social reality itself are viewed as being symbolically constructed through the processes of ongoing interaction. The norms, standards, and expectations that guide human behavior are not imposed on individuals from without but emerge gradually from within the group itself. As people interact with each other, common meanings are established among them. Society, therefore, is primarily the persistence over time of shared definitions of the situation.

## THE LABELING PROCESS

The interactionist perspective on deviance, often referred to as *labeling theory*, has developed from the more general social-psychological approach of symbolic interactionism. Labeling theory emphasizes that social definitions are powerful forces in the formation of individual behavior, particularly because of their impact on the individual's conception of self. When a given behavior has been called into question, the pressures leveled against the actor affect his or her identity. If the community reacts toward certain persons as though they were deviant, they may come to identify themselves as such. The major importance of this perspective, then, is in its intensified focus on the creation of deviant identities through processes of symbolic interaction.

Edwin M. Lemert (1951) was the first to develop these ideas into a systematic explanation of how deviance is caused. He began with the general assumption that people behave in ways that are influenced by and appropriate to their own social and cultural situations. Societies are differentiated by class, race, age, sex, geographical location, and the like. Within these various collectivities, people acquire behaviors that reflect group-specific norms and values. Like Émile Durkheim and W. I. Thomas before him, therefore, Lermert saw the inevitability of behavioral variation in differentiated society. Those behaviors that conflict with dominant norms and expectations are likely to result in social penalties, rejection, and segregation. These reactions are dynamic factors that may increase, decrease, or condition the form of the initial difference or deviation (Lemert, 1951: 22).

At any given time, an individual occupies a number of statuses in the community. The roles associated with these positions shape his or her public and personal identity. Positions related to employment, education, family life, and the like locate the person in the community and, at the same time, provide role requirements and expectations for behavior. Identification with these roles is central to the individual's conception of self. Thus, for example, persons come to view themselves in terms of their occupational and educational achievements, marital status, and religious affiliations and to organize their lives around the attendant roles.

Deviations are also important criteria for assigning status, and they may become active roles as well (Lemert, 1951: 75–78). The likelihood of this occurring depends on the repetition and visibility of the deviant acts, and the severity with which they are sanctioned. Under these circumstances, integration of the existing legitimate roles may be disrupted, and identity and behavior may be reorganized around a new deviant role.

Sometimes people adopt roles in which deviations that were previously defined negatively are given more socially acceptable expression, as when ex-convicts and former alcoholics and drug addicts utilize their deviations by assuming leadership roles in self-help and treatment organizations. Here, a history of proscribed behavior provides access to legitimate opportunities for role performance. In other cases, a person may assume a deviant role and organize life and identity accordingly. Lemert refers to this latter outcome as *secondary deviation* and distinguishes it from original, or *primary*, deviation.

## Primary and Secondary Deviation

Lemert's distinction between primary and secondary deviation is central to an understanding of the behavioral consequences of societal reaction. Primary deviations are original, specific, and often transient incidents of rule violation that may result from accident, experimentation, or group pressure. They include both physical and mental attributes as well as behavior. Deviations of this type are universal; that is, everyone at some time or other possesses characteristics or engages in actions that may elicit social sanction. Such deviations remain primary as long as they are viewed as incidental to the individual's total situation. When they become the basis of societal response, the individual becomes increasingly aware of the deviation and may compulsively organize his or her life around it. The end product of this process may be the adoption of a deviant role, or secondary deviation.

> Deviations remain *primary deviations* or symptomatic and situational as long as they are rationalized or otherwise dealt with as functions of a socially acceptable role.... [However,] when a person begins to employ ... deviant behavior or a role based upon it as a means of defense, attack, or adjustment to the overt and covert problems created by the consequent societal reaction, ... [the] deviation is secondary. [Lemert, 1951: 75–76]

The sequence of interaction leading to secondary deviation is roughly as follows:

> (1) primary deviation; (2) social penalties; (3) further primary deviation; (4) stronger penalties and rejections; (5) further deviation, perhaps with hostilities and resentment beginning to focus upon those doing the penalizing; (6) crisis reached in the tolerance quotient, expressed in formal action by the community stigmatizing of the deviant; (7) strengthening of the deviant conduct as a reaction to the stigmatizing and penalties; (8) ultimate acceptance of deviant social status and efforts at adjustment on the basis of the associated role. [Lemert, 1951: 77]

Consistent with the symbolic interactionist approach, labeling theory emphasizes the effects of the reactions of others on the development of self and behavior. Very generally, attributions of conformity result in conformist identities that, in their turn, are influential in producing socially acceptable behavior. Conversely, imputations of deviance produce identities and behaviors that fit these responses.

Reactions to deviance occur at several different levels. *Self responses* are based on the individual's own definitions of the situation. These definitions are acquired through early socialization and reaffirmed in the routine interaction of everyday life. Persons who find themselves involved in deviance may call upon these definitions to interpret their own behavior. For example, the adolescent or young adult male who has learned in childhood the stereotype of the homosexual may, if he has a homosexual experience, rely on the popular imagery to attribute meaning to his situation.

*Anticipated responses,* a second level of reaction to deviance, emerge from the information the individual has obtained from previous experiences of people's reactions to the deviation. Thus, for example, earlier observations of negative reactions to homosexuality may lead persons who engage in such behavior to expect similar treatment. This predictive process is based on an assumption of continuity in the social response.

*Perceived responses,* a third form of reaction, involve assigning meaning to the behavior of others. This attribution includes an assessment of the actions of others as they conform to shared symbols. To be meaningful as a symbol of rejection, for example, the epithet "queer" must be understood by the person to whom it is applied. Symbols of this type acquire meaning through ongoing social interaction. In addition, however, perceived responses may involve a person's projecting self responses and anticipated responses onto others. The deviant who is familiar with the stereotype of homosexuality and who expects rejection from others may interpret their gestures as negative, regardless of how they were intended.

Self responses, anticipated responses, and perceived responses all involve the deviant's subjective evaluation of the reactions of others. There are also *objective responses* to deviance. These may occur in both primary and secondary group settings. *Primary group reactions* are those which take place in the family, peer group, and neighborhood or small community. *Secondary group reactions* are found in the impersonal contacts that characterize public settings. Finally, there may be formal reactions to deviance—the *organizational responses* of such official processing agencies of social control as the police, the courts, probation and parole agencies, correctional institutions, and organizations for the blind, the deaf, and the mentally defective.

## The Social Response and Secondary Deviation

The movement from primary to secondary deviance involves a number of factors central to the labeling process, including (1) the highly salient nature of the deviant status, (2) the attribution to that status of a distinct role defined in terms of the public stereotype, and (3) the negative redefinition of other statuses and identifications of the deviant. The cumulative effect is that the deviation comes to take precedence over other aspects of an individual's life and to serve as the guiding force for subsequent behavior.

**Deviance as a Master Status.** The designation of persons as deviant involves assigning them to a new status with an institutionalized set of role expectations. Regardless of the other positions an individual may occupy, the status of deviant remains the *master status*—the major source of identification. People assigned to this position will be publicly identified as deviant, and will come to identify themselves as such, *before* other identifications are made (Becker, 1963: 31–34; see also Figure 4–1).

Self-conscious identification with the deviant status often results in paranoid-like behavior patterns (Scott and Lyman, 1968). The stigmatized position in which deviant individuals find themselves may

**FIGURE 4–1   Deviance as a Master Status**

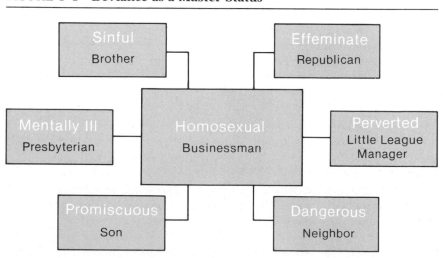

The assignment of deviance as a master status and the associated role expectations act to disrupt identity based on the integration of legitimate social positions.

heighten their sensitivity to the language, cues, and gestures of others. Interaction that is routine for the normal person frequently becomes difficult for the deviant, who may respond intensely to reactions so subtle that they are almost imperceptible to others. In this heightened-awareness context, the deviant's suspicion of the motives and actions of others is likely to result in accusation and aggression. This suspicion is not unfounded but rather is in accordance with the deviant's perception of the deteriorating interaction that accompanies the disvalued status.

An individual identified as deviant has increasing difficulty engaging in meaningful group participation (Lemert, 1962a). As toleration for the nonconformer evaporates, strategies emerge to isolate him or her from the reciprocal communication essential for a normalized role (Davis, 1961). This cycle of suspicion and exclusion undermines the deviant's ability to maintain a conception of self based on the integration of more socially acceptable statuses. Legitimate positions that the deviant may occupy become for others as well as self mere pretense, a front for what is essentially true. The result is a restructuring of the self around the highly salient deviant status.

**Stereotyping.**   Public stereotypes also play an important role in the creation of secondary deviance. There is abundant evidence that such stereotypes exist in the general population (Nunnally, 1961; Simmons, 1965; Scheff, 1966; Scott, 1969; Reed and Reed, 1973; Hess and Mariner, 1975). People do, in fact, tend to use highly stereotypical characterizations to describe deviants. Furthermore, individual descriptions of specific deviations are remarkably similar in content (Guskin, 1963; Simmons, 1965; Reed and Reed, 1973) and remain stable over time (Cauthen et al., 1971).

Deviance-specific stereotypes have emerged from studies of such diverse behaviors as drug use, sexual deviance, political radicalism (Simmons, 1965), mental illness (Nunnally, 1961; Scheff, 1966) and blindness (Scott, 1969). Such conceptions are perpetuated in everyday interaction and in the mass media characterizations in comic strips, television, newspapers, books, songs, and advertising. Thus, even the very young become familiar with the stereotypes, which are reaffirmed throughout adulthood (Cain, 1964; Scheff, 1966: 64).

The expectations associated with deviant positions are prescribed by these *public stereotypes*. Based on the possession of a single deviant trait, the individual is attributed a role defined in terms of the popular conception. Deviations, then, have a generalized symbolic value in that people assume the nonconformer possesses other undesirable traits thought to be associated with the deviant one (Becker, 1963: 31–34; Goffman, 1963: 5). On the basis of the original and specific deviation the individual may be assigned a wide range of imperfections. Thus, to be

**TABLE 4–1  Public Stereotypes of Deviants**

| Marijuana Smokers | % | Beatniks [Hippies] | % | Adulterers | % | Homosexuals | % | Political Radicals | % |
|---|---|---|---|---|---|---|---|---|---|
| Looking for kicks | 59 | Sloppy | 57 | Immoral | 41 | Sexually abnormal | 72 | Ambitious | 61 |
| Escapist | 52 | Non-conformist | 46 | Promiscuous | 36 | Perverted | 52 | Aggressive | 47 |
| Insecure | 49 | Escapist | 32 | Insecure | 34 | Mentally ill | 40 | Stubborn | 32 |
| Lacking self-control | 41 | Immature | 28 | Lonely | 32 | Maladjusted | 40 | Non-conformist | 32 |
| Frustrated | 34 | Individualistic | 27 | Sinful | 31 | Effeminate | 29 | Impulsive | 28 |
| Excitement seeking | 29 | Lazy | 27 | Self-interested | 29 | Lonely | 22 | Dangerous | 28 |
| Nervous | 26 | Insecure | 26 | Lacking self-control | 28 | Insecure | 21 | Individualistic | 26 |
| Maladjusted | 24 | Irresponsible | 20 | Passionate | 24 | Immoral | 15 | Self-interested | 23 |
| Lonely | 22 | Self-interested | 18 | Irresponsible | 22 | Repulsive | 14 | Intelligent | 22 |
| Immature | 21 | False lives | 16 | Frustrated | 21 | Frustrated | 14 | Irresponsible | 21 |
| Weakminded | 17 | Artistic | 16 | Immature | 16 | Weakminded | 12 | Conceited | 15 |
| Irresponsible | 15 | Maladjusted | 14 | Sensual | 14 | Lacking self-control | 12 | Imaginative | 14 |
| Mentally ill | 13 | Harmless | 13 | Over-sexed | 13 | Sensual | 11 | Excitement-seeking | 9 |
| Pleasure-loving | 11 | Imaginative | 12 | Sexually abnormal | 12 | Secretive | 11 | | |
| Dangerous | 11 | Lonely | 11 | Pleasure-loving | 12 | Over-sexed | 10 | | |
| | | Imitative | 10 | False lives | 11 | Dangerous | 10 | | |
| | | Frustrated | 10 | Maladjusted | 11 | Sinful | 10 | | |
| | | Happy-go-lucky | 9 | | | Sensitive | 10 | | |

N = 134

Source: J. L. Simmons, "Public Stereotypes of Deviants," *Social Problems* 13 (Fall 1965): 227.

"crazy" is to be wild, erratic, and dangerous, and "helplessness, dependency, melancholoy, docility, gravity of inner thought, aestheticism [are the] things that commonsense views tell us to expect of the blind" (Scott, 1969: 4).

Treating persons as though they were generally rather than specifically deviant produces a self-fulfilling prophecy, as Thomas Scheff (1966) has described in his discussion of mental illness. The existence of a widely diffused stereotype of insanity ensures that persons who perceive themselves being defined and reacted to as insane are likely to be aware of the role expectations that accompany that status. In essence, the stereotype is a summary of the characteristics assumed relevant to the deviation. The stereotype, learned in childhood and routinely reinforced in everyday interaction, underlies the responses of both society and the deviant. In this regard, stereotypic definitions and reactions cause labeled individuals eventually to organize their identity and behavior around the stereotype of the deviation.

> In a crisis, when the deviance of an individual becomes a public issue, the traditional stereotype of insanity becomes the guiding imagery for action, both for those reacting to the deviant and, at times, for the deviant himself. When societal agents and persons around the deviant react to him uniformly in terms of the traditional stereotypes of insanity, his amorphous and unstructured rule-breaking tends to crystallize in conformity to these expectations, thus becoming similar to the behavior of other deviants classified as mentally ill, and stable over time. The process of becoming uniform and stable is completed with the traditional imagery becomes a part of the deviant's orientation for guiding his own behavior. [Scheff, 1966: 82]

**Concurrent and Retrospective Interpretation.** The individual's more general identity may also lose validity as a result of others' attempting to neutralize their conflicting information about him or her by reinterpreting his or her past as well as current situation and behavior to fit the deviation. Such reinterpretation allows others to establish biographical continuity. The result is to invalidate other bases of identity and to give increased meaning to the deviation.

The formal actions of official processing agencies illustrate this process. The often dramatic and ceremonial nature of criminal sanctions, involuntary commitment, and various organizational approaches to deviance and disability may have the effect of publicly denouncing the legitimacy of persons at whom such action is directed. Like abrupt rites of passage, these reactions suddenly remove individuals from their more socially acceptable positions in the community and transfer them into distinct deviant roles.

The other person becomes in the eyes of his condemners literally a different and new person . . . the former identity stands as accidental; the new identity is the "basic reality." What he is now is what, "after all," he was all along. [Garfinkel, 1956: 421–422]

Although the public ceremony is important in dramatizing the fact of deviance, it is important to consider the consequences of such action for less formal responses (Lemert, 1967: 42–60). Labels may have limited impact if they are not highly publicized and the information not widely circulated. There is little evidence to suggest, for example, that military dismissal of homosexuals influences either their identity or behavior. Although such action "may be very traumatic in the short term, . . . *generally* its long-term effects . . . are not readily apparent" (Williams and Weinberg, 1971: 181).

Some deviant labels are more widespread in their consequences than others, and this should be recognized. . . . It seems that less than honorable discharge . . . [is] restricted in its effects; in other words, the mere fact that a person is officially labeled deviant does not tell us much unless we know the nature of the label and its disruptive potential for those who carry it. With regard to this latter point, we need to know the conditions under which the stigmatic potential of deviant labels is realized. For the majority of [homosexuals,] . . . managing the stigma of their discharge . . . [does] not pose insurmountable problems. This we feel is due mainly to the nature of the label itself having little influence outside of certain occupations and appearing on the official records of few of the organizations that circumscribe a person's life. [Williams and Weinberg, 1971: 183]

This suggests that the immediate results of isolated formalized reactions may subside. Full appreciation of the labeling process, therefore, requires that the patterned and recurrent experiences of rejection that occur in more informal encounters also be given careful consideration. While formal reactions alone may not be sufficient to cause secondary deviation, however, conceptual developments at this level contribute much to an understanding of the phenomenon at the informal level. Thus, for example, concurrent and retrospective interpretation of deviants is not limited to public ceremonies but applies to informal reactions as well. In much the same way that prosecutors amass information to demonstrate the criminality of defendants, or psychiatrists the insanity of their patients, people who routinely interact with deviants—community acquaintances, work associates, and the like—also reassess the individual in light of the new information regarding the deviation. Persons asked to recount the circumstances that led to their recognizing that an acquaintance was homosexual, for example, tended to reinterpret the:

individual's past behavior in the light of the new information concerning his sexual deviance. . . . The subjects indicate that they reviewed their past interactions with the individuals in question, searching for subtle cues and nuances of behavior which might give further evidence of the alleged deviance. This retrospective reading generally provided the subjects with just such evidence to support the conclusion that "this is what was going on all the time." [Kitsuse, 1962: 253]

*Retrospective accounts by the New York Times of the life of Lee Harvey Oswald, alleged assassin of President John F. Kennedy, illustrate the interpretive processes that bring consistency to deviant labels.*

## Oswald, as Boy, Had Mental Test

Lee H. Oswald, accused assassin of President Kennedy, underwent a court-ordered psychiatric examination here in 1953, when he was 13 years old. . . .

[A] psychiatrist's report in the case had found that Oswald showed schizophrenic tendencies and was "potentially dangerous." . . . Oswald's mother had found him ungovernable.

Last night . . . , the present principal of [the junior high school Oswald attended] said in a telephone interview that one of Oswald's teachers had described him as a "belligerent, hostile youngster who was withdrawn and had no friends to speak of."

The teacher said Oswald was a boy "who would lash out at anyone who offended him.". . .

The principal added that there was no evidence of emotional disturbance on Oswald's record at the school.

Source: *New York Times,* December 1, 1963, pp. 1, 57.

## Oswald Was "Loner," Ex-Marine Recalls

Lee H. Oswald was a "loner" who did not have friends in the Marines, a Milwaukee man who served with him said . . . today. . . .

He remembers Oswald as quiet, serious and "trying to find himself.". . .

"The rest of us used to wrestle and horse around, but he would have his bunk in the corner and stay there, reading a book," he said. "He didn't have any friends."

"I didn't know the names of Senators or where they were from, but he could rattle them off, and he knew their ideals and what they stood for." . . .

Source: *New York Times,* December 2, 1963, p. 41.

# Judges Asked Aid for Oswald at 13

Lee H. Oswald's probation officer . . . said yesterday that four judges in Bronx Children's Court had recommended when Oswald was 13 years old that he receive intensive psychiatric treatment. . . .

Oswald watched television all day long, . . . [he] found. His mother, who had a job, was out of the house most of the day. The boy had been taunted by schoolmates for having a Southwestern drawl and for wearing blue jeans. . . .

[The probation officer said] "There are a lot of children like Lee Oswald in this city, fatherless children who feel unloved and have to act out." . . .

Source: *New York Times*, December 3, 1963, p. 34.

# Oswald Below Average in Junior High

Lee H. Oswald made below-average grades when he was a junior high school student [in New Orleans] in 1955, but his instructors saw no evidence of maladjustment. . . .

The record on file at Warren Easton High School showed that Oswald, as a teen-ager, was a poor speller, had an immature handwriting and commanded little attention from his teachers. . . .

Asked [on a personal history form] if he had any close friends in the school, he wrote in "No." The next question was "If so, name two." Oswald wrote in two names. The names, however, were erased, presumably by him. . . .

Source: *New York Times*, December 3, 1963, p. 34.

# Mental Study of Oswald at 13 Found Him Angry

A psychiatric examination of Lee H. Oswald, performed 10 years ago, revealed a quiet, subdued youth who:

Was potentially dangerous.

Was given to violence and had fantasies involving violence.

Had a hatred for authority—fixed on a father symbol.

Was resentful of persons who had fathers.

Had much hidden anger, although outwardly was a calm youth. . . .

It was learned that the examination report, at least three pages long, described young Oswald as a schizoid personality.

What was meant by that, according to the report, was that he had an unruffled, seclusive personality. . . .

Oswald's father died before the youth was born, and this led to his vengeful feelings toward those persons who had fathers, the report indicated.

This led in part to Oswald's schizoid personality, which the report said, meant that he had an underlying hidden, almost passive, tendency toward aggression. . . .

Source: *New York Times,* December 4, 1963, p. 18.

# Ex-Marine Lieutenant Calls Oswald "Wise Guy"

A former Marine lieutenant says Lee H. Oswald was a "wise guy" who went out of his way to annoy people. . . .

[He] described Oswald as in revolt "against any kind of authority." Oswald liked, he said, to ask officers to explain relatively obscure situations in foreign affairs, "to show off his superior political knowledge." . . .

Source: *New York Times,* December 4, 1963, p. 18.

Through retrospective (Schur, 1971: 52–56) and concurrent interpretation, then, people come to view deviators in a new light. "The ramifications of such rereading . . . are basic to the way in which the labeling process 'creates' deviants. . . . The potential force of . . . [re]interpretation lies in the attendant social refusal to validate . . . [legitimate] identity" (Schur, 1971: 53, 56). Thus, the deviant individual finds it increasingly difficult to maintain a conception of self other than that based on the deviance, because the reinterpretation involves a negative redefinition of the otherwise legitimate criteria on which he or she might construct a self-definition. As the alternative, socially acceptable roles are diminished, the deviant identity comes to take precedence.

The major determinants of deviant identity, then, are (1) the creation of deviance as a master status, (2) assignment to this status of a distinct role defined by a negative stereotype, and (3) a negative redefinition of the individual's other identities through concurrent and retrospective interpretation. Their cumulative effect is to introduce a consistent definition of deviance to an otherwise heterogeneous configuration of the elements that comprise the lives of most individuals and ultimately to the interaction between deviants and nondeviants.

The processes associated with labeling are the means by which members of society justify the proscription and negative sanction of deviant conduct. Penalizing people who were seen to possess valued attributes would produce cognitive dissonance. Thus, a definition of the deviant cannot contain both valued and disvalued characteristics. Placing the nonconformer into the master status, applying the stereotype, and engaging in retrospective and concurrent interpretation redefine legitimate attributes and allow others to act toward the deviant with little ambivalence.

The labeling process severely limits the roles that the deviant might otherwise assume, a restriction that further prescribes the nature and boundaries of subsequent interaction. The social-psychological impact is for the individual to become engulfed in the deviant role, to define himself or herself almost solely in terms of the cultural expectations attached to that role (Schur, 1971: 69–70).

## RESEARCH ON LABELING

Concepts central to the labeling theory of social deviance point to the importance of the interaction between self and others in the construction of deviance careers. The research tradition generated by this approach has focused on two distinct areas—variations in the reactions of others to nonconformity and the impact of these reactions on self-concept and behavior.

### Factors That Affect the Social Response

As discussed in the preceding section, reactions to deviance may occur at a number of different levels. Research on the social response, however, has focused on the informal reactions in primary groups and public encounters and the formal responses of organizations for social control. The findings indicate that reactions to deviance are influenced by the nature of the interaction between the deviant and others as well as by the social and personal characteristics of each.

**Informal Labeling.**   Intimate primary groups generally are reluctant to reject members whose behaviors deviate from acceptable patterns. Rather, they make substantial efforts either to persuade errant members to conform (Orcutt, 1973) or to deny that the behavior in question exceeds socially approved limits (Schwartz, 1957). Only when the nonconformity threatens to disrupt the ongoing activities of the group will steps be take to censure the offender's behavior.

Secondary groups, however, are more likely to reject nonconformity. Unlike primary ties, secondary associations are characterized by limited knowledge of the other; the attribution of deviance, therefore, becomes important information for determining group responses.

Rejection of the nonconformer is also predicated on a number of social and personal factors. The visibility of the deviation, the sex and physical attractiveness of the actor, and especially the nonconformer's social class mediate the responses. Deviations that are most visible, and therefore most disruptive of social activities, are most likely to elicit negative reactions (Mechanic, 1962; Phillips, 1963; Farrell and Morrione, 1974). More allowances are generally made for the deviations of females and physically attractive people (Phillips, 1963; Dion, 1972). Lower-class persons whose definitions of deviance are similar to those of the middle classes are more rejecting of deviants than are their higher-status counterparts (Kitsuse, 1962; Dohrenwend and Chin-Shong, 1967; Farrell and Morrione, 1974). In addition, the personal characteristics of lower-class individuals and the circumstances under which they conduct their behavior are more likely to bring their deviations to the attention of conforming others (see Leznoff and Westley, 1955; Myerhoff and Myerhoff, 1964). Thus, insofar as lower-class deviations are character-ized by increased intensity (Terry, 1967), frequency (Mechanic, 1962; Terry, 1967), visibility (Mechanic, 1962; Stinchcombe, 1963), and un-favorability of the place and situation in which they occur (Terry, 1967), these behaviors will elicit more negative responses.

**Formal Labeling.**   We have seen that reactions to deviance may also involve the application of formal labels. That is, once behaviors have been brought to the attention of social control agencies, those agencies may invoke procedures and sanctions that formally designate certain in-dividuals deviant, delinquent, or criminal.

The likelihood that formal labeling will take place is, as with in-formal labeling, dependent on a number of factors. Many persons regularly violate social and legal norms. Whether it is inappropriate public behavior, illicit sexual encounters, or systematic tax evasion, some behavior of most persons at one time or another makes them potential candidates for official sanction. Yet, relatively few are actually hospitalized or imprisoned. Official intervention seems to be affected by the original informal reaction and by institutionalized selection pro-cedures as well as by the nature and visibility of the behavior itself.

Organizations for the official control of deviance have limited resources. As more and more behaviors have come to be viewed as needing treatment, the proportion of persons who can be processed decreases. The mental health movement, for example, has been active in expanding definitions of mental disease to include ever-larger categories of behaviors. Most people experiencing "problems of living"—dif-ficulties in adjusting to social and employment situations—are now con-sidered to need treatment. Changing conceptions of drug and alcohol abuse, sexual deviation, hyperactivity in children, learning disability, and marital discord as emotional and behavioral disorders that require specialized treatment are cases in point.

## American Psychiatric Association Classification Changes

The psychiatric definition of mental illness has expanded considerably. The diagnostic categories that follow exemplify the kinds of behavior that have come to be viewed as pathological within the last two decades.

Alcohol intoxication
Caffeine intoxication
Cannabis abuse (hashish, marijuana)
Cocaine abuse
Tobacco use disorder
Psychosexual dysfunctions
    with inhibited sexual desire
    with inhibited sexual excitement
    with inhibited female orgasm
    with inhibited male orgasm
    with premature ejaculation
Ego-dystonic homosexuality
Specific reading disorder
Specific arithmetic disorder
Separation anxiety disorder
Shyness disorder
Introverted disorder of childhood
Academic underachievement disorder
Specific academic or work inhibition
Pathological gambling
Temporary insomnia
Somnambulism

Source: American Psychiatric Association, *Diagnostic and Statistical Manual of Mental Disorders*, 3d ed. (Washington, D.C., American Psychiatric Association, 1980).

Particularly illustrative are the changing definition and treatment of homeless men. Until the late 1940s, the hobo was a common figure on the U.S. landscape. Transient, poor, and inclined to use too much alcohol, hobos moved from town to town in railroad boxcars, camping at regular sites along the way. They subsisted by performing menial jobs or simply by begging from door to door. Although they were excluded from mainstream community activity and often ostracized by the children and adults with whom they came into contact, hobos were not regarded as mentally ill or seriously criminal. Rather, they were believed to be an inevitable part of society. In time, however, the hobo became the target of changing concerns regarding the life-style that characterized his situation. Today, one third of all arrests in the United States are for public intoxication, and mental hospital wards are occupied by many whose primary maladjustment is homelessness.

The criminal justice system too has seen rapid growth in the number of activities classified as illegal. Laws to regulate transportation, manufacturing, production and distribution of food and drugs, and the management of entrusted funds and laws to prohibit child abuse, hijacking, and rioting, for example, did not exist until the twentieth century. The proliferation of criminal definitions has resulted in an expanding population of potential candidates for legal treatment. The resources available for such processing, however, preclude full enforcement. Official agencies must select only certain offenders and offense types to receive legal sanction. In arriving at these decisions, agencies rely on the informal reactions of conforming others. For example, most hospitalizations for symptoms of mental disorder occur with the deviant's family acting as the complainant (Haney and Miller, 1970; Gove and Howell, 1974). Similarly, most arrests are made in response to citizens' requests for assistance; a study of police mobilizations in Boston, Chicago, and Washington, D.C., showed that 86 percent resulted from dispatches to calls for help by private citizens, while only 14 percent were responses to incidents witnessed by police in the field (Black and Reiss, 1967). Since formal agencies depend on the reactions of the general population to guide their selection of individuals for treatment, official labels reflect public definitions of deviance (Mechanic, 1962). These definitions, as well as their institutional manifestations, may be based primarily on popular stereotypes of crime and deviance.

**Stereotypes and the Official Response.**  As we have seen, stereotypes exist throughout society (Nunnally, 1961; Simmons, 1965; Scheff, 1966; Scott, 1969; Reed and Reed, 1973; Hess and Mariner, 1975). These stereotypes not only shape public attitudes and behavior toward deviants but also guide the choice of individuals who are to be so defined. People who possess characteristics associated with the stereotype of a particular deviation are most likely to be identified and reacted to as deviant (Simmons, 1965). Furthermore, since minority groups, lower-class persons, and males more closely approximate the stereotypes of many types of deviation, these groups are especially susceptible to their application (Simmons, 1965).

Popular beliefs about deviants are also found at the organizational level and may influence the application of formal labels. "Organizational practices, particularly the selection and processing of individuals by formal agencies of control, often reflect common public stereotypes or more specific organizational ideologies grounded in stereotyped thinking" (Schur, 1971: 51). Thus, for example, facial stereotypes of the murderer, robber, and traitor have been found to affect evaluations of guilt in each of these criminal categories (Shoemaker et al., 1973). Similarly, in the case of homosexuality:

> the crucial factor influencing legal processing in not whether individuals are known to be engaging in homosexual activity, but rather if they appear to be homosexual in a stereotypic sense. . . . Such highly visible behavior may invite the intervention of police who tend to operate on "normal" (stereotypic) cases and convince them of guilt once they have apprehended the individual. The fact that [a person] does not display [for example] overt and effeminate behavior may [even] raise the more basic question in the minds of some as to whether [the person] is in fact homosexual. [Farrell and Hardin, 1974: 134–135]

The importance of appearance also emerges in the case of shoplifting, where the conventionality of the dress of shoplifters has been shown to exert a major influence on reporting levels (Steffensmeier and Terry, 1973). The involuntary hospitalization of black and lower-class populations (Gibbs, 1962; Rushing, 1971) and the more frequent selection for legal treatmet of lower-status delinquents (Goldman, 1963; Piliavin and Briar, 1964) and adult offenders (Westley, 1953; Skolnick, 1966; Reiss, 1968; Black, 1970; Green, 1970; Marshall and Purdy, 1972) also reflect official reliance on deviance stereotypes. In these situations, where the circumstances and behavior of the actor are ambiguous, agents frequently rely on the popular conceptions of nonconformity in making treatment decisions (Wahrman, 1970; Marshall and Purdy, 1972; Dion, 1972).

It appears, therefore, that stereotypes do operate as guiding imageries for action in the treatment of deviance. They are the "means for categorizing persons and the complement of attributes felt to be ordinary and natural for members of . . . [deviant] categories," allowing others "to deal with [such persons] . . . without special attention or thought" (Goffman, 1963). Law-enforcement situations seem to be particularly prone to the use of such categorizations. Where constraints of time, personnel, and the sheer number of individuals who must be processed will not allow full enforcement or extensive investigation, officials are likely to depend on shorthand methods to make administrative decisions. These methods include inspection of the offender and the offense for conformity to the popular conception of criminality (see also Hawkins and Tiedeman, 1975).

**Informal Response to Formal Labels.**    Once the official label has been applied, informal responses to the deviant may become increasingly negative. Incidental deviance has become official. The formal label, therefore, may, under certain circumstances, act as a permanent stigma that discredits any attempt by the individual to return to a more legitimate status.

# The Painted Bird

*Jerzy Kozinski*

The devastating effects of social stigma are symbolically conveyed in the following passage from Jerzy Kozinski's *The Painted Bird.*
[When Lekh (the protagonist of the story) became angry, he would stare solemnly at the captured birds in their cages.] Finally, after prolonged scrutiny, he would choose the strongest bird, tie it to his wrist, and prepare stinking paints of different colors which he mixed together from the most varied components. When the colors satisfied him, Lekh would turn the bird over and paint its wings, head, and breast in rainbow hues until it became more dappled and vivid than a bouquet of wildflowers.

Then we would go into the thick of the forest. There Lekh took out the painted bird and ordered me to hold it in my hand and squeeze it lightly. The bird would begin to twitter and attract a flock of the same species which would fly nervously over our heads. Our prisoner, hearing them, strained toward them, warbling more loudly, its little heart, locked in its freshly painted breast, beating violently.

When a sufficient number of birds gathered above our heads, Lekh would give me a sign to release the prisoner. It would soar, happy and free, a spot of rainbow against the backdrop of clouds, and then plunge into the waiting brown flock. For an instant the birds were confounded. The painted bird circled from one end of the flock to the other, vainly trying to convince its kin that it was one of them. But, dazzled by its brilliant colors, they flew around it unconvinced. The painted bird would be forced farther and farther away as it zealously tried to enter the ranks of the flock. We saw soon afterwards how one bird after another would peel off in a fierce attack. Shortly the many-hued shape lost its place in the sky and dropped to the ground. When we finally found the painted bird it was usually dead. Lekh keenly examined the number of blows which the bird had received. Blood seeped through its colored wings, diluting the paint and soiling Lekh's hands. . . .

One day he trapped a large raven, whose wings he painted red, the breast green, and the tail blue. When a flock of ravens appeared over our hut, Lekh freed the painted bird. As soon as it joined the flock a desperate battle began. The changeling was attacked from all sides. Black, red, green, blue feathers began to drop at our feet. The ravens flew amuck in the skies, and suddenly the painted raven plummeted to the fresh-plowed soil. It was still alive, opening its beak and vainly trying to move its wings. Its eyes had been pecked out, and fresh blood streamed over its painted feathers. It made yet another attempt to flutter up from the sticky earth, but its strength was gone.

Jerzy Kozinski, *The Painted Bird*, in *The Manufacture of Madness*, Thomas Szasz (New York: Harper & Row, 1970), pp. 291–292.

The continued rejection of deviants following official processing is, of course, related to the persistence of the original behavior. Individuals who display symptoms of serious mental disorder, for example, are responded to negatively, independent of the source or nature of the official labels applied to them (Phillips, 1963; Bord, 1971; Kirk, 1974; Loman and Larkin, 1976, Larkin and Loman, 1977). However, official processing may also influence the community response. In the case of societal reaction to mental disorders, research has shown that an individual who exhibits given types of behavior is increasingly rejected as he or she is described alternately as having sought no help, seen a clergyman, a physician, a psychiatrist, and finally as having been admitted to a mental hospital (Phillips, 1963). Although the behavior itself has an independent effect, a normal person who is described as having been in a mental hospital is rejected more than a person whose behavior is characteristically psychotic but who has sought no help. Therefore, people labeled deviant may be rejected for reasons other than the seriousness of their behavior (see also Caetano, 1974; Weissbach and Zagon, 1975; Loman and Larkin, 1976; Larkin and Loman, 1977). Once a person is formally placed in a specific deviance category, formerly ambiguous conduct crystallizes in the eyes of others. In this instance, all the actor's behaviors come to be viewed with suspicion and to be seen as confirming the applicability of the label.

As we have already noted, people may not only react negatively to labeled deviants, but they may also withhold from them the opportunity to conform. In a study of the employability of criminal offenders, four employment folders were constructed that were identical in all respects except for variations in criminal record (Schwartz and Skolnick, 1962). The first folder indicated that the applicant had been convicted and sentenced for assault; the second, that the individual had been tried for the offense but acquitted. The third included not only a statement of acquittal but a letter from the judge certifying the value of the presumption of innocence, and the fourth showed no criminal record. Of the twenty-five prospective employers who received the fourth folder, nine expressed interest in the applicant. This was considered to be the best possible employment response which could be expected for all other applicants. Six of the twenty-five employers who received dossiers containing presumption-of-innocence letters made job offers; three out of twenty-five would have considered hiring those acquitted of their offenses; and only one out of twenty-five employers would have considered those with records of criminal conviction (see Table 4–2). A replication of this study yielded similar results (Buikhuisen and Dijksterhuis, 1971). The opportunities for employment, in this case, for juveniles, were again much greater for persons without records, even though the other information provided to the prospective employers was identical.

A formal label is more likely to stigmatize its bearer if it is specific and visible rather than diffuse and marginally relevant to ongoing social activities. For example, a man on probation as a convicted felon, given the restrictions attending voting, residence, employment, and interpersonal associations, will be more stigmatized than a man with a less than honorable discharge from the military. In the latter case, formal action may have been the product of a wide range of behaviors and is less relevant in the routine of everyday interaction (Williams and Weinberg, 1971).

Labels will also be more effective sources of stigma within secondary, rather than primary, associations (Freeman and Simmons, 1961; Ericson, 1977). Like behavioral deviations themselves, official labels constitute only one aspect of the interaction that characterizes primary ties—the individual is among intimates a parent, sibling, provider, and friend in addition to being an officially designated deviant. Within secondary groups, however, where interaction with the deviant is more uni-dimensional, knowledge that an individual has been formally processed may determine all succeeding evaluations of the deviant and his or her behavior. Thus, for example, the more socially distant a person is from a released prisoner, the more likely he or she is to treat the individual as fundamentally stigmatized (Ericson, 1977). In other words,

**TABLE 4–2. Effect of Four Types of Legal Folder on Job Opportunities**

|  | No Record | Acquitted With Letter | Acquitted Without Letter | Convicted |
|---|---|---|---|---|
| Interest in hiring | 9 | 6 | 3 | 1 |
| No interest in hiring | 16 | 19 | 22 | 24 |
| Total | 25 | 25 | 25 | 25 |

Source: Adapted from Richard D. Schwartz and Jerome H. Skolnick, "Two Studies in Legal Stigma," *Social Problems* 10 (Fall 1962): 137.

when they have little other information, people rely on the "ex-convict" status for interactional cues that are based on the stereotype of the label. The effects of this practice may include neighbors' not allowing the ex-offender to associate with their sons and daughters, prospective employers' erecting barriers to job opportunities, the police continuing to watch for signs of additional crime, and probation officers' providing constant reminders to past events (Ericson, 1977).

Reactions to formal labels also show subcultural variations. We have seen that individuals who conform to popular images of crime and deviance are more often officially labeled as deviant. Insofar as members of the lower classes and minority populations fit these stereotypes, they will tend to be disproportionately selected for deviance processing. At the same time, lower-class people, because of continued economic isolation and social discrimination, are to some extent marginal to dominant definitions of nonconformity. Therefore, although lower-status persons are more frequently labeled, these labels may have little impact on the subsequent responses of people within the deviant's own socio-cultural setting (Freeman and Simmons, 1961; Mercer, 1965). Thus, for example, lower-status children who are diagnosed as retarded and placed in institutions are more quickly released to their families than are similarly diagnosed higher-status children (Mercer, 1965). That is, higher-status parents more frequently agree with the official definitions of retardation, and are more pessimistic about the prognosis for their children outside the institu-

**TABLE 4–3.  Factors That Affect the Application of Deviant Labels**

|  | Application of Deviant Labels | Withholding of Deviant Labels |
|---|---|---|
| Level of organization of reacting others | Formal | Informal |
| Group setting of interaction | Secondary Public encounters | Primary Intimate relations |
| Visability of the deviation | Overt | Covert |
| Physical characteristics of the deviant | Unattractive | Attractive |
| Social characteristics of the deviant | Male Lower status | Female Higher status |
| Conformity of the deviant's behavior to the public stereotype | Stereotypic | Nonstereotypic |

tion. Since lower-status families tend to be less impressed by the professional definition of this disability, their subsequent behavior toward the child will often be less affected by the label. The definitions of deviance differ across social and racial contexts, and the reactions of others to formally applied labels vary accordingly.

In summary, then, the labeling perspective on social deviance envisions nonconformity as the consequence of the successful application of a label. The informal and formal reactions of others to the behavior in question is an important part of this process. Whether or not persons will be thought deviant depends on the visibility of their behavior, their age, sex, and physical characteristics, and the context within which they are evaluated. In this regard, persons in secondary group encounters and those from the lower social classes will more likely be evaluated negatively. Responses will also be rejecting if the individual conforms to the popular stereotype of the deviation. Since such stereotypes have become institutionalized in the selection procedures of agencies of social control, they may also contribute to the decision to apply formal labels.

Officially designating a person as deviant may, in turn, increase the negative reactions experienced by this individual in future encounters. Such a designation, that is, may operate as a master status and significantly reduce the possibility of interaction on more legitimate bases. Response to the formal label will vary depending on the nature of the label itself, as well as on the relationship of the audience to the actor and the socio-cultural context in which the interaction occurs. People in primary association with the labeled deviant will generally be more accepting than will those in secondary associations. In addition, if the deviant's significant others are socially and culturally marginal, they will less often accept the label as meaningful information.

**TABLE 4–4 Factors that Affect Social Responses to Formally Labeled Deviants**

|  | Rejection of Deviant | Acceptance of Deviant |
|---|---|---|
| Characteristics of the label | Specific<br>Relevant to ongoing interaction | Diffuse<br>Irrelevant to ongoing interaction |
| Group setting of interaction | Secondary<br>Public encounters | Primary<br>Intimate relations |
| Position of the deviant's group affiliations in the larger society | Integrated | Marginal |

## THE SOCIAL RESPONSE AND
## DEVIANCE OUTCOMES

As we have seen, labeling theorists argue that rejection of the nonconformer may increase his or her behavioral deviation through the symbolic communication of expectations of deviance and the simultaneous isolation of the individual from legitimate roles. According to Lemert (1951), nonconformity that is severely sanctioned may be incorporated as part of the *me* of the individual. The result may be the disrupton of the individual's legitimate roles and the reorganization of his or her life around the deviant identity. As we have seen, Lemert referred to this outcome as secondary deviation and suggested that it develops as a means of adjustment to the problems created by society's reaction to the original or specific (primary) deviation.

Tests of Lemert's argument, however, have been limited. The empirical model usually proposed assumes a direct relationship between the application of formal sanctions and increased behavioral deviation. Although some evidence confirms the existence of such a relationship (Gold and Williams, 1969; Meade, 1974;[1] Farrington, 1977), other research does not (Williams and Weinberg, 1971; Fisher, 1972; Klein, 1974).[2]

The most outstanding feature of these studies, in addition to the contradictory nature of their findings, is their systematic exclusion of the reference group—those to whom we compare ourselves and to whom we look for reward and personal identity. Contrary to its development in both symbolic interactionism and labeling theory, the concept of reacting others has typically been operationalized in the research as meaning those who apply official sanction: the police, the courts, and the prisons.

It may be recalled that the major assumption of symbolic interactionism is that *self-concept develops out of a process of ongoing communication between the individual and significant others.* According to Cooley and Mead, we cannot conceive of the self independently but only through interaction with those in association with us. This assumption is also central to the labeling theory of deviance. Here too we find attention to the role of significant others in the process of deviance creation. Thus, for Lemert (1951), assuming a deviant role implies associational learning. "There must be a spreading corroboration of a socio-pathic self-conception and societal reinforcement at each step in the process" (Lemert, 1951: 77). Such corroboration depends on more than the negative reactions of agents of social control.[3] Deviance is created not only when the actor is propelled into the role of the outsider but also when the actor is attracted to people willing to define the behavior in question in more positive terms.

Becoming a marijuana user, for example, involves more than the formal or informal assignment of an individual to a deviant status (Becker, 1963).

> Before engaging in the activity on a more or less regular basis, the person has no notion of the pleasures to be derived from it; he learns these in the course of interaction with more experienced deviants. He learns to be aware of new kinds of experiences and to think of them as pleasurable. . . . The individual *learns*, in short, to participate in a subculture organized around the particular deviant activity. [Becker, 1963: 31]

Through such group associations, behavior defined negatively by society takes on a more positive character; new rationales for continuing the behavior are acquired; and individuals learn how to engage in the deviation with a "minimum of trouble" and to evade enforcement officials with techniques established by "earlier pioneers" (Becker, 1963: 39). Theoretical developments in other areas, such as the study of nudism (Weinberg, 1966), stuttering (Lemert, 1962b), homosexuality (Farrell and Morrione, 1975), and blindness (Scott, 1969) have also focused on the associational factor in the acquisition of deviant behavior.

The importance of group associations may even be seen in the case of insanity. Persons comprising the treatment setting—physicians, hospital personnel, and other patients—reward the individual for conforming to their conceptions of mental illness. This group support transforms initially undifferentiated deviance into more uniform and stable mental disorder (Scheff, 1966: 84–87).

Labeling theorists, then, have indeed been aware of the importance of referent others in the construction of deviant careers. They have emphasized not only the perceived or real responses of legitimate society but also the individual's identification and association with deviant groups. Persistent nonconformity is viewed as a product both of the negative sanctions imposed by the larger society and of the rewards provided by people with whom the individual interacts more intimately.

Empirical investigations that have included the concept of significant others have consistently studied it only in terms of conforming others. The original, nondeviant referents of mother, father, and close personal friends have been exclusively used as the audience that evaluates and affects the self-evaluations of labeled deviants (Reckless et al., 1956, 1957; Dintz et al., 1958; Scarpitti et al., 1960; Burkett, 1972; Kaplan, 1976; Hepburn, 1977). Although the responses of these groups may be a necessary factor in deviance causation, the nature of interaction with nonconforming others may likewise be crucial. That is, both deviant and nondeviant groups may serve as referents for identity and behavior. The neglect of the former in empirical investigations of labeling theory may account for the lack of support generated for the perspective.

Furthermore, the assumption that the response of legitimate groups is a sufficient condition for a person's taking a deviant role may not be applicable to many forms of deviance, insofar as deviant role models are not readily available in legitmate groups. In this situation, deviants must rely on the expectations of nondeviants as transmitted to them through interpersonal encounters or through official designation of their behavior as falling outside the limits of legitimate group requirements. The only information that individuals have about their deviations is that acquired from the messages contained in these responses and from their own definitions of the situation learned through prior socialization. At this stage, they may not have other deviants to imitate, to model themselves after in their attempts to establish meaningful roles as defined by the larger society. For this they must eventually shift reference associations from those who have labeled and responded to them as deviant to those who accept them as equals and who have adopted similar roles for themselves as a result of like experiences in the community at large. In this manner, the deviant becomes familiar with the nature of the role and, at the same time, acquires the knowledge, symbols, and support necessary for its enactment. This is an interpretive process based both on the responses encountered in the larger society and on the more intimate interactions within the deviant group.

In general, then, reference groups, with their values, beliefs, and attitudes, provide the standards by which individuals evaluate themselves. As persons are identified as deviant by conforming referents, they may shift their attachments to groups more sympathetic towards the deviant identity.

> The [deviant] is in search of self-validation or of some groups or social systems that will be a "good" looking-glass so the self can be mirrored as a "good" self or a worthy self. If self-acceptance is based upon "other" acceptance of the self and if the legitimate social system produces only negative images of self and persons in the system, needs for self-validation through love and acceptance will arise in the individual that are not met by the legitimate social system. The [deviant] will then reject the legitimate social system for any system that offers an opportunity for fulfillment of his needs. [Chapman, 1966, 379]

The support provided by other deviants has obvious consequences for continued nonconformity. A person who is accepted by a group that rewards individuals precisely *because* they are deviant may become further committed to the deviant role.

The few studies that have included a measure of deviant association support this argument. Labeled deviants do positively evaluate persons who represent their own marginal status (Chapman, 1966; Moriarty, 1974). In addition, behavior after labeling appears to be influenced by people who share the deviant attribute (Ageton and Elliott, 1974;[4] Moriarty, 1974; Newton and Shelden, 1975; Farrell and Nelson, 1976). This supports the idea that individuals whose behavior has been questioned by more conforming groups may develop new attachments to others similarly disvalued. When this occurs, the organization of behavior and identity around the deviation may be virtually assured.

# The Social Response, Reference Association, and Homosexual Deviance

*Ronald A. Farrell and James F. Nelson*

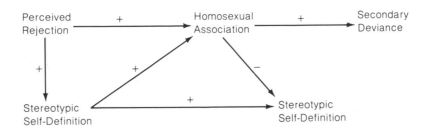

If persons perceive others reacting to them in terms of the homosexual stereotype, they may incorporate the stereotype as part of their self-definition. These responses, and the accompanying feelings of stigma, are likely to produce stress. As an adaptation, individuals may shift their reference associations to homosexual groups. While providing for a more positive identity, the ultimate outcome of these associations is often secondary deviance.

Source: Ronald A. Farrell and James F. Nelson, "A Causal Model of Secondary Deviance: The Case of Homosexuality," *Sociological Quarterly* 17 (Winter 1976): 109, 116.

Theoretical developments within the labeling approach to deviant behavior are clear. The role of referent others in the deviance-defining process is multiple; they not only apply labels, but they also respond to individuals once the labels have been applied. The nature of this latter response will determine subsequent behavior on the part of those labeled.

Following public recognition of nonconformity, negotiations between labeled deviants and their significant others may result in one of several outcomes. First, the original primary reference group may continue to accept the individual on the basis of the nondeviant identity. By refusing to recognize the legitimacy of external evaluations of the behavior of one of its members, primary groups may fail to treat the nonconformer in terms of the expectations implied by the label. Thus, for example, many youngsters regarded in their communities as "good boys" have histories of contact with legal authorities. Parents, teachers, and friends continue to think of them as essentially good, as do the boys themselves (Reckless et al., 1956, 1957; Foster et al., 1972). In like manner, homosexuals are typically accepted by primary others. What rejection they do experience comes from those with whom they are less intimately associated. Furthermore, homosexuals who are rejected in public encounters are able to maintain essentially nondeviant identities if they perceive acceptance in primary group relations (Farrell, 1972: 85–95, 99–101).

The greater acceptance of deviance by primary groups is a product of the nature of the interaction that occurs in such settings. Intimate associations involve extensive knowledge of the other person and are characterized by an empathy not usually found in secondary encounters. This more complete understanding and mutual identification take precedence over the public's stereotypic definition of the deviant. The continued acceptance of the nonconformer and the invalidation of the label that follows from this interaction render the behavioral consequences of public labeling ineffective. Deviation in this instance may be expected to remain at its primary level.

Although significant others are reluctant to reject one of their members, continued acceptance may be in terms of the imputed deviance. In this instance, the labeled nonconformer will not experience alienation from the original reference group but will find the deviant status validated by these associations. Such an outcome is similar to that described by Kai Erikson in his study of schizophrenia in the military (Dentler and Erikson, 1959). In the study, described in Chapter 2 of this book, army recruits resisted elimination of pre-institutionalized psychotics from their training units. While recognizing that the nonconformers were not capable of performing daily army routines, the groups erected protective shells around them lest military authorities become aware of the deviants' behavior. Similarly, wives of psychotic spouses have been found to exert great effort in maintaining the original relationship. Defining the bizarre behavior to require institutional intervention was denied as long as accommodation within the family could be maintained (Schwartz, 1957). Finally, in a study of perceptions of stigma among apprehended juveniles, the youths did not appear to perceive any loss of esteem among their families. Many of the parents already regarded their sons as prone to trouble and expressed no surprise at the latest instance of delinquency (Foster et al., 1972). Here, no change in parental reaction followed the children's being officially designated deviant. When the response of significant others involves such acceptance of the deviance, the labeled individual will tend toward an intensification of and commitment to the behavior. In this instance, the support of primary others is instrumental in propelling the individual toward a pattern of secondary deviation.

The third possible response of primary groups is, of course, to reject the labeled deviant. It is this course of action that is implied in most research on labeling. On the basis of this rejection, it is further presumed that additional deviant behavior will ensue. Commitment to nonconformity following primary group rejection, however, is itself uncertain.

Given the individual's need for associations conducive to the maintenance of a positive self-concept (Chapman, 1966), rejection by his or her original reference group may produce stress (Parsons, 1951; Cohen, 1955, 1959) and may therefore generate the need to adapt. Such adaptation may involve selecting a new reference group, whose response to the labeled deviant is itself variable.

In one instance, the adopted referent others may accept the nonconformer on a nondeviant basis; this is the purpose of such group-support organizations as Weight Watchers and Alcoholics Anonymous. While maintaining that the essential identity of their members remains forever "fat" or "alcoholic," they try to convert *discrediting stigma* into *discreditable stigma*[5] (Goffman, 1963; Roman and Trice, 1968; Trice and Roman, 1970; Warren, 1974; Laslett and Warren, 1975). Drug rehabilitation programs, religious organizations, and many more informal associations perform a similar function. By relating to the deviant on the basis of a more legitimate status, these groups may prevent the individual from reorganizing his or her life and identity around continued deviation.

Individuals who are rejected by the original primary others may also develop associations with people who accept them in terms of the deviant label. This subcultural adaptation (Cohen, 1955, 1959) involves the interaction of individuals who share similar problems of adjustment to the stigmatizing label and who, through their interaction, can offer each other a more positive evaluation of the deviant role. The concept of subcultural association has long occupied an important position in explorations of deviant behavior (Hooker, 1956; Short, 1957; Reiss, 1961; Einstadter, 1969; Adams, 1973). As we have seen, however, its utilization in research on labeling has been limited. The evidence available indicates that enculturation of labeled nonconformers to deviant subcultures may result from perceived societal rejection (Farrell and Nelson, 1976, 1978). Individuals who perceive such rejection may adapt to the stigma by shifting reference associations to deviant groups. While these associations provide collective support, their ultimate outcome may be further identification with the deviant role and the eventual development of secondary deviation.

The varying response patterns of significant others to designated deviance and the implications of such responses for future behavior are illustrated in Table 4–5.

In sum, the research dealing with the impact of the social response on self-concept and behavior appears to have abandoned its link with labeling theory and antecedent developments in symbolic interactionism. In its emphasis on significant others, the interactionist perspective includes as its most basic assumption the notion of referent identification and association. It is through the ongoing processes of such communicative interaction that symbolic realities are constructed and reconstructed. In this manner, individuals come to attach meaning to the behaviors of self and others. Such a premise lies so close to the heart of the interactionist perspective as to have become an assumption taken for granted within the approach.

Labeling research, however, while positing the importance of the reactions of others in the development of deviant careers, has overlooked the role of referent identifications and associations in this process. The consequences of labeling for the deviant depend upon the several patterns of interaction with people whose acceptance of deviant attributes and behaviors are themselves variable.

**TABLE 4–5 Behavioral Consequences of the Nature of Referent Identification and Association and Group Acceptance**

| Nature of Group Acceptance | Nature of Referent Identification and Association | |
| --- | --- | --- |
| | Identification and Association with Original Group | Identification and Association with Adopted Group |
| Acceptance as nondeviant | Primary deviance | Primary deviance |
| Acceptance as deviant | Secondary deviance | Secondary deviance |

## CONCLUSION

The interactionist perspective suggests that personal identity and behavior are socially constructed through communication with significant others. An important part of this process is the assignment of status and role. If persons are designated as deviant, the community's response will be guided by that definition; and the individual will be subject to the expectations commonly associated with the deviation. The major factors operating in this process are (1) the saliency, or importance, of the disvalued status as a source of identification; (2) the stereotypic role that prescribes the position and serves as a basis of response for self and others; and (3) the ongoing reassessment of legitimate identities through concurrent and retrospective interpretation. Once the definition has been applied, interaction becomes structured in terms of the deviation. As a result, the individual is engulfed in the deviant role and tends to organize life around it.

Whether initial, or primary, deviance elicits a negative social response depends on (1) the visibility of the deviation, (2) the personal and social characteristics of the actor, (3) the social distance between the deviant and reacting others, and (4) the extent to which the individual and his or her behavior approximate the public stereotype. If the community's response results in the application of a formal label, the deviant may become the object of increased societal rejection. This intensified response is most likely to occur (1) in secondary group encounters, (2) when the label is publicly communicated, and (3) in interaction with groups who concur with the official label.

The effect of societal reaction on the individual's identity and behavior is dependent on his or her reference identifications. Reference groups who do not treat the individual in terms of the label will impede movement toward secondary deviation. Those, on the other hand, who rely on the public definition in their interaction with the nonconformer will reinforce deviant involvement. Rejection or acceptance of the label may emanate from either original or adopted reference groups.

## NOTES

1. Meade (1974) points out, however, that his own positive findings are only suggestive of the labeling hypothesis. Without an analysis of the subjective states of sanctioned individuals, alternative explanations of the original relationship remain unchallenged. Those persons eventually labeled may in fact be more committed to lives of deviance. Such a possibility constitutes an equally plausible explanation of the available supportive evidence. Until it and similar competing hypotheses can be eliminated, labeling theory remains untested.

2. Related research shows little direct effect of formal sanction on criminal attitudes (O'Connor, 1970; Harris, 1975). Furthermore, contrary to labeling-theory assumptions, such a sanction as incarceration can actually perform a rehabilitative function for those whose delinquent orientations are already low and who are sentenced to resocialization-oriented institutions (O'Connor, 1970). Rehabilitation also seems to be the outcome for those whose period of confinement is relatively brief (Harris, 1975). Labeling predictions are supported, however, when delinquency oriented youth are detained in custodial halls (O'Connor, 1970) and when persons are sentenced to longer periods of incarceration (Harris, 1975).

3. Lemert emphasized that "groups become instrumentally important in those forms of deviance which require for the systematic or continued activiation goods and services provided through others through specifically organized relationships" (1967: 47). Examples of these behaviors are homosexuality, prostitution, gambling, systematic criminality, and political radicalism. Maintaining the identity necessary to sustain such behavior is also said to be facilitated by such contact.

4. Ageton and Elliott (1974) point out, however, that the influence of deviant peers on an individual may occur before the public label has been applied.

5. According to Goffman (1963), stigma may be either discrediting or discreditable. Discrediting stigma are attributes or characteristics that are clearly visible in social interaction—for example, bodily disfigurements; impairments of speech, hearing, or sight; and skin color. Discreditable stigma, on the other hand, while not immediately detectable, have the potential for becoming salient information. A history of arrest or hospitalization and addiction to drugs or alcohol are discreditable to the extent that their discovery may affect subsequent interaction.

## REFERENCES

Adams, Reed
  1973  Differential Association and Learning Principles Revisited. Social Problems 20 (Spring): 458–470.
Ageton, Suzanne S., and Delbert S. Elliott
  1974  The Effects of Legal Processing on Delinquent Orientations. Social Problems 22 (October): 87–100.
American Psychiatric Association
  1980  Diagnostic and Statistical Manual of Mental Disorders. Third ed. Washington, D.C.: American Psychiatric Association.
Becker, Howard S.
  1963  Outsiders. New York: Free Press.
Black, Donald J.
  1970  Production of Crime Rates. American Sociological Review 35 (August): 733–748.
Black, Donald J., and Albert J. Reiss, Jr.
  1967  Patterns of Behavior in Police and Citizen Transactions. *In Studies in Crime and Law Enforcement in Major Metropolitan Areas*, Vol. 2, Field Surveys III. President's Commission on Law Enforcement and Administration of Justice. Washington, D.C.: Government Printing Office.

Bord, Richard J.
 1971  Rejection of the Mentally Ill: Continuities and Further Developments. Social Problems 18 (Spring): 496–509.
Buikhuisen, Walter P., and Fokle P. H. Dijksterhuis
 1971  Delinquency and Stigmatization. British Journal of Criminology 11 (April): 185–187.
Burkett, Steven R.
 1972  Self-Other Systems and Deviant Career Patterns: The Small Group Situation. Pacific Sociological Review 15 (April): 169–183.
Caetano, Donald F.
 1974  Labeling Theory and the Presumption of Mental Illness in Diagnosis: An Experimental Design. Journal of Health and Social Behavior 15 (September): 253–260.
Cain, Albert C.
 1964  On the Meaning of "Playing Crazy" in Borderline Children. Psychiatry 27 (August): 278–289.
Cauthen, Nelson R., Ira E. Robinson, and Herbert H. Krauss
 1971  Stereotypes: A Review of the Literature 1926–1968. Journal of Social Psychology 84 (June): 103–125.
Chapman, Ivan
 1966  Race and Self-Concept of Delinquents and Non-Delinquents. Sociological Quarterly 7 (Summer): 373–379.
Cohen, Albert C.
 1955  Delinquent Boys. New York: Free Press.
 1959  The Study of Social Disorganization and Deviant Behavior. In Sociology Today. Robert K. Merton, Leonard Broom, and Leonard S. Cottrell, eds. pp. 461–484. New York: Basic Books.
Cooley, Charles Horton
 1902  Human Nature and the Social Order. New York: Charles Scribner's Sons.
Davis, Fred
 1961  Deviance Disavowal: The Management of Strained Interaction by the Visibly Handicapped. Social Problems 9 (Fall): 120–132.
Dentler, Robert A., and Kai T. Erikson
 1959  The Functions of Deviance in Groups. Social Problems 7 (Fall): 98–107.
Dinitz, Simon, Walter C. Reckless, and Barbara Kay
 1958  A Self Gradient Among Potential Delinquents. Journal of Criminal Law, Criminology, and Police Science 49 (September–October): 230–233.
Dion, Karen K.
 1972  Physical Attractiveness and Evaluation of Children's Transgressions. Journal of Personality and Social Psychology 24 (November): 207–213.
Dohrenwend, Bruce P., and Edwin Chin-Shong
 1967  Social Status and Attitudes Toward Psychological Disorder: The Problem of Tolerance of Deviance. American Sociological Review 32 (June): 417–433.
Einstadter, Werner J.
 1969  The Social Organization of Armed Robbery. Social Problems 17 (Summer): 64–83.

Ericson, Richard V.
  1977  Social Distance and Reaction to Criminality. British Journal of Criminology 17 (January): 16–29.
Farrell, Ronald A.
  1972  Societal Reaction to Homosexuals: Toward a Generalized Theory of Deviance. Ph.D. dissertation, University of Cincinnati.
Farrell, Ronald A., and Clay W. Hardin
  1974  Legal Stigma and Homosexual Career Deviance. In Crime and Delinquency: Dimensions of Deviance. Marc Riedel and Terence P. Thornberry, eds. Pp. 461–484. New York: Praeger.
Farrell, Ronald A., and Thomas J. Morrione
  1974  Social Interaction and Stereotypic Responses to Homosexuals. Archives of Sexual Behavior 3 (September): 425–442.
  1975  Conforming to Deviance. In Social Deviance. Ronald A. Farrell and Victoria Lynn Swigert, eds. Pp. 375–387. Philadelphia: J. B. Lippincott.
Farrell, Ronald A., and James F. Nelson
  1976  A Causal Model of Secondary Deviance: The Case of Homosexuality. Sociological Quarterly 17 (Winter): 109–120.
  1978  A Sequential Analysis of Delinquency. International Journal of Criminology and Penology 6 (August): 255–268.
Farrington, David P.
  1977  The Effects of Public Labelling. British Journal of Criminology 17 (April): 112–125.
Fisher, Sethard
  1972  Stigma and Deviant Careers in School. Social Problems 20 (Summer): 78–83.
Foster, Jack Donald, Simon Dinitz, and Walter C. Reckless
  1972  Perceptions of Stigma Following Public Intervention for Delinquent Behavior. Social Problems 20 (Fall): 202–209.
Freeman, Howard E., and Ozzie G. Simmons
  1961  Feelings of Stigma Among Relatives of Mental Patients. Social Problems 8 (Spring): 312–321.
Garfinkel, Harold
  1956  Successful Degradation Ceremonies. American Journal of Sociology 61 (March): 420–424.
Gibbs, Jack P.
  1962  Rates of Mental Hospitalization: A Study of Societal Reaction to Deviant Behavior. American Sociological Review 27 (December): 782–792.
Goffman, Erving
  1963  Stigma: Notes on the Management of Spoiled Identity. Englewood Cliffs, New Jersey: Prentice-Hall.
Gold, Martin, and Jay R. Williams
  1969  National Study of the Aftermath of Apprehension. Prospectus, A Journal of Law Reform 3 (December): 3–12.
Goldman, Nathan
  1963  The Differential Selection of Juvenile Offenders for Court Appearance.

New York: National Research and Information Center, National Council on Crime and Delinquency.

Gove, Walter R., and Patrick Howell
1974  Individual Resources and Mental Hospitalization: A Comparison and Evaluation of the Societal Reaction and Psychiatric Perspective. American Sociological Review 39 (February): 86–100.

Green, Edward
1970  Race, Social Status, and Criminal Arrest. American Sociological Review 35 (June): 476–490.

Guskin, Samuel
1963  Dimensions of Judged Similarity Among Deviant Types. American Journal of Mental Deficiency 68 (September): 218–224.

Haney, C. Allen, and Kent S. Miller
1970  Definitional Factors in Mental Incompetency. Sociology and Social Research 54 (July): 520–532.

Harris, Anthony R.
1975  Imprisonment and the Expected Value of Criminal Choice: A Specification and Test of Aspects of the Labeling Perspective. American Sociological Review 40 (February): 71–87.

Hawkins, Richard, and Gary Tiedeman
1975  The Creation of Deviance: Interpersonal and Organizational Determinants. Columbus, Ohio: Charles E. Merrill.

Hepburn, John R.
1977  Official Deviance and Spoiled Identity: Delinquents and Their Significant Others. Pacific Sociological Review 20 (April): 163–179.

Hess, Albert G., and Dorothy A. Mariner
1975  On the Sociology of Crime Cartoons. International Journal of Criminology and Penology 3 (August): 253–265.

Hooker, Evelyn
1956  A Preliminary Analysis of Group Behavior of Homosexuals. Journal of Psychology 42: 217–225.

Kaplan, Howard
1976  Self Attitudes and Deviant Response. Social Forces 54 (June): 788–801.

Kirk, Stuart A.
1974  The Impact of Labeling on Rejection of the Mentally Ill: An Experimental Study. Journal of Health and Social Behavior 15 (June): 108–117.

Kitsuse, John I.
1962  Societal Reaction to Deviant Behavior: Problems of Theory and Method. Social Problems 9 (Winter): 247–256.

Klein, Malcolm W.
1974  Labeling, Deterrence, and Recidivism: A Study of Police Dispositions of Juvenile Offenders. Social Problems 22 (December): 292–303.

Kozinski, Jerzy
1970  The Painted Bird. In The Manufacture of Madness. Thomas Szasz. Pp. 291–292. New York: Harper & Row.

Larkin, William, and L. A. Loman
1977  Labeling in the Family Context: An Experimental Study. Sociology and Social Research 61 (January): 192–203.

Laslett, Barbara, and Carol A. Warren
  1975  Losing Weight: The Organizational Promotion of a Behavior Change. Social Problems 23 (October): 69–80.
Lemert, Edwin M.
  1951  Social Pathology: A Systematic Approach to the Theory of Sociopathic Behavior. New York: McGraw-Hill.
  1962a Paranoia and the Dynamics of Exclusion. Sociometry 25 (March): 2–25.
  1962b Stuttering and Social Structure in Two Pacific Island Societies. Journal of Speech and Hearing Disorders 27 (February): 3–10.
  1967  Human Deviance, Social Problems and Social Control. Englewood Cliffs, New Jersey: Prentice-Hall.
Leznoff, Maurice, and William Westley
  1955  The Homosexual Community. Social Problems 3 (April): 257–263.
Loman, L. Anthony, and William E. Larkin
  1976  Rejection of the Mentally Ill: An Experiment in Labeling. Sociological Quarterly 17 (Autumn): 555–560.
Marshall, Harvey, and Ross Purdy
  1972  Hidden Deviance and the Labeling Approach: The Case for Drinking and Driving. Social Problems 19 (Spring): 541–553.
Mead, George Herbert
  1934  Mind, Self and Society. Chicago: University of Chicago Press.
Meade, Anthony C.
  1974  The Labeling Approach to Delinquency: State of the Theory as a Function of Method. Social Forces 53 (September): 83–91.
Mechanic, David
  1962  Some Factors in Identifying and Defining Mental Illness. Mental Hygiene 46 (January): 66–74.
Mercer, Jane
  1965  Social System Perspective and Clinical Perspective Frames of Reference for Understanding Career Patterns of Persons Labeled as Mentally Retarded. Social Problems 13 (Summer): 18–34.
Myerhoff, H. L., and B. G. Myerhoff
  1964  Field Observation of Middle Class Gangs. Social Forces 42 (March): 328–336.
Moriarty, Thomas
  1974  Role of Stigma in the Experience of Deviance. Journal of Personality and Social Psychology 29 (June): 849–855.
Newton, Charles H., and Randall G. Shelden
  1975  The Delinquent Label and Its Effects on Future Behavior: An Empirical Test of Lemert's Levels of Deviance. International Journal of Criminology and Penology 3 (August): 229–241.
Nunnally, J. C., Jr.
  1961  Popular Conceptions of Mental Health. New York: Holt.
O'Connor, Gerald
  1970  The Impact of Initial Detention upon Male Delinquents. Social Problems 18 (Fall): 194–199.
Orcutt, James D.
  1973  Societal Reaction and the Response to Deviation in Small Groups. Social Forces 52 (December): 259–267.

Parsons, Talcott
1951 The Social System. New York: Free Press.
Phillips, Derek L.
1963 Rejection: A Possible Consequence of Seeking Help for Mental Disorders. American Sociological Review 28 (December): 963–972.
Piliavin, Irving, and Scott Briar
1964 Police Encounters with Juveniles. American Journal of Sociology 70 (September): 206–214.
Reckless, Walter C., Simon Dinitz, and Ellen Murray
1956 Self Concept as an Insulator Against Delinquency. American Sociological Review 21 (December): 744–746.
1957 The "Good" Boy in a High Delinquency Area. Journal of Criminal Law, Criminology, and Police Science 48 (August): 18–26.
Reed, John P., and Robin S. Reed
1973 Status, Images, and Consequence: Once a Criminal Always a Criminal. Sociology and Social Research 57 (July): 460–472.
Reiss, Albert J., Jr.
1961 The Social Integration of Queers and Peers. Social Problems 9 (Fall): 102–120.
1968 Police Brutality: Answers to Key Questions. Transaction 5 (July/August): 10–19.
Roman, Paul M., and Harrison M. Trice
1968 The Sick Role, Labeling Theory and the Deviant Drinker. International Journal of Social Psychiatry 14 (Autumn): 245–251.
Rushing, William
1971 Class, Culture, and "Social Structure and Anomie." American Journal of Sociology 76 (March): 857–872.
Scarpitti, Frank R., Ellen Murray, Simon Dinitz, and Walter C. Reckless
1960 The "Good" Boy in a High Delinquency Area: Four Years Later. American Sociological Review 25 (August): 555–558.
Scheff, Thomas J.
1966 Being Mentally Ill. Chicago: Aldine.
Schur, Edwin M.
1971 Labeling Deviant Behavior: Its Sociological Implications. New York: Harper & Row.
Schwartz, Charlotte
1957 Perspectives on Deviance—Wives' Definitions of Their Husbands' Mental Illness. Psychiatry 20 (August): 275–291.
Schwartz, Richard D., and Jerome H. Skolnick
1962 Two Studies of Legal Stigma. Social Problems 10 (Fall): 133–142.
Scott, Marvin B., and Stanford M. Lyman
1968 Paranoia, Homosexuality and Game Theory. Journal of Health and Social Behavior 9 (September): 179–187.
Scott, Robert A.
1969 The Making of Blind Men. New York: Russell Sage.
Shoemaker, Donald J., Donald R. South, and Jay Lowe
1973 Facial Stereotypes of Deviants and Judgements of Guilt or Innocence. Social Forces 51 (June): 427–433.

Short, James F., Jr.
  1957  Differential Association and Delinquency. Social Problems. 4 (January): 233–239.
Simmons, J. L.
  1965  Public Stereotypes of Deviants. Social Problems 13 (Fall): 223–232.
Skolnick, Jerome H.
  1966  Justice Without Trial: Law Enforcement in Democratic Society. New York: John Wiley and Sons.
Steffensmeier, Darrell J., and Robert M. Terry
  1973  Deviance and Respectability: An Observational Study of Reactions to Shoplifting. Social Forces 51 (June): 417–426.
Stinchcombe, Arthur L.
  1963  Institutions of Privacy in the Determination of Police Administrative Practice. American Journal of Sociology 69 (September): 150–159.
Swigert, Victoria Lynn and Ronald A. Farrell
  1978  Referent Others and Deviance Causation: A Neglected Dimension in Labeling Research. *In* Crime, Law, and Sanction. Marvin D. Krohn and Ronald L. Akers, eds. Pp. 59–72. Beverly Hills: Sage Publications.
Terry, Robert M.
  1967  The Screening of Juvenile Offenders. Journal of Criminal Law, Criminology, and Police Science 58 (June): 173–181.
Trice, Harrison M., and Paul Michael Roman
  1970  Delabeling, Relabeling, and Alcoholics Anonymous. Social Problems 17 (Spring): 538–546.
Wahrman, Ralph
  1970  Status, Deviance, and Sanctions. Pacific Sociological Review 13 (Fall): 229–240.
Warren, Carol A. B.
  1974  The Use of Stigmatizing Social Labels in Conventionalizing Deviant Behavior. Sociology and Social Research 58 (April): 303–311.
Weinberg, Martin S.
  1966  Becoming a Nudist. Psychiatry 29 (February): 15–24.
Weissbach, Theodore A., and Gary Zagon
  1975  The Effect of Deviant Group Membership upon Impressions of Personality. Journal of Social Psychology 95 (April): 263–266.
Westley, William A.
  1953  Violence and the Police. American Journal of Sociology 59 (July): 34–41.
Williams, Colin, and Martin S. Weinberg
  1971  Homosexuals and the Military. New York: Harper & Row.

# 5

## Status Frustration and Adaptation to Strain

According to the interactionist perspective, individuals whose behavior or attributes contravene established norms may be labeled and rejected by society. When they perceive these reactions from their reference groups, they may internalize the public definition of their situation. In this manner, nonconformers may come to think of themselves as generally, rather than specifically, deviant.

It can be further argued that the social response and subsequent self-labeling produce stress and a tendency toward some mode of adaptation. Adaptation is not necessarily a rational and systematic process but might better be characterized as a semiconscious effort to reduce strain. In this regard, Lemert has noted that:

> the law of effect is a simple idea that people beset with problems posed for them by society will choose lines of action they expect to be satisfactory solutions to the problems. If the consequences are those expected, the likelihood that the action or generically similar action will be repeated is increased. If the consequences are unsatisfactory, unpleasant, or make more problems than they solve, then the pattern of action will be avoided. [1967: 54]

*Anomie theory* elaborates the causes of strain and the process of adapting to it. This perspective regards deviance as an adaptation to the stress that occurs when conformity to normative expectations is strongly motivated but difficult to attain. A critical element in this process is the ambivalence that develops regarding these expectations. This uncertainty opens the way for a deviant adaptation by reducing the impact of the norms that promote conforming behavior.

## ANOMIE AND THE REGULATION
## OF BEHAVIOR

The concept of *anomie* was developed by Émile Durkheim (1897) to refer to the lack of normative regulation that sometimes exists within social systems. A product of rapid social change, such normlessness results in increased nonconformity among group members. Durkheim first used the concept to explain suicide patterns. He observed that, although individuals take their own lives for any number of personal and psychological reasons, suicide may also be understood in terms of the nature of the social system in which it occurs. In particular, Durkheim argued that societies are differentiated in two important ways: (1) in the degree to which the members of a collectivity are integrated into the institutions and interpersonal networks that comprise social life, variations in which produce either *altruistic* or *egoistic* suicide, and (2) in the force with which behavior and expectations are regulated, a condition affecting the extent of *anomic* suicide.

Altruistic suicides are more likely to take place when the social system is highly integrated, as is typical of *folk society.* Members participate fully in the community and share equally in its responsibilities and rewards. In this situation the welfare of the group takes precedence over the individual member. It sometimes happens, therefore, that individuals will end their lives to protect the collectivity. At one time, for example, aged or infirm Eskimos who could no longer contribute to the sustenance of the village would sacrifice themselves for the welfare of the others. Occasionally, altruistic suicides are also found in modern society. The fireman who rushes into a burning building to save others, the combat soldier who willingly sacrifices his life so that his companions might live, or the aging father who acts on the belief that he has become a burden to his family are illustrative of altruistically motivated suicides. However, since urban industrial societies preclude the level of integration conducive to altruistic suicide, this behavior is more typically associated with smaller, less-developed social systems.

Excessive integration may result in the total immersion of individuals in the group. Obversely, social ties may become so weak that persons lose their sense of membership with the community. In the former instance, individuals may be said to have everything to die for; in the latter, they have nothing to live for. Durkheim termed the self-inflicted death of those cut off from the institutions and activities of the larger society *egoistic suicide;* it is more likely to be found in modern, complex society. As nuclear families replace extended kinship networks and multigenerational communities succumb to highly mobile residential patterns, many people find themselves without meaningful social relationships.

The influence of the lack of social integration on suicide rates can be seen in a number of areas. The incidence of suicide among persons who are single, childless, or unemployed is higher than among people who have more group ties. Similarly, Protestants have higher suicide rates than Roman Catholics. Catholicism, with its hierarchical control of religious belief and its prescriptions for religious observance, integrates its members into the institution more fully than do the various Protestant sects, in which the faithful are more often encouraged to manage their own religious expressions and have less required participation in organized ritual. This difference in integration into the institutions is reflected in the suicide rates of the two groups.

Both altruistic and egoistic suicide depend upon the degree of social integration. Highly integrated collectivities are characterized by altruistically motivated suicides; where integration is weak, egoistic suicides predominate.

The third type of suicide, *anomic suicide*, is most relevant to the present discussion. Some people may take their own lives when they perceive an absence of norms by which to guide their behavior. Among animals, regulation of the needs necessary for survival occurs *homeostatically*—internal biological controls ensure that the organism obtains what it needs for continued existence. The functions of sleep, sexual activity, obtaining nourishment, elimination, and self-protection are reflexive in nature and do not require conscious deliberation for their fulfillment. Humans also possess biological needs, but after they are met most activities are directed toward goals that are socially determined. These goals have no natural, homeostatically controlled limits. Rather, the pursuit of such aspirations as power, prestige, and wealth is virtually never-ending. Since the ultimate goal is located in infinity, efforts to attain it will yield no progress. "Even our glances behind and our feeling of pride at the distance covered can cause only deceptive satisfaction, since the remaining distance is not proportionately reduced. To pursue a goal which is by definition unattainable is to condemn oneself to a state of perpetual unhappiness" (Durkheim, 1897: 248).

Since needs and desires are socially derived, their regulation must also emanate from outside the individual. It is society that provides the moral force necessary to moderate human appetites by prescribing a range of expectations appropriate to its members. Furthermore, the limits of aspiration are often group-specific and depend upon the social status of the individual. Thus,

> a certain way of living is considered the upper limit to which a workman may aspire in his efforts to improve his existence, and there is another limit below which he is not willingly permitted to fall unless he has seriously demeaned himself. Both differ for city and country workers, for the domestic servant and the day-laborer, for the business clerk and the of-

ficial. . . . Likewise the man of wealth is reproved if he lives the life of a poor man, but also if he seeks the refinements of luxury overmuch. [Durkheim, 1897: 249]

Through normative regulation of individual aspirations, the anarchy of unbridled expectations is avoided.

Sometimes, however, rapid social change disrupts normative controls. Through social or economic catastrophe, or an unexpected boon, once-familiar limits suddenly become inapplicable. In the absence of normative regulation and with little to guide their behavior, individuals under stress may turn to suicide. Historical illustrations of this phenomenon are plentiful. Military conquest, internal revolutions, the failure of the stockmarket, or the discovery of gold, for example, may render traditional norms ineffective. "When society is disturbed by some painful crisis or by beneficient but abrupt transitions, it is momentarily incapable of exercising . . . [its limiting] influence; thence come the sudden rises in the curve of suicides. . . . [Durkheim, 1897: 252]

In addition to the normlessness that frequently attends social crisis, a more chronic form of anomie has accompanied the economic growth of modern industrial society (Durkheim, 1897). As industry has continued to expand into new markets and to increase its capacity to offer mass-produced luxuries at lower prices, expectations of producer and consumer alike have soared. At the same time, religion has lost much of its ability to encourage the subordination of worldly interests to everlasting riches, and government has served to protect rather than control industry's expanding influence. With material success moving steadily beyond the reach of the ability to achieve, many individuals are left with heightened but unfulfilled aspirations.

Durkheim was primarily concerned with a generalized condition of normlessness produced by changes in the social system. Later theorists, however, have dealt with a form of anomie that affects various segments of the population differently. Particular groups and individuals experience the normative deregulation that makes conformity difficult.[1] At the same time, they are under pressure from those who are relatively unaffected by the problem to conform to behavioral norms. Thus, in addition to describing the sources of normative deregulation, more recent anomie theorists have focused on individual adaptations to this structural condition.

## STRUCTURAL MALINTEGRATION AND DEVIANT ADAPTATIONS

Robert K. Merton (1938), the first contemporary theorist to apply the concept of anomie to a more general theory of deviant behavior, focused on problems of social structure as they contribute to nonconformity.

Merton described society as comprising two parallel structures: culturally defined goals and institutionalized means for their attainment. Ideally, these components are sufficiently well integrated so that persons can achieve the goals to which they are encouraged to aspire. Greater emphasis on one set of normative expectations, however, indicates a malintegration of the means-goals structure.

Two hypothetical examples illustrate the extremes of structural malintegration. A social system that encouraged the acquisition of valued objects at any cost would most closely approximate a state of anarchy—a war of all against all for personal gain. A society that commanded absolute adherence to the rules of performance, on the other hand, would approach totalitarian stagnation. In most instances, the imbalance of cultural emphasis on means and goals is one of degree. This imbalance has been conceptualized by Merton as producing social structural strain which may lead to anomie, or normlessness.

Merton illustrates this thesis through a discussion of structured inequality and the emphasis on the acquisition of wealth in U.S. society. Regardless of class position, people are encouraged to attain material success. The great American promise is that anyone, through hard work and personal sacrifice, not only can but is morally obligated to achieve this goal. U.S. folklore is replete with rags-to-riches heroes who confirm this belief. The progress of immigrants, the life of Abraham Lincoln, the heroes of Horatio Alger, and the portrayals of early industrialists in educational materials, the media, and political speeches are examples.

# Advice to a Young Tradesman

*Benjamin Franklin*

The way to wealth, if you desire it, is as plain as the way to market. It depends chiefly on two words, industry and frugality; that is, waste neither time nor money, but make the best use of both. Without industry and frugality nothing will do, and with them everything. He that gets all he can honestly and saves all he gets (necessary expenses excepted), will certainly become rich, if that Being who governs the world, to whom all should look for a blessing on their honest endeavours, doth not, in his wise providence, otherwise determine.

An Old Tradesman.

Source: Benjamin Franklin, "Advice to a Young Tradesman," in *Poor Richard's Almanac*, 1757 (New York: David McKay Company, 1963), pp. 45–46.

# Ragged Dick

*Horatio Alger*

"I hope, my lad, you will prosper and rise in the world. You know in this free country poverty in early life is no bar to a man's advancement. I haven't risen very high myself," [Mr. Whitney] added, with a smile, "but have met with moderate success in life; yet there was a time when I was as poor as you."

"Were you, sir," asked Dick, eagerly.

"Yes, my boy, I have known the time I have been obliged to go without my dinner because I didn't have enough money to pay for it."

"How did you get up in the world," asked Dick, anxiously.

"I entered a printing-office as an apprentice, and worked for some years. Then my eyes gave out and I was obliged to give that up. Not knowing what else to do, I went into the country, and worked on a farm. After a while I was lucky enough to invent a machine, which has brought me a great deal of money. But there was one thing I got while I was in the printing-office which I value more than money."

"What was that, sir?"

"A taste for reading and study. During my leisure hours I improved myself by study, and acquired a large part of the knowledge which I now possess. Indeed, it was one of my books that first put me on the track of the invention, which I afterwards made. So you see, my lad, that my studious habits paid me in money, as well as in another way."

"I'm awful ignorant," said Dick, soberly.

"But you are young, and, I judge, a smart boy. If you try to learn, you can, and if you ever expect to do anything in the world, you must know something of books."

"I will," said Dick, resolutely. "I ain't always goin' to black boots for a livin'."

"All labor is respectable, my lad, and you have no cause to be ashamed of any honest business; yet when you can get something to do that promises better for your future prospects, I advise you to do so. Till then earn your living in the way you are accustomed to, avoid extravagance, and save up a little money if you can."

"Thank you for your advice," said our hero. "There aint many that takes an interest in Ragged Dick."

"So that's your name," said Mr. Whitney. "If I judge you rightly, it won't be long before you change it. Save your money, my lad, buy books, and determine to be somebody, and you may yet fill an honorable position."

"I'll try," said Dick. "Good-night sir." . . .

"Good-by, my lad," said Mr. Whitney. "I hope to hear good accounts of you sometime. Don't forget what I have told you. Remember that your future position depends mainly upon yourself, and that it will be high or low as you choose to make it."

He held out his hand, in which was a five-dollar bill. Dick shrunk back.

"I don't like to take it," he said. "I haven't earned it."

"Perhaps not," said Mr. Whitney; "but I give it to you because I remember my own friendless youth. I hope it may be of service to you. Sometime when you are a prosperous man, you can repay it in the form of aid to some poor boy, who is struggling upward as you are now."

"I will, sir," said Dick, manfully.

Source: Horatio Alger, Jr., "Ragged Dick," in *Struggling Upward: And Other Works* (New York: Crown Publishers, 1945), pp. 203–205.

The institutionalized means for achieving material success in our society include educational and occupational advancement. Although these opportunities are proclaimed to be available to all, the U.S. class system and the limitations placed on those at the lower-status level preclude equal advancement. Members of the lower classes most likely to experience stress are those who have internalized societal goals but lack legitimate means to attain them.

The differential distribution of rewards does not in itself lead to stress. In caste-stratified systems, for example, differences in status and wealth among the strata are more pronounced than in class societies. Since there are few common goals to which all groups aspire, however, there is less feeling of deprivation. A class system such as that in the United States, on the other hand, with its emphasis on universal achievement and mobility, is more likely to engender stress when goal attainment is blocked. This sense of deprivation is a precipitating factor in the development of anomie and deviant behavior.

People who aspire to unattainable goals may develop feelings of *frustration* and *ambivalence* toward related values and attempt to adjust to this stress through some mode of adaptation. Because of the ambivalence that surrounds frustrated achievement, the likelihood of the adaptation being deviant is increased.

Particular adaptations to frustration depend upon the relative degree to which group members have internalized the means or the goals of the social system. The degree of internalization is a result of the extent to which each has been emphasized during prior socialization. That is, cultural goals and their institutionalized means of attainment may not have received equal attention during earlier learning experiences. Some individuals may have been exposed to a greater emphasis on the goal or achievement and less emphasis on how to attain it, while others may have acquired a commitment to correct performance that exceeds their interest in the acquisition of particular ends. In other words, for some the game must be won, for others it must be played well.

Based on the strength of internalized commitment to means and goals, Merton proposed the five possible adaptations to stress depicted in Table 5–1.

**TABLE 5–1  Five Adaptations to Stress**

|  | Cultural Goals | Institutionalized Means |
|---|---|---|
| I. Conformity | + | + |
| II. Innovation | + | − |
| III. Ritualism | − | + |
| IV. Retreatism | − | − |
| V. Rebellion | ± | ± |

Note: ( + ) signifies acceptance, ( − ) signifies elimination, and ( ± ) signifies rejection and substitution of now goals and means.

Source: Robert K. Merton, "Social Structure and Anomie," *American Sociological Review* 3 (1938 October): 676.

Individuals may be strongly motivated to conform to both the institutionalized means and the cultural goals. Within every society and among all social groups, this adaptation—*conformity*—is the one most frequently encountered. "It is, in fact, only because behavior is typically oriented toward the basic values of the society that we may speak of a human aggregate as comprising a society" (Merton, 1957: 141).

It may be argued that some forms of conformity constitute deviant adaptations, although this is not explicit in Merton's discussion. Some people cling to prescribed rules for goal achievement, despite continued frustration. Compulsive conformity to normative expectations may be seen in those who hold two and sometimes three jobs in the belief that, although personal property has not yet arrived, just a bit more effort will achieve it. This behavior is not proscribed, but neither is it a successful solution to frustration. Conformity in this case represents a compulsive performance orientation that is never quite satisfied.

The second mode of adaptation proposed by Merton is *innovation*, which involves adhering to the culturally defined goals but abandoning the legitimate means to attain them. Examples include robbery, burglary, prostitution, and other forms of predatory crime. Thus, innovation is an adaptation which involves material gain through illegitimate means.

*Ritualism*, Merton's third category, refers to excessive attention to means without a corresponding commitment to goals. In other words, some people seem to become so involved with *how* to do something that they lose sight of *why* they are doing it. This kind of behavior is often neurotic and counterproductive. The authoritarian father who beats his small boy for not learning his prayers properly, the nurse who refuses emergency care for a patient who does not have sufficient insurance coverage, or the professor who insists on "covering the material" regardless of the interest or clarity with which it is presented are all cases in point.

People who forgo both the means and the goals of the social system are said to have adapted through *retreatism*. Individuals in this adjustment category are, given early socialization emphases, equally imbued with both the goals and means. In spite of their failure to achieve, they are unable to depreciate one over the other. In their attempts to resolve frustration, they withdraw from situations that demand this choice. People who make the retreatist adaptation are "in the society but not of it. . . . In this category are *some* of the activities of psychotics, psychoneurotics, chronic autists, pariahs, outcasts, vagrants, vagabonds, tramps, chronic drunkards and drug addicts" (Merton, 1938: 677).

Individuals who reject institutionalized goals and means and who also propose alternative values and strategies for achievement comprise Merton's fifth category, *rebellion*. Included here are revolutionaries and agents of social change. "Rebellion occurs when emancipation from the reigning standards, due to frustration or to marginalist perspectives, leads to the attempt to introduce a 'new social order' " (Merton, 1938: 678).

Conformity, innovation, ritualism, retreatism, and rebellion refer to ways of adapting to social structural malintegration[2] (or anomie) and not to the personality types of the individuals who are trying to adapt. Particular individuals may, and often do, try several adaptation strategies in their attempts to reduce stress. Thus, drug addicts may have first dealt with their inability to achieve through innovative means, and compulsive conformists who recognize that their continuing failure lies not within themselves but in the social structure may turn to rebellion.

The concept of structural imbalance is applicable to a wide variety of culturally defined goals. Merton's focus on pecuniary success is an illustration, and a powerful one, of one means-goals dimension that can produce anomie and the need to adapt. Since, in U.S. society, certain portions of the population have limited opportunities for achievement, stress and the likelihood of deviant adaptations among these groups will be heightened. Class- and race-related inequality implies that the lower social strata will be most vulnerable in this regard. However, since there is a general cultural emphasis on the accumulation of wealth, individuals at all status levels will tend toward some form of adaptation when this goal is frustrated. This is the normal response of persons whose access to a valued object is thwarted. The white-collar criminal and the lower-class burglar, the mentally ill, and the drug- or alcohol-addicted from all social classes have similar motivations. When the social system promotes goal achievement above and beyond the legitimate avenues to those goals, alternative performance strategies will emerge.

## INTERPERSONAL STRAIN AND
## INDIVIDUAL ADJUSTMENT

The application of anomie theory at the level of interpersonal relationships was first offered by Talcott Parsons (1951). According to Parsons, deviance is an adaptation to the frustrations of unrewarding interaction. It is an individual personality adjustment to the stress that arises when the actions of others toward the individual do not conform to the norms governing the relationship. If others persist in such actions and if the individual is not able to cope through normal means, a deviant adaptation is the likely outcome.

Parsons begins with the observation that an interpersonal relationship is in equilibrium when the persons involved comply with the rules pertaining to that relationship. Give the reciprocity of rights and obligations upon which close associations are built, conformity on the part of group members will result in mutual satisfaction.

The importance of conformity to the individual is based on three interrelated factors. First, cultural rules, or norms, prescribe the conduct of participants in all relationships. Persons who form associations, whether friendships, work groups, or marriages, have through prior socialization internalized the relevant norms as part of their own needs. Second, within social relationships there are also mutually agreed-upon expectations for conduct that develop from ongoing interaction and that may be unique to specific associations. The importance of these expectations lies in the reciprocity essential to persistent relationships. The ability of individuals to execute their own roles depends upon the reciprocation of others. As with cultural norms, this interdependency of role expectations becomes part of the needs of group members. Finally, as the individual continues to interact with others, they become objects of *cathexis*, or personal attachment. They are the people to whom the individual looks for reward and positive sanction. These attachments, along with the internalization of cultural norms and role expectations, mean that the failure of others to fulfill their obligations will *strain*, or disturb, the equilibrium of the relationship (see Figure 5–1). Such disequilibrium frustrates the needs of the individual and motivates him or her toward some mode of adaptation.

There are several nondeviant modes of adjustment to strain. The individual may try to *persuade the other person to change* the behavior in question so that it conforms to the rules of their relationship. Or the individual may utilize the defense mechanism of *repression* to deny the other's nonconforming behavior. In this way, needs no longer being satisfied are psychologically inhibited. A third adaptation is for the individual to legitimize the behavior of the other by *redefining* the norms and expectations of the relationship. Here, actions previously con-

**FIGURE 5–1   Equilibrium and Disequilibrium in Social Relationships**

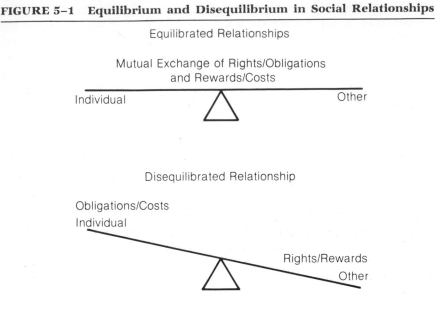

sidered violations are neutralized or reinterpreted as conforming to the rules of the interaction. Finally, one may seek to reduce stress by *transferring cathexis,* or attachment, to others who will fulfill internalized expectations. If these measures are not, or cannot, be employed, the individual may become ambivalent toward the relationship and restructure the situation through some deviant mode of adaptation.

In the deviant adaptation, the individual remains within the relationship and maintains a commitment to its norms and expectations as well as to the other as a cathected object. The situation is one of continued frustration, but the relationship cannot be easily abandoned because it has been internalized. By maintaining the commitment to the relationship while resenting its costs, the individual may develop feelings of ambivalence about it. This unstable state may result in excessively passive or aggressive behavior, referred to by Parsons as *passivity* and *activity,* respectively.

An additional element in the deviant adaptation is for the individual to repress one side of the ambivalence. He or she may repress the negative feelings, for example, if the need for the relationship is so great that it is worth enduring the frustrations produced by the other's behavior. Even though the individual has a negative feeling toward the other, he or she will compulsively conform to the norms of the association so as not to risk further disturbance. This defensive contradiction in behavior is referred to as *reaction formation.* The emergent personality trait is termed *conformative dominance*, which means that the tendency to conform will be dominant—in order to compensate for the anxiety engendered by the relationship, the individual engages in exaggerated and inappropriate compliance. Overaccommodation, deference, and, in general, behaviors that are in opposition to the actor's true feelings are a defensive response intended to preserve relationships with significant others.

If, on the other hand, the positive feelings regarding a relationship are repressed, the person may deny the importance of the relationship. In other words, he or she will maintain an attachment to the other person but will not express it overtly and will refuse to conform to the norms of the association. This behavior is motivated by the need to prevent depreciation of the self in light of the continued commitment to an unrewarding relationship. This defensive position is referred to as *alienative dominance* and involves a resistence to the norms and expectations governing interaction. In this instance the individual may become compulsively nonconformist.

Individuals may develop any one of several deviant orientations, depending on whether they are active or passive and whether they possess a conformative or an alienative dominance in their personalities. The various possibilities may be depicted in terms of the four-way classification shown in Table 5–2. For example, one who shows both passivity and conformative dominance will be inclined toward compulsive acquiescence. This person will be obsessively concerned with conformity to group norms and the expectations of others. The individual characterized by activity and alienative dominance, on the other hand, will be rebellious and will tend to defy regulations.

A final dimension of Parsons' theory deals with the target of the initial frustration. If the individual has experienced stress because relationship norms have been violated, this frustration will produce nonconformity directed toward *norms*. Alternatively, if stress has occurred when the other person did not meet the individual's particular expectations or provide anticipated rewards, this frustration will lead to difficulties in relating to other people, referred to by Parsons as *social ob-*

**TABLE 5–2   Deviant Orientations**

|  | Activity | Passivity |
|---|---|---|
| Conformative dominance | Compulsive performance | Compulsive acquiescence |
| Alienative dominance | Rebelliousness | Withdrawal |

Source: Talcott Parsons, *The Social System* (New York: Free Press, 1951): 257.

*jects.* The introduction of this dimension produces the eight adaptations shown in Table 5–3.

When the conformative element is dominant and there is a high level of activity, we find the following:

1. If the focus is on social objects, the individual tries to dominate other people, placing them in positions where it is difficult for them to do anything but fulfill his or her expectations.
2. If the focus is on norms, the individual expresses a compulsive need to enforce rules on others.

Domination of the conformative component with passivity will result in the following:

1. If social objects are the focus, the person is submissive to the demands of others. He or she seeks to preserve the relationship by acquiescing to the other person's every wish.
2. If norms are the objects of frustration, the person displays a compulsive need to observe the rules.

Conformative dominance, whether active or passive, may be seen to produce much of the same behavior discussed by Merton under his categories of innovation and ritualism.

Alienative dominance with activity will produce the following:

1. The person engages in aggressive behavior toward others when the frustration is with social objects.

**TABLE 5–3  Parsons' Eight Modes of Deviant Adaptation to Stress**

|  | Activity | | Passivity | |
|---|---|---|---|---|
|  | Focus on social objects | Focus on norms | Focus on social objects | Focus on norms |
| Conformative dominance | Compulsive performance | | Compulsive acquiescence | |
| | Dominance | Compulsive enforcement | Submission | Perfectionist observance |
| Alienative dominance | Rebelliousness | | Withdrawal | |
| | Aggression | Incorrigibility | Compulsive independence | Evasion |

Source: Adapted from Talcott Parsons, *The Social System* (New York: Free Press, 1951) 259.

2. The person displays incorrigibility, a flaunting of the rules for its own sake, if the focus is on norms.

Much of what is considered criminal behavior falls into these two categories. Whether such behaviors are directed toward others in the form of abusive and assaultive acts or toward normative expectations of the system in the form of truancy or vandalism, their basis is found in adjustive mechanisms oriented toward preserving the self.

Finally, when alienative dominance is combined with passivity, we find the following:

1. When social objects are the focus, the individual is compulsively independent, thereby avoiding exposure to the incongenial expectations of others.
2. The individual is evasive and seeks to escape from situations in which expectations and sanctions are operative, if norms are the primary cause of the strain.

In these cases, the behavioral adaptations are similar to Merton's rebellion and retreatism.

In addition to its deleterious effect on the personality, an important aspect of the deviant adaptation is its negative impact on future interaction. Such adjustive reactions precipitate additional denial of rewards by the other person (referred to by Parsons as *alter*), which further frustrates the individual *(ego)* and leads to increased strain.

> It is here that we have the focus of the well-known vicious circle in the genesis of deviant behavior patterns, whether they be neurotic or psychosomatic illness, criminality or others. It may be presumed that the reaction of ego to the change in alter's behavior, which resulted in resort to adjustive and defensive mechanisms involving ambivalence, will be in some way complementary to the change alter introduced. For example, alter, instead of recognizing the merit of a piece of work ego has done, may have shown marked disapproval. . . . Ego reacted to this with resentment which, however, he repressed and became compulsively anxious to secure alter's approval. This compulsive element in ego's motivation makes him excessively "demanding" in his relation to alter. He both wants to be approved, to conform, and his need for approval is more difficult to satisfy because of his anxiety that alter may not give it. This in turn has its effect on alter. Whatever his original motivation to withhold the approval ego expected, ego has now put him in a position where it is more difficult than it was before for him to fulfill ego's expectations; the same level of approval which would have sufficed before is no longer sufficient. . . . The tendency will be to drive alter to approve even less, rather than more as ego hopes. This will still further increase the strain on ego and intensify his resentment, hence, if the alienative component does not break

through, it will add to the compulsiveness of his motivation to seek approval through conformity with alter's expectations. The pressure of ego's conflict may also of course lead to cognitive distortion so that he thinks that alter's expectations are more extreme than they really are, and that therefore he is being held to intolerable standards. [Parsons, 1951: 255–256; see also Figure 5–2.]

## THE SUBCULTURAL SOLUTION

An important contribution of anomie theory is its explanation of the development of the deviant subculture. Albert K. Cohen combined Merton's concept of blocked achievement with Parsons' ideas on adjustment to interpersonal strain to explain the origins of lower-class delinquency. He argued that delinquent behavior is a subcultural solution to the child's problem of achieving status within middle-class reference groups.

The delinquent subculture, according to Cohen (1955), consists of norms and behavioral expectations that exist apart from the larger social system. Primarily a lower-class male phenomenon, the delinquent subculture is characterized by an emphasis on nonutilitarian, malicious, and negativistic behavior. That is, delinquency is not usually oriented toward particular goals, such as the acquisition of property, but occurs "for the hell of it," as nonutilitarian game or sport. Similarly, members of delinquent groups seem to take pleasure in nonconformity simply because it produces discomfort for others. It is a malicious violation of taboos, a flaunting of rules for its own sake. Most generally, delinquent activities and the norms upon which they are based are negativistic, or in direct opposition to those of "respectable" adult society.

Support for this thesis lies in Cohen's observation that the behaviors of delinquent groups are highly versatile. Although crime against property is particularly favored, it takes no special form. In addition, as the opportunities arise, other types of delinquency are readily adopted. Group members show little evidence of planning or budgeting for long-range goals. Rather, their short-run hedonism is reflected in their "hanging around," "waiting for something to happen," and impulsivity. Finally, while the group is intensely cohesive and exercises a great deal of informal pressure on each of its members, it is also fiercely autonomous. The members actively resist interference from external authority. Religious organizations, teachers, law-enforcement officials, and even parents are unwelcome sources of restraint that are resisted if not actively condemned.

The delinquent subculture is the result of mutual problem-solving by individuals who share similar difficulties in adjustment. Human be-

**FIGURE 5–2  Deviant and Nondeviant Adaptations to the Stress of Social Relationships**

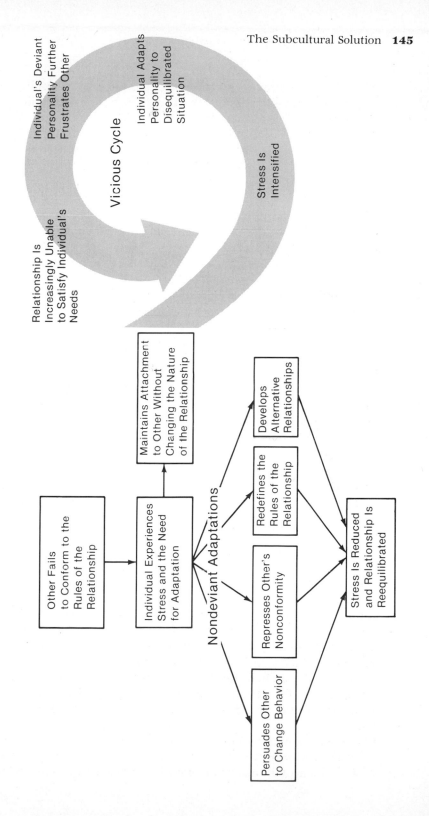

ings depend upon others for reward and personal reinforcement. This dependence exerts pressure on all persons to solve problems in ways that are acceptable to those to whom they look for reward. Should these problems not be solvable in a manner acceptable to this group, individuals are more likely to find a group sympathetic to their needs than to employ strategies repugnant to referent others. The emergence of this new reference group depends upon the "effective interaction . . . of a number of actors with similar problems of adjustment" (Cohen, 1955: 59). The subcultural norms that guide their behavior are the result of a mutual, exploratory construction of an alternative solution to stress.

Particularly relevant in the genesis of delinquent subcultures is the problem of status achievement. A person's ability to achieve status, or respect in the eyes of others, depends upon the evaluative criteria employed by his or her group. People who lack the characteristics or abilities necessary to acquire status under one set of criteria may gravitate to one another and "jointly establish new norms, new criteria of status which define as meritorious the characteristics they *do* possess, the kinds of conduct of which they are capable" (Cohen, 1955: 66).

In U.S. society, the dominant criteria by which people are evaluated reflect the norms and life-style of the middle classes. The middle-class obligation to strive and to achieve includes such values as ambition, the possession of a high level of aspiration; individual responsibility, a reliance on self and personal resources; the cultivation and possession of skills for achievement; the ability to defer present gratification for future rewards; rationality as reflected in forethought, planning, and budgeting; the cultivation of such interpersonal skills as manners, courtesy, and personality; control of physical aggression; the belief that recreation should be constructive rather than aimless; and, especially, respect for property.

In Cohen's view, one consequence of a social system that places a high premium on equality and achieved status is that the same criteria for evaluation are used in assessing all social groups. Since the people doing the evaluating tend to represent the middle-class viewpoint, middle-class performance criteria are most often employed. The middle-class home, then, is more likely to train the child to compete successfully for status in terms of these dominant norms, and lower-class children are frequently found to be deficient. To the extent that lower-class children care what middle-class persons think of them or to the extent that they have internalized the dominant values, they may feel ashamed and uncomfortable.

One situation in which all children come together to compete for status is the school system. Because this institution represents and espouses dominant norms, it assesses youngsters in terms of the middle-class measuring rod. Many lower-status children do not have the skills to compete successfully. Differences in verbal ability, aggression, familiarity with classroom etiquette, and aspirations will be reflected in performance ratings by teachers and classmates alike. In this situation, as in all encounters with the middle-class world, lower-class children are likely to find themselves at the bottom of the status hierarchy. They will feel stress and experience a need to adapt if (1) higher-status groups constitute a meaningful reference, (2) the persons who are evaluating them are important to them, (3) their prior socialization has been to middle-class norms, and (4) they evaluate themselves in terms of the dominant standards.

Cohen (1959: 462–474) argues that three options are available to lower-class children who are experiencing the stress of status frustration. First, they can persist in trying to conform despite continuing frustration. In this case, they maintain a commitment to middle-class values in spite of their inability to perform adequately. Since this option does not remove the source of the stress, it is not a satisfactory solution. A second choice is for the children to stop caring about middle-class rejection and continue to behave in ways that are familiar. Insofar as the lower-class youths have internalized middle-class norms and find little social support for their behavior, this attempt to "go it alone" is also likely to fail as an adaptation to stress. Finally, they may attempt to deal with their frustration by employing a subcultural solution, which involves renouncing middle-class referents and the standards they represent.

An important part of the subcultural adaptation is *reaction formation* (Cohen, 1955). That is, since middle-class norms are not easily extinguished, they must be suppressed—in this case, by being made the object of active, malicious hostility. The lower-class child deals with the norms and values internalized through earlier socialization by expressing overt contempt for the middle-class way of life. Reaction formation, therefore, accounts for the nonutilitarian, malicious, and negativistic behavior that characterizes the delinquent subculture. By neutralizing the effects of middle-class norms, the lower-class child successfully relieves the stress of being evaluated in their terms.

The delinquent subculture, then, is a product of "those very values which respectable society holds most sacred. The same value system, impinging upon children differently equipped to meet it, is instrumental in generating both delinquency and respectability" (Cohen, 1955: 137).

The subcultural solution to status frustration is not limited to delinquent juveniles. Rather, wherever there is prolonged interaction among individuals trying to adjust to their failure to achieve, subcultural norms will develop. This phenomenon is illustrated by the emergence of the inmate culture of the prison community (Sykes, 1958). Imprisonment is an extremely painful experience, and adaptations by the prisoners to the strain are limited by the restrictive nature of the institution. Inmates are unable to escape either physically or psychologically. They lack the cohesion to carry out an insurrection that is bound to fail and have little faith in a peaceful compromise with prison officials. Therefore, they turn to one another to alleviate their deprivations and construct a "society of captives" based on a system of norms and standards for behavior that define the nature of relationships among prisoners, the attitudes appropriate toward both the guards and the outside world, and the rewards and obligations that attend the members of the prison. In this way, the subculture offers the most satisfying solution available to withstanding the pains of imprisonment with the least amount of difficulty. It "provides the prisoner with a meaningful social group with which he can identify himself and which will support him in his battles against his condemners. (Sykes, 1958: 107).

# The Prison Subculture and Homosexuality

*Gresham M. Sykes*

As group experiences come to differ more and more from those of the larger community of which the group is a part—as new patterns of behavior arise demanding evaluation and interpretation—the language of the group begins to change. . . . The society of captives exhibits a number of distinctive tags for the distinctive social roles played by its members in response to the particular problems of imprisonment. . . . [Among them are the argot roles related to homosexuality.]

The inmates . . . recognize and label a variety of homosexual acts, such as sodomy, fellatio, transvestism, frottage, and so on, although the labels of the inmates are not those of the medical profession or modern psychiatry. And the inmates, too, attempt to distinguish the "true" sexual pervert and the prisoner driven to homosexuality by his temporary deprivation. In the world of the prison, however, the extent to which homosexual behavior involves "masculinity" and "femininity" would appear to override all other considerations and it is this which provides the main basis for the classification of sexual perversion by the inmate population. Homosexuals are divided into those who play an active, aggressive role, i.e. a "masculine" role by the stern standards of the prisoners, and those who play a more passive and submissive part. The former are termed *wolves;* the latter are referred to as *punks* and *fags.*

Now it is true that the society of captives does draw a line between *punks* and *fags*. "Punks," it is said, "are made, but *fags* are born." And in this curt aphorism the inmates are pointing to a difference between those who engage in homosexuality because they are coerced into doing so or because male prostitution is a means of winning goods and services in short supply and those who engage in homosexuality because it is preferred. But this division of passive homosexual roles on the basis of motive or genesis is accompanied by—and overshadowed by—the idea that *punks* and *fags* differ in the kind of femininity involved in their sexual aberration. The *fag*—the man who engages in homosexuality because "he likes it" or because "he wants to," according to the prisoners—is a man with a womanly walk and too-graceful gestures; he may, on occasion, dye his underclothing, curl his hair, or color his lips with homemade lipstick. As one inmate, much given to thoughtful analysis, has explained, "The *fag* is recognizable by his exaggerated, feminine mannerisms. The *fag*—they call him a *queen* on the West Coast—employs the many guiles for which females are noted, like playing 'stay away closer' or 'hard to get but gettable.' " The *fag*, in short, fills the stereotype of the homosexual as it is commonly held in the free community. He has forfeited his claim to masculinity not only by his reversal of the sexual role per se but also by taking on the outward guise of women.

The *punk,* on the other hand, submits to the importunities of the more active, aggressive homosexuals without displaying the outward signs of femininity in other aspects of his behavior. His forfeiture of masculinity is limited to the homosexual act. But even though the *punk* does not exhibit those mannerisms characterized as feminine by the inmate population, he has turned himself into a woman, in the eyes of the prisoners, by the very act of his submission. His is an inner softness or weakness; and, from the viewpoint of the prisoners, his sacrifice of manhood is perhaps more contemptible than that of the *fag* because he acts from fear or for the sake of quick advantage rather than personal inclination. In the words of the inmate quoted above, "A *punk* can't fend off the pressure of older, tougher men who may have bullied him, grilled him, put the arm on him in some other institution. He's basically morally weak to begin with, but because he has no source of finances the older, tougher cons ply him with cigarettes, candy, extra food supplies, and maybe even hooch. The weaker ones usually make a deliberate trade, but in some cases the kid may be told that he's not getting it for nothing. He's told he's got to pay up and since he hasn't got the money he's given an alternative—he'll get beaten up or he'll have to submit to an unnatural act. *Punks* are cowards."

The society of captives, then, distinguishes between *punks* and *fags* partly on the basis of differences in the causes or origins of their passive homosexuality. But, more importantly, both *punks* and *fags* fail to be men—the former because they lack an inner core of "toughness" and the latter because they assume the overt, obvious symbols of womanhood. Both are set off from the more active, aggressive, "masculine" *wolf.*

The stress of the "masculinity" of the *wolf's* role is reinforced by the fact that many inmates believe his part in a homosexual relationship to be little more than a search for a casual, mechanical act of physical release. Unmoved by love, indifferent to the emotions of the partner he has coerced, bribed, or seduced into a liaison, the *wolf* is often viewed as simply masturbating with another person. By thus stripping the *wolf* of any aura of "softness," of sentiment or affection, his homosexuality loses much of the taint of effeminacy which homosexuality often carries in the free community. His perversion is a form of rape and his victim happens to be a man rather than a woman, due to the force of circumstances.

It would appear, therefore, that . . . inmates . . . have changed the criteria by which an individual establishes his claim to the status of male. Shut off from the world of women, the population of prisoners finds itself unable to employ that criterion of maleness which looms so importantly in society at large—namely, the act of heterosexual intercourse itself. Proof of maleness, both for the self and for others, has been shifted to other grounds and the display of "toughness," in the form of masculine mannerisms and the demonstration of inward stamina, now becomes the major route to manhood. These are used by the society at large, it is true; but the prison, unlike the society at large, must rely on them exclusively. In short, there are primary and secondary sexual characteristics in terms of social behavior just as there are primary and secondary sexual characteristics in terms of biological attributes; and the inmates have been forced to fall back on the secondary proof of manhood in the area of personal relations, i.e., "toughness," since the primary proof, in the form of heterosexual intercourse, is denied them. And the reliance on the secondary proof of manhood is so great that the active, aggressive homosexual—the *wolf* —almost manages to escape the stigma of his perversion.

By the standards of the free community, the prisoner's definition of masculine behavior may seem excessive with its emphasis on callousness, its flinty indifference to the more tender aspects of human relationships. It is perhaps understandable, however, in light of the fact that the definition of masculine behavior in a society composed exclusively of men is apt to move to an extreme position. But more important . . . is the fact that by changing the criteria of maleness, the prisoners have erected a defense against the threat posed by their involuntary celibacy. The path to manhood has been reopened. However difficult to achieve or however harsh its mode of expression, "toughness"—and thus manhood—is at least possible. The anxieties generated by isolation from women and homosexuality lose something of their sting, since the individual's conception of himself as a male no longer depends so completely on his sexual activity. The *fag* and the *punk* must, of course, still bear the burden of the "softness" and the *wolf*—no matter how "tough" he may be—cannot entirely avoid the attitudes commonly elicited by his perversion. But for homosexuals and non-homosexuals alike, the emphasis placed by the society of captives on the accompaniments of sexuality rather than sexuality itself does much to transform the problem of being a man in a world without women.

Source: Gresham M. Sykes, *The Society of Captives: A Study of a Maximum Security Prison* (New Jersey: Princeton University Press, 1958), pp. 86, 95–99.

Subcultural norms are shaped by and remain intimately linked to the larger society. Within the black, lower-class neighborhoods of urban areas, for example, may be found relatively stable collections of males who, unemployed and separated from their families, spend many hours of seemingly aimless interaction with one another (Liebow, 1967). This subculture phenomenon is not so much a product of norms and values that spring from lower-class life as it is a response to structurally induced failure.

These "streetcorner men" are not cut off from the values, sentiments, and beliefs of the larger society; rather, through continuous exposure to the dominant culture, they are painfully aware of its expectations. In this regard, both employment and stable marital ties are crucial to the self-evaluations of these men. Yet, the lower-class male is usually unskilled; and since his father before him as well as his friends are likely to have failed at their jobs, he expects to do the same. The menial nature of any job he gets is held in contempt by the larger society, and he feels the same way about it. His expectation for failure and his contempt for the job usually result in his quitting or being fired.

Marital relationships of a streetcorner man may be described in similar terms. He marries early because that is what men are supposed to do. Again, however, he expects the marriage to fail as did those of his father and friends. Since his wife is also familiar with the divorces and separations of her mother and her friends, the prophecy is soon fulfilled.

Increasingly, the individual who fails in terms of these larger societal criteria turns to the streetcorner and to those who permit him to be a man:

> From this perspective, the streetcorner man does not appear as a carrier of an independent cultural tradition. His behavior appears not so much as a way of realizing the distinctive goals and values of his own subculture, or of conforming to its models, but rather as his way of trying to achieve many of the goals and values of the larger society, of failure to do this, and of concealing his failure from others and from himself as best he can.
>
> Thus, many similarities between the lower class Negro father and son (or mother and daughter) . . . result . . . from the fact that the son goes out and independently experiences the same failures, in the same areas, and for much the same reasons as his father. What appears as a dynamic, self-sustaining cultural process is, in part at least, a relatively simple piece of social machinery which turns out, in rather mechanical fashion, independently produced look-alikes. [Liebow, 1967: 222–223]

Adjustment to failure, then, is interpersonally oriented; people who share similar problems of status and goal attainment look to each other for solutions. Once a social system has systematically induced the need for alternative behavior, it also generates the need for a system of roles and definitions to support that behavior. The resultant culture (subordinate to the larger culture of which it is a part) is a system of shared symbols, communicated through the process of interaction, out of which subculturally sanctioned roles, definitions, and personal identities emerge. Within this circle of significant others, the individual learns the identity and behavior appropriate to his or her role. The subculture, therefore, performs the same function as any other reference group. The same processes of interaction and shared meaning operate within the cultures of both deviant and nondeviant groups.

## RELATIVE DEPRIVATION: A CRITICAL CONTINGENCY

We have seen that strain and the need to resolve it arise when aspirations to desired goals exceed the opportunities for their attainment. According to anomie theory, U.S. society emphasizes certain common goals more than it emphasizes prescribed means to achieve them. Moreover, means for goal attainment are not equally available to the various social classes. Thus, lower-status individuals are more vulnerable to structural malintegration than people in higher-status groups.

This does not mean, of course, that crime and deviance occur exclusively in the lower classes or that all lower-status persons are subject to the strain toward adaptation. In fact, people who occupy the lowest status positions conform most of the time; and a great deal of behavioral deviation can be found within the highest class levels. Relative to their proportion in the population, persons from the most prestigious occupational categories, such as business executives, dentists, and physicians, have the highest incidence of alcoholism (McCord and McCord, 1960), suicide (Powell, 1958; Breed, 1963; Dublin, 1963), and drug addiction (Winick, 1961; Chambers, 1971). In addition, we are only beginning to recognize the extent of white-collar and corporate criminality, which is the exclusive property of the middle and upper classes.

Although the official statistics indicate that the incidence of crime and deviance is higher in the poor and working classes, we must keep in mind that these statistics are indices of conventional criminality. Burglary, robbery, aggravated assault, and the like are lower-class offenses. There are few comparable measures of the business, professional, and political activities that comprise middle-class crime. Even the reportedly higher incidence of conventional crime among lower-status groups must be interpreted with caution; whether this pattern is a product of class variations in nonconformity or of the greater frequency with which lower-class crimes are detected and sanctioned remains an empirical question.

There is little question that the opportunities for goal achievement are unequally distributed. For reasons of class, race, age, and sex, many people are restricted in their access to education, occupation, and other opportunities. Relatively few people achieve the high levels of accomplishment enjoyed by a small portion of the population. In spite of inequities, however, people remain surprisingly conformist in their behavior.

It appears that the *perception* of blocked goals relative to the level of aspiration, rather than the objective state of restricted opportunity, underlies the development of stress and the tendency toward deviant adaptation. Such levels of aspiration and perceptions of achievement are not uniformly distributed throughout society. Lower-status groups generally place less emphasis on traditional success goals; and at the same time, their awareness of blocked achievement is limited (Hyman, 1953; Empey, 1956; Lipset and Bendix, 1959; Wilson, 1959; Mizruchi, 1964; Wendling and Elliott, 1968; Rushing, 1971). When a person fails to achieve in terms of his or her *own* aspirations, stress *will* develop. Since achievement expectations tend to be specific to the various status levels of society, the concept of *relative deprivation* emerges as central to anomie theory.

In assessing progress toward goals, people generally evaluate themselves in terms of the achievements of others within their personal reference networks. They believe they are "doing well" if their achievements come reasonably close to those of the people with whom they compare themselves. When these comparisons reveal failure to measure up to the successes of others or when self-evaluations are made in terms of persons who occupy higher social positions, people may feel deprived and experience the need to adapt. Thus, for example, officially designated delinquents are more likely to perceive a lack of legitimate opportunities for goal attainment than are nondelinquent youths of the same social class (Landis and Scarpitti, 1965; Short et al., 1965). This suggests that delinquents, in assessing their situation, apply higher standards than nondelinquents. A great deal depends, therefore, on the norms internalized by particular individuals. Middle-class values and expectations may indeed permeate all social levels, but insofar as groups tend to develop norms commensurate with their life situations, the effects of the dominant standards may be minimized.

Additional support for this thesis comes from observations of culturally marginal individuals. When aspirations and expectations are compared across groups varying in ethnic origin, persons whose earlier socialization was influenced by the ethnic culture are less likely to evaluate themselves in terms of society's dominant culture (Wendling and Elliott, 1968; Rushing, 1971). It appears, therefore, that it is the culturally influenced subjective interpretation of an individual's position that underlies stress, rather than any objective disparity between his or her goals and available means for their attainment (Rushing, 1971).

The importance of comparisons becomes most visible during periods of social change. For example, one of the consequences of blacks' attempts to improve their social and political positions in the United States was that blacks more frequently compared themselves with whites at all class levels. The black-power movement called increasing attention to the opportunities and goals of people who had formerly not been part of their reference group. Increasingly conscious of achievements that were previously the reserve of the white majority, blacks have increasingly come to adopt dominant success themes as their own (Stephenson, 1957; Antonovsky and Lerner, 1959; Rosen, 1959; Gist and Bennett, 1963; Wendling and Elliott, 1968).

A similar phenomenon has emerged with regard to the changing status of women. Partly because of the feminist movement, many women have come to compare their goal achievements with those of men. Where marriage, family, and home have traditionally sufficed as valued objects for most women, occupation, income, and independence have emerged as alternative aspirations. Where the means for achievement have not kept pace with expanding goals, increases in the level of stress and deviance may be expected.[3]

An unfavorable comparison of self with others in the reference group generally leads to a sense of relative deprivation and feelings of frustration. This frustration constitutes a problem that presses for solution. People who are unsuccessful in their attempts to conform may adopt some form of deviant behavior. If the source of the frustration is removed, however, the deviant solution may be avoided or terminated.

## AVOIDING THE DEVIANT SOLUTION

As we have seen, anomie theory argues that some lower-class children become delinquent because they cannot measure up to the middle-class standards that predominate in the U.S. school system. If the status deprivation experienced at school is indeed related to delinquency, such behavior will be greater among adolescents who stay in school than among those who drop out. This appears to be precisely the case (Elliott, 1966). As shown in Table 5–4, the rate of official contact with law enforcers is substantially greater for boys in school (4.95) than for those who drop out before graduation (2.75). The highest delinquency referral rate occurred among lower-class drop-outs before they left school (8.70). This same group had the lowest rate of official contact after dropping out. By escaping the stresses associated with the inability to per-

**TABLE 5–4  Delinquent Referral Rate[a] Among Boys
in and out of School**

| | In School | | | Out of School |
| SES Areas | Graduates | Dropouts[b] | Subtotal | Dropouts[b] |
| --- | --- | --- | --- | --- |
| Lower | 4.13 | 8.70 | 4.96 | 2.42 |
| Higher | 4.92 | 4.95 | 4.92 | 4.63 |
| Total | 4.34 | 8.03 | 4.95 | 2.75 |

[a]Number of referrals per 10,000 in-school or out-of-school days.

[b]These are the same individuals during two different time periods.

Source: Delbert S. Elliott, "Delinquency, School Attendance and Dropout," *Social Problems* 13 (Winter 1966): 312.

form according to middle-class expectations and by returning to a group to which they are better able to conform, lower-class youngsters can avoid the delinquent outcome.

There is no comparable effect on middle-class delinquents. Since dropping out of school does not remove them from the normative reference group within which their behaviors are assessed, the source of their frustration remains. School attendance, therefore, has no appreciable effect on their behavior.

Stress may also arise when lower-status persons aspire to the traditional goals of economic achievement. In this case, expanding their opportunities for access to the legitimate social structure can provide alternatives to illegitimate courses of action. Such a finding emerged in a study of sixty boys with histories of "serious and persistent" juvenile offenses (Odell, 1974). The boys, all adjudicated delinquent, were divided into four groups representing various strategies of supervised probation. The first group was organized around a traditional casework approach. Caseworkers were expected to take whatever action they felt necessary to serve the needs of their clients. The second group participated in a program of intensive counseling for the boys and their parents. The counseling sessions supplemented regular casework. The third group emphasized the educational and occupational advancement of probationers. The boys were enrolled in a high-school equivalency diploma program and, at its completion, were provided jobs by local employers. Boys who desired additional education were enrolled in vocational or junior colleges. Finally, a fourth group was placed in the high-school equivalency program alone. That is, after receiving their diplomas, these boys did not receive job placement or further education. Boys were evaluated at three-month intervals for a period of nine months.

As shown in Table 5–5, referrals for additional delinquent offenses differed markedly among groups. The recidivism rate showed the

**TABLE 5–5  Recidivism by Three-Month Periods**
**(in percentages; noncumulative)**

| Groups | 3 Months | 6 Months | 9 Months |
|---|---|---|---|
| I. Traditional casework | 38.5% | 33.4% | 20.0% |
| II. Intensive counseling | 35.7 | 23.0 | 27.3 |
| III. Educational and occupational placement | 6.7 | 0.0 | 6.7 |
| IV. Education | 7.2 | 0.0 | 7.2 |
|  | $x^2 = 7.518$ | $x^2 = 10.454$ | $x^2 = 3.124$ |
|  | $P < .05$ | $P < .02$ | $P < .30$ |

Source: Brian Neal Odell, "Accelerating Entry into the Opportunity Structure: A Sociologically Based Treatment for Delinquent Youth," *Sociology and Social Research* 58 (April 1974): 315.

greatest variation between the traditional and counseling programs, on the one hand, and the educational and job placement programs, on the other. Access to opportunities for educational and occupational advancement appreciably reduced the likelihood of the delinquent alternative.

Access to legitimate opportunities has a similar impact on adult offenders. Ex-prisoners, as part of an experimental project designed to facilitate the transition from prison to society, were assigned to one of several income assistance and job placement programs (Berk et al, 1980). Periodic interviews of participants revealed that, during the twelve months following their release, ex-offenders who secured employment or received income supplements had fewer difficulties with the law than those without such resources. Once again, therefore, the availability of legitimate opportunities obviated illegitimate adaptations.

## CONCLUSION

Anomie theory provides additional dimensions toward a general theory of deviant behavior. The theoretical perspectives discussed in the preceding chapters have emphasized the social functions of deviance and the processes by which such behavioral categories become established within a social system and within the personal identities of its members. Adding to these perspectives, anomie theory points to the relationship that exists between the goals-means structure of a system and the individual behavior of the system's members.

Anomie theory proposes that opportunities for approved behavior are unequally distributed. Because an important criterion in such distribution is social class, the system precludes the full or satisfying participation of certain members. If those affected have internalized the norms of the system, they may feel deprived and may need to adapt.

Adaptations to stress often involve a shift in reference identifications to groups wherein the attainment of status and a more positive identity can be realized. If the norms of these groups are at variance with those of the larger society, deviant behavior is the likely outcome.

It is apparent that the concept of *referent others* is important to our understanding of nonconformity at a number of stages. Others not only apply the standards by which we assess ourselves, they also provide and withhold the opportunities for continued conformity. Other people determine the level of stress we experience, depending on how important their opinions are to us. Finally, insofar as others share our adjustment problems, they will help shape adaptations to them.

Reference associations are also central to the theory of social and cultural support. A discussion of this perspective and its explanation of the role of subcultural associations as they shape deviance and conformity is the focus of Chapter 6.

## NOTES

1. The concept of anomie has been measured in terms of a wide range of criteria. Included among them are such varied phenomena as rates of residential overcrowding, home ownership, marital status, educational achievement (Bordua, 1958), family value confusion and disorganization (Jaffe, 1969), and the marriageability of females (Sandhu and Allen, 1969). The validity of such factors as measures of anomie, however, is dubious. Although these indicators appear to be positively associated with nonconformity, their relationship to normlessness can only be inferred.

2. For expansions of these possible modes of adaptation, see Dubin (1959) and Harary (1966).

3. An empirical question as yet unexplored is whether the increasing crime rates reported for females are related to their adoption of males as status referents.

## REFERENCES

Alger, Horatio, Jr.
  1945 Ragged Dick. *In* Struggling Upward: And Other Works. New York: Crown Publishers.
Antonovsky, Aaron, and Melvin J. Lerner
  1959 Occupational Aspirations of Lower Class Negro and White Youth. Social Problems 7 (April): 132–138.

Berk, Richard A., Kenneth J. Lenihan, and Peter H. Rossi
  1980  Crime and Poverty: Some Experimental Evidence from Ex-Offenders. American Sociological Review 45 (October): 766–786.
Breed, Warren
  1963  Occupational Mobility and Suicide Among White Males. American Sociological Review 28 (April): 179–188.
Bordua, David
  1958  Juvenile Delinquency and "Anomie": An Attempt at Replication. Social Problems 6 (Winter): 230–237.
Chambers, Carl D.
  1971  Differential Drug Use Within the New York State Labor Force. Narcotic Addiction Control Commission, State of New York.
Cohen, Albert K.
  1955  Delinquent Boys. New York: Free Press.
  1959  Reference Group Identification and Deviant Behavior. In Sociology Today. Robert K. Merton, ed. Pp. 462–474. New York: Basic Books.
Dubin, Robert
  1959  Deviant Behavior and Social Structure: Continuities in Social Theory. American Sociological Review 24 (April): 147–164.
Dublin, Louis I.
  1963  Suicide: A Sociological and Statistical Study. New York: Ronald Press.
Durkheim, Émile
  1897  Suicide. John A. Spaulding and George Simpson, trans. New York: Free Press, 1951.
Elliott, Delbert S.
  1966  Deliquency, School Attendance and Dropout. Social Problems 13 (Winter): 307–314.
Empey, Lamar T.
  1956  Social Class and Occupational Aspirations: A Comparison of Absolute and Relative Measurement. American Sociological Review 21 (December): 703–709.
Franklin, Benjamin
  1757  Advice to a Young Tradesman. In Poor Richard's Almanac. New York: David McKay, 1963.
Gist, Noel P., and William S. Bennett, Jr.
  1963  Aspirations of Negro and White Students. Social Forces 42 (October): 40–48.
Harary, Frank
  1966  Merton Revisited: A New Classification for Deviant Behavior. American Sociological Review 31 (October): 693–697.
Hyman, Herbert H.
  1953  The Value Systems of Different Classes: A Social Psychological Contribution to the Analysis of Stratification. In Class, Status and Power. Reinhard Bendix and Seymour M. Lipset, eds. Pp. 426–442. Glencoe, New York: Free Press.
Jaffe, Eliezer D.
  1969  Family Anomie and Delinquency: Development of the Concept and

Some Empirical Findings. British Journal of Criminology 9 (October): 376–388.

Landis, Judson R., and Frank R. Scarpitti
1965 Perceptions Regarding Value Orientation and Legitimate Opportunity: Delinquents and Non-Delinquents. Social Forces 44 (September): 83–91.

Lemert, Edwin M.
1967 Human Deviance, Social Problems and Social Control. Englewood Cliffs, New Jersey: Prentice-Hall.

Liebow, Elliot
1967 Tally's Corner: A Study of Negro Streetcorner Men. Boston: Little, Brown and Company.

Lipset, Seymour M., and Reinhard Bendix
1959 Social Mobility in Industrial Society. Berkeley: University of California Press.

McCord, William, and Joan McCord
1960 Origins of Alcoholism. Stanford, California: Stanford University Press.

Merton, Robert K.
1938 Social Structure and Anomie. American Sociological Review 3 (October): 672–682.
1957 Social Theory and Social Structure. Glencoe, New York: Free Press.

Mizruchi, Ephraim H.
1964 Success and Opportunity. Glencoe, New York: Free Press.

Odell, Brian Neal
1974 Accelerating Entry into the Opportunity Structure: A Sociologically-Based Treatment for Delinquent Youth. Sociology and Social Research 58 (April): 312–317.

Parsons, Talcott
1951 The Social System. New York: Free Press.

Powell, Elwin H.
1958 Occupation, Status and Suicide: Toward a Redefinition of Anomie. American Sociological Review 23 (April): 131–139.

Rosen, Bernard C.
1959 Race, Ethnicity, and the Achievement Syndrome. American Sociological Review 24 (February): 47–60.

Rushing, William A.
1971 Class, Culture, and "Social Structure and Anomie." American Journal of Sociology 76 (March): 857–872.

Sandhu, Harjit, and Donald E. Allen
1969 Female Delinquency: Goal Obstruction and Anomie. Canadian Review of Sociology and Anthropology 6 (May): 107–110.

Short, James F., Ramon Rivera, and Ray A. Tennyson
1965 Perceived Opportunities, Gang Membership, and Delinquency. American Sociological Review 30 (February): 56–68.

Stephenson, Richard M.
1957 Mobility Orientation and Stratification of 1000 Ninth Graders. American Sociological Review 22 (April): 204–212.

Sykes, Gresham M.
  1958   The Society of Captives: A Study of a Maximum Security Prison. New Jersey: Princeton University Press.
Wendling, Aubrey, and Delbert S. Elliott
  1968   Class and Race Differentials in Parental Aspirations and Expectations. Pacific Sociological Reveiw 11 (Fall): 123–133.
Wilson, Alan B.
  1959   Residential Segregation of Social Classes and Aspirations of High School Boys. American Sociological Review 24 (December): 836–845.
Winick, Charles
  1961   Physician Narcotic Addicts. Social Problems 9 (Fall): 174–186.

# 6

## Social and Cultural Support and Behavioral Commitment

The preceding chapter dealt with the development of social structural and interpersonal strain and the processes by which persons adapt to them. Central to the discussion was the concept of the *reference group,* which determines the extent to which a person internalizes the cultural expectations of the larger society. These referent others also influence the development of personal needs and the degree to which individuals experience stress when these needs go unsatisfied. Successful adaptation to stress depends upon the individual's ability to choose a new reference group supportive of his or her situation.

The reference group is also an important concern to *social and cultural support theory.* In association with significant others, individuals acquire the role models that influence their behavior. The process is the same for conformity and nonconformity alike; both are products of a defining social environment, and both are transmitted through the interactional dynamics of group life.

An underlying assumption of social and cultural support theory is that society is composed of groups whose definitions of acceptable conduct vary. Individuals acquire stable behavior patterns through exposure to these definitions. Deviance, then, is a product of sustained interaction within groups having a preponderance of definitions favorable to nonconformity. The structure, process, and content of this interaction is discussed in the pages that follow.

### THE ROLE OF IMITATION

A basic process in the acquisition of behavior is *imitation* (Tarde, 1912). Through the example of others, individuals become capable of participating in society. Imitation can be seen readily in the play of small children. Dressing in the clothing of their parents, youngsters mimic the roles they will assume as adults. Similarly, by taking on the conduct and character of literary and popular figures, children become familiar with the range of performance and sentiment expected of members of the culture.

Imitation, however, is not restricted to children. The stereotypic college professor with beard, pipe, elbow patches, and long, thoughtful pauses; the business executive with gray flannel suit, Mercedes sedan, and home in the exurbs; and the suburban mother with artificially wood-paneled station wagon, latest fashion casuals, and home decor inspired by *Better Homes and Gardens* are all cases in point.

Although sexual behavior and eating are physiologically motivated, they also involve imitation. Cultural codes concerning the appropriate objects and techniques of sexual expression and the proper foods and techniques of food preparation and eating are precisely defined by societies and must be learned by the individual participants.

The same process of imitation operates in the case of nonconformity. Individuals become aware of the varieties and methods of deviation by the example of those who have come before them. A spectacular but authentic example is the following description of a homicide:

> The case involves a 24-year-old male who, during a homosexual encounter, took the life of his 35-year-old victim. Accounts of the event indicated that the defendant had read Frederick Wertham's *The Show of Violence* (1949) several years previous to the crime, and had become obsessed with one of the murders. Residing out of state, he bought a bus ticket to the city in which the crime was committed, for the express purpose of reenacting Wertham's description of the homicide. Having arrived at his destination, he purchased an ice pick and returned to the bus station to select a victim. He was shortly solicited by a homosexual, who took him to his apartment. Following sexual relations, [and in the manner described by Wertham,] the defendant plunged the ice pick into the skull of the victim, and beat him with a plaster statuette. He then ransacked the room to make it appear that the victim had been killed in the course of a robbery. [Swigert et al., 1976: 394–395]

Even the decision to commit suicide may be influenced by imitation. It has been observed, for example, that newspaper coverage of self-inflicted death is followed immediately by a sharp rise in the suicide rate (Phillips, 1974; see also Figure 6–1). People use the behavior of others to guide their own lines of action. If people commit suicide by following the example of others, it is possible that they steal or do not steal, assault or do not assault, because of imitation (Tarde, 1912).

**FIGURE 6-1   Fluctuation in the Number of Suicides Before, During and After the Month of the Suicide Story**

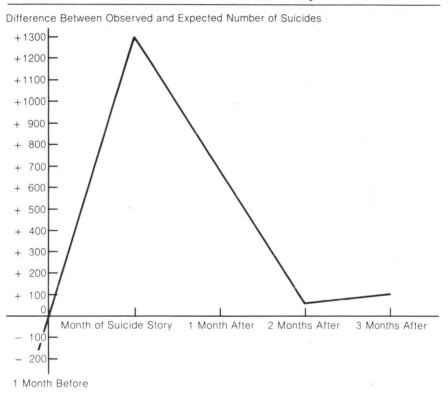

Difference Between Observed and Expected Number of Suicides

Source: David P. Phillips, "The Influence of Suggestion on Suicide: Substantive and Theoretical Implications of the Werther Effect," *ASR,* Vol. 39, June 1974, Figure 1 on p. 343 *only.*

# They Started with Babies

Jonestown, Guyana—When the Rev. Jim Jones learned Saturday that Rep. Leo J. Ryan had been killed but that some members of the congressman's party had survived, Jones called his followers together and told them that the time had come to commit the mass suicide they had *rehearsed several times before.*

"They started with the babies," administering a potion of Kool-aid mixed with cyanide, Odell Rhodes recalled yesterday when I revisited Jonestown to view the horrifying sight of . . . [nearly a thousand] bodies— men, women and children, most of them grouped around the altar where Jones himself lay dead.

Rhodes is . . . [a] survivor of Jonestown who witnessed a part of the suicide rite before managing to escape. He was helping Guyanese authorities identify the dead yesterday.

Most of those who drank the deadly potion served to them by a Jonestown doctor, . . . and by nurses, did so willingly, Rhodes said. Mothers would give the cyanide to their own children before taking it themselves, he said.

But others who tried to escape were turned back by armed guards who ringed the central pavilion where the rite was carried out, Rhodes said. They were then forced to drink the poisoned Kool-aid and shortly after the mass killing began, Rhodes said, "it just got all out of order. Babies were screaming, children were screaming and there was mass confusion."

It took about five minutes for the liquid to take its final effect. Young and old, black and white, grouped themselves, usually near family members, often with their arms around each other, waiting for the cyanide to kill them.

They would go into convulsions, their eyes would roll upward, they would gasp for breath and then fall dead, Rhodes said.

All the while, Jones was talking to them, urging them on, explaining that they would "meet in another place." Near the end, Rhodes said, Jones began chanting, "mother, mother, mother"—an apparent reference to his wife who lay dead not far from the altar.

Yesterday, a stilled Jonestown looked much as it must have moments after the mass suicide ended two days earlier. The bodies were where they had fallen, the half-empty vat of cyanide-laced Kool-aid was still on the table near the altar in the open air pavilion. The faces of the dead bore the anguished expressions of their terrible deaths.

More than 390 of the bodies were grouped around the altar, many of them arm-in-arm. They were so thickly bunched together that it was impossible to see the ground beneath them.

Source: *Washington Post*, November 21, 1978, p. 1. [Emphasis added.]

## DIFFERENTIAL ASSOCIATION AND SOCIALIZATION TO DEVIANCE

Edwin Sutherland's theory of *differential association* provides a systematic explanation of the learning processes that underlie deviance. This theory assumes that human behavior is shaped by a supportive social and cultural environment. Based on this assumption, Sutherland (1947: 6–8) developed a series of nine propositions related to crime:

1. *"Criminal behavior is learned."* Nonconformity is not inherited, nor is it invented as a solution to normlessness. Persons become capable of engaging in deviant acts only after they have learned to do so.

2.  *"Criminal behavior is learned in interaction with other persons in a process of communication."* This communication is both verbal and nonverbal, and includes direct tutelage as well as the language of gestures. Through the example of others and their expressions of approval and encouragement, the individual acquires the normative definitions and behaviors that comprise group culture.

3.  *"The principal part of the learning of criminal behavior occurs within intimate personal groups."* These are the primary associations of the family, neighborhood, community, and peer group. The communication of norms and values within these settings will generally take precedence over information emanating from the more impersonal sources of mass media and public encounters.

4.  *"When criminal behavior is learned, the learning includes (a) techniques of committing the crime, which are sometimes very complicated, sometimes very simple; [and,] (b) the specific direction of motives, drives, rationalizations, and attitudes."* Most crimes require a minimum level of skill for their execution. Many criminal techniques are widely diffused and readily available through nondeviant associations, such as the skills associated with shoplifting and many forms of illicit sexual behavior. Other \methods, however, are acquired only through the learning environments of deviant subcultures. Included here, for example, are professional auto theft, counterfeiting, and the marketing of stolen goods.

Furthermore, all human behavior takes place within a framework of motives, drives, rationalizations, and attitudes. These forces compel and justify action for the conformer and deviant alike. The offender may pursue crime with the same zeal and commitment with which the conformist pursues higher education or religious salvation. The direction of the learning may be different, but the processes are the same.

5.  *"The specific direction of motives and drives is learned from definitions of the legal codes as favorable or unfavorable."* Society is composed of a plurality of social groups. The norms and values of some collectivities will coincide with legal codes; those of others will vary from them considerably. But none of the subgroups will fully comply *ambiguity* with or totally contravene the law. The several populations will have varying ratios of deviant and nondeviant definitions.

6.  *"A person becomes delinquent because of [exposure to] an excess of definitions favorable to violation of law over definitions unfavorable to violation of law."* That is, when more definitions in a subgroup favor deviance than favor conformity, the behavior of group members will be similarly oriented.

This is the principle of differential association. It refers to both criminal and anti-criminal associations and has to do with counteracting forces.

> When persons become criminal, they do so because of contacts with criminal patterns and also because of isolation from anti-criminal patterns. [Sutherland, 1947: 6]

The applicability of this proposition is most apparent in the case of career criminality, in which persons systematically organize their lives around illegal activities such as professional theft, prostitution, and confidence games. Individuals may adopt such behaviors because of their association in subcultural groups wherein these patterns predominate.

It must be noted, however, that more respected groups also espouse norms that encourage violation of the law. Thus, among some white-collar professionals, income tax evasion is considered an acceptable deviation. Their beliefs regarding the unfairness of government taxation or the universality and harmlessness of padded expense accounts and undisclosed incomes facilitate tax fraud. In this instance, an excess of group definitions regarding violation of a specific legal code leads to its infraction.

7. *"Differential associations may vary in frequency, duration, priority, and intensity."* Whether persons become deviant as a result of exposure to criminal definitions depends upon these four factors. The *frequency* with which individuals encounter deviant patterns and the *duration* or length of time involved will affect the degree to which criminal norms are internalized. Further, associations that occur early in life—that have *priority*—are more influential in shaping behavior than those that develop later; prior learning experiences within the family and neighborhood are particularly important determinants of stable behavior patterns. Finally, *intensity*, the importance the individual attaches to the associations, affects their influence; associations that are also reference groups will have a greater impact than less significant ones.

8. *"The process of learning criminal behavior by association with criminal and anticriminal patterns involves all of the mechanisms that are involved in any other learning."* In effect, this statement is a summary of all preceding propositions. The explicit emphasis is on socialization and the learning processes that shape conformity and deviance alike.

9. *"While criminal behavior is an expression of general needs and values, it is not explained by . . . them . . . since noncriminal behavior is [also] an expression of the same needs and values."* The satisfaction of internalized needs and values is a necessary condition for deviant behavior. It is not, however, a sufficient condition, nor is it unique to nonconformity.

Thieves generally steal in order to secure money, but likewise honest laborers work in order to secure money. . . . The happiness principle, striving for social status, the money motive, or frustration . . . explain lawful behavior as completely as they explain criminal behavior. They are similar to respiration, which is necessary for any behavior but which does not differentiate criminal from noncriminal behavior. [Sutherland, 1947: 7–8]

To put it simply, Sutherland argued that criminal behavior is acquired through interaction in groups that have more criminal than noncriminal definitions. Whether the individual internalizes these definitions depends upon the importance of such associations within the individual's total network of social relationships.

# Prisonization

*Donald Clemmer*

We may use the term *prisonization* to indicate the taking on in greater or less degree of the folkways, mores, customs, and general culture of the penitentiary. . . . Every man who enters the penitentiary undergoes prisonization to some extent. The first and most obvious integrative step concerns his status. He becomes at once an anonymous figure in a subordinate group. A number replaces a name. He wears the clothes of the other members of the subordinate group. He is questioned and admonished. He soon learns that the warden is all-powerful. He soon learns the ranks, titles, and authority of various officials. And whether he uses the prison slang and argot or not, he comes to know its meanings. Even though a new man may hold himself aloof from other inmates and remain a solitary figure, he finds himself within a few months referring to or thinking of keepers as "screws," the physician as the "croaker" and using the local nicknames to designate persons. He follows the examples already set in wearing his cap. He learns to eat in haste and in obtaining food he imitates the tricks of those near him.

After the new arrival recovers from the effects of the swallowing-up process, he assigns a new meaning to conditions he had previously taken for granted. The fact that food, shelter, clothing, and a work activity had been given him originally made no especial impression. It is only after some weeks or months that there comes to him a new interpretation of these necessities of life. This new conception results from mingling with other men and it places emphasis on the fact that the environment *should* administer to him. . . .

In various other ways men new to prison slip into the existing patterns.

They learn to gamble or learn new ways to gamble. Some, for the first time in their lives, take to abnormal sex behavior. Many of them learn to distrust and hate the officers, the parole board, and sometimes each other, and they become acquainted with the dogmas and mores existing in the community. . . . In the highest or greatest degree of prisonization the following factors may be enumerated:

1. A sentence of many years, thus a long subjection to the universal factors of prisonization.
2. A somewhat unstable personality made unstable by an inadequacy of "socialized" relations before commitment, but possessing, none the less, a capacity for strong convictions and a particular kind of loyalty.
3. A dearth of positive relations with persons outside the walls.
4. A readiness and a capacity for integration into a prison-primary group.
5. A blind, or almost blind, acceptance of the dogmas and mores of the primary group and the general penal population.
6. A chance placement with other persons of a similar orientation.

Source: Donald Clemmer, *The Prison Community* (New York: Holt, Rinehart and Winston, 1958), pp. 299–302.

Later theorists elaborated Sutherland's differential association thesis by incorporating principles of behavioral psychology. In particular, the concept of *operant conditioning*—the strengthening of an existing response through reinforcement—helps to specify the general learning mechanisms referred to in the eighth proposition (Jeffrey, 1965).

The reinforcements for criminal behavior are both social and material. The support of reference associations contributes to the formation and stability of behavior, and so do the material gains acquired through the criminal act. Crimes that involve the illegal acquisition of property are reinforced by these material gains; crimes of violence against persons are gratifying insofar as a hated person is injured or removed. Similarly, illicit sexual activities are the product of prior conditioning in the sexual area, and drugs and alcohol are reinforcers because of their physiological effects.

Although there are reinforcements for criminal behavior, there is also the possibility of punishment. "An act of robbery produces money; it also may produce being shot at by the victim or the police, being arrested, being imprisoned" (Jeffrey, 1965: 295). For criminal behavior to occur, the reinforcements for nonconformity must seem to exceed the possibility of punishments.

# A Differential Association–Reinforcement Theory of Criminal Behavior

[Robert Burgess and Ronald Akers (1968) have systematically reformulated the propositions of Sutherland's theory by utilizing the principles of operant conditioning. Since the concepts of learning theory are readily testable, their use in a reformulation of differential association provides a more accurate and useful tool for the analysis of criminal behavior.]

| Sutherland's Statements | Reformulated Statements |
|---|---|
| 1. Criminal behavior is learned.<br>8. The process of learning criminal behavior by association with criminal and anticriminal patterns involves all of the mechanisms that are involved in any other learning. | 1. Criminal behavior is learned according to the principles of operant conditioning. |
| 2. Criminal behavior is learned in interaction with other persons in a process of communication. | 2. Criminal behavior is learned both in nonsocial situations that are reinforcing or discriminative and through that social interaction in which the behavior of other persons is reinforcing or discriminative for criminal behavior. |
| 3. The principal part of the learning of criminal behavior occurs within intimate personal groups. | 3. The principal part of the learning of criminal behavior occurs in those groups which comprise the individual's major source of reinforcements. |
| 4. When criminal behavior is learned, the learning includes (a) techniques of committing the crime, which are sometimes very complicated, sometimes very simple; (b) the specific direction of motives, drives, rationalizations, and attitudes. | 4. The learning of criminal behavior, including specific techniques, attitudes, and avoidance procedures, is a function of the effective and available reinforcers, and the existing reinforcement contingencies. |

| Sutherland's Statements | Reformulated Statements |
|---|---|
| 5. The specific direction of motives and drives is learned from definitions of the legal codes as favorable or unfavorable. | 5. The specific class of behaviors which are learned and their frequency of occurrence are a function of the reinforcers which are effective and available, and the rules or norms by which these reinforcers are applied. |
| 6. A person becomes delinquent because of an excess of definitions favorable to violation of law over definitions unfavorable to violation of law. | 6. Criminal behavior is a function of norms which are discriminative for criminal behavior, the learning of which takes place when such behavior is more highly reinforced than noncriminal behavior. |
| 7. Differential associations may vary in frequency, duration, priority, and intensity. | 7. The strength of criminal behavior is a direct function of the amount, frequency, and probability of its reinforcement. |
| 9. While criminal behavior is an expression of general needs and values, it is not explained by those general needs and values since noncriminal behavior is an expression of the same needs and values. | 9. (Omit from theory.) |

Source: Robert L. Burgess and Ronald L. Akers, "A Differential Association–Reinforcement Theory of Criminal Behavior," *Social Problems* 14 (Fall 1968): 146–147.

The utility of general learning principles in elaborating social and cultural support theory has been demonstrated in a study of marijuana and alcohol use among adolescents (Akers, et al., 1979). The findings indicated that individual variations in behavior were strongly influenced by exposure to role models whose own approach to drugs and alochol can be imitated, by the relative frequency of association with using and abstinent peers and adults, by the pattern with which use is rewarded or punished, and by the weight of positive and negative definitions which the individual encounters (Akers, et al., 1979: 639). Together, differential imitation, association, reinforcement, and definition were able to explain 68 percent of the difference between marijuana using and asbtinent juveniles and 55 percent of the difference between adolescents who used alcohol and those who did not (Akers, et al., 1979: 642).

## SPATIAL DISTRIBUTION
## OF DEVIANCE DEFINITIONS

Socialization to criminal and other deviant norms is made possible by the *differential distribution of values* in society. That is, society is made up of different groups separated by space and cultural variations. Within some of these groups, norms and values develop that are in opposition to the standards of the dominant society. Participation in such groups will lead to the acquisition of motives and behaviors defined as deviant by the society in general.

Clifford Shaw and Henry McKay (1942) pointed out that within urban areas the opportunities to partcipate in delinquent groups are also differentially distributed. They observed from earlier studies that most urban areas are made up of a series of concentric zones radiating outward from the center of the city (Park, et al., 1925). The first zone, the *central business district*, consists of banks, stores, theaters, hotels, public transportation facilities, and government office buildings. The second, the *zone in transition*, is characterized by a combination of the expanding business district and the abandoned dwellings of people who have fled to locations further from the city's heart. Buildings that were once the homes of the wealthy have been converted into the tenements and small businesses that make up the slums and ghettos of many U.S. cities. The *zone of working-class homes*, the third area, contains the older, relatively inexpensive housing of people who were able to leave the zone in transition. The fourth area, largely a *residential zone*, is composed of small businesses and professional offices and a large number of privately owned single-family homes. Finally, the *commuter zone* comprises suburban towns of more affluent families whose working population travels to the city.

Evidence generated by the study of the spatial distribution of offenders within these several areas of Chicago (Shaw, 1929) and six other major cities—Philadelphia, Richmond, Cleveland, Birmingham, Denver, and Seattle (Shaw and McKay, 1931)—during the 1920s and 1930s revealed that: (1) offense rates decreased steadily from the areas immediately outlying the center of the city to suburban communities (this pattern for Chicago is illustrated in Figure 6–2); (2) the high-rate areas were characterized by physical deterioration, by a declining population, and by conditions generally regarded to be indicators of social disorganization, such as poverty and physical and mental illness; (3) rates in high-offense areas remained high in spite of changes in ethnic composition over time; and finally (4) offenders who resided in high-rate areas were most likely to become *recidivists*, that is, to develop records of repeated criminality.

**FIGURE 6–2  Concentric Zones of Chicago**

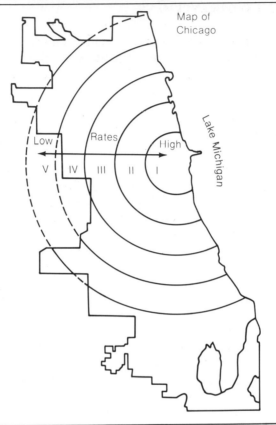

The greater incidence of delinquent and criminal behavior in the
slums near the center of the city is the product of the existence there of
competing systems of values (Shaw and McKay, 1942). This *normaitve
heterogeneity* results when religious, educational, and recreational institutions migrate from the urban slum into the middle-class suburb,
leaving behind only the vestiges of their original forms. Since these
organizations are designed to protect and perpetuate a stable value
system, attitudes and behaviors are likely to be homogeneous in communities in which they are prevalent. The absence of these control institutions in delinquent areas has opened the way for the development
of deviant traditions that are intergenerationally transmitted. The
result is an ongoing exposure of members of these communities to an
excess of normative definitions favorable to violation of the law.

# PERFORMANCE STRUCTURES
# FOR NONCONFORMITY

Social and cultural support theorists have focused on the social relationships that foster the *acquisition of norms* conducive to nonconformity (Sutherland, 1947; Shaw and McKay, 1942). According to Richard Cloward and Lloyd Ohlin (1960), the availability of opportunities to *engage in* deviant behavior are also important; persons must have access not only to the social environments for learning deviant roles but those for executing them as well. Access depends upon a variety of factors, such as age, sex, and social class.

While motivation for deviant behavior, then, may be a product of association in groups supportive of nonconformity, association is not in itself sufficient to explain the behavior. Opportunities to enact deviant roles are also necessary (Cloward and Ohlin, 1960; Palmore and Hammond, 1964). Criminal behavior, for example, depends upon access to the means of committing a crime. If the means are not available in an individual's environment, he or she is not likely to become criminal.[1] Similarly, if a person lives in a community where it is difficult to obtain drugs or where the means for expressing violence are not present, drug use or violent behavior is less likely to occur. The type of deviant behavior that does develop, therefore, depends upon the particular illegitimate opportunities available within a given community. Cloward and Ohlin (1960) maintain that the persistence of such opportunity structures over time may result in stable *criminal, conflict,* and *retreatist subcultures.*

The *criminal subculture* is made possible by the high degree of integration of age levels in the community and by an integration of legitimate and illegitimate roles. Older criminals are visible and readily accessible to younger delinquents. This contact between age groups facilitates the younger group's entry into the illegitimate opportunity structure. Members of conventional society are also important for the persistence of criminality; bail bondsmen, lawyers, fences, law enforcement officials, and the like provide the supportive milieu and services that allow the criminal to continue to operate.

*Conflict subcultures,* however, are more likely to flourish where transiency and instability are predominant. These communities cannot provide opportunities for either legitimate or illegitimate learning and performance. Here, people may attempt to achieve status through the use of violence.

> Adolescents seize upon the manipulation of violence as a route to status not only because it provides a way of expressing pent-up angers and

> frustrations but also because they are not cut off from access to violent means by vicissitudes of birth. . . . The principal prerequisites for success are "guts" and the capacity to endure pain. [Cloward and Ohlin, 1960: 175]

The conflict subculture, therefore, develops in response to a lack of access to criminal means.

The *retreatist subculture* is populated by failures from both the criminal and conflict subcultures as well as from the legitimate world. Persons who continue to cling to achievement aspirations under conditions of failure in both the legitimate and illegitimate opportunity structures may adapt through the use of drugs. Even here, however, the persistence of such behavior depends on social and cultural support. The individual must maintain contact with the subculture to secure a regular supply of drugs as well as to learn the effects of the substance, the skills for obtaining and using it, and the techniques for avoiding detection.

## PATTERNS IN ASSOCIATIONAL LEARNING

Nonconformers do tend to associate with people whose norms, values, and behavior, like theirs, reflect criminal definitions (Glueck and Glueck, 1950; Short, 1957, 1958, 1960; Reiss and Rhodes, 1964; Stanfield, 1966;Voss, 1969; Jensen, 1972; Liska, 1973). Repeated explorations of delinquency, for example, have shown that juveniles who are most seriously involved in law-violating behavior more often describe their friends as delinquent; those least involved associate with others who are more conforming (Short, 1960; Voss, 1964; Stanfield, 1966). Furthermore, the frequency, priority, duration, and intensity of delinquent associations tend to further specify the extent of delinquent involvement. Thus, the juvenile whose interactions with nonconforming associates are frequent, began early in life, have remained stable over a long period of time, and are seen as important will most likely be committed to delinquency (Short, 1957, 1958; Glaser, 1960; Voss, 1964, 1969).

That does not mean, however, that delinquency is necessarily a group activity. Although some forms of juvenile nonconformity involve the participation of several children, others do not (for a review of the relevant literature see Erickson, 1971; and Hindelang, 1971). Thus, while property destruction, drinking, and marijuana smoking tend to be group activities, illicit sexual behavior, theft, and heroin use are more often performed apart from others.[2]

The importance of differential association in the acquisition of criminal behavior patterns is illustrated by Sutherland (1937) in his study, *The Professional Thief.* Professional theft is more than the illegal appropriation of other people's property; it is a "way of life and a social institution" (Sutherland, 1937: vii). The techniques of professional thievery involve an emphasis on wits, front, and talking ability; thieves who must rely on manual dexterity or physical force are regarded as amateurs. Proper techniques for planning and executing the crime, disposing of the goods, and fixing the case if arrest occurs are acquired only through association with more experienced thieves. An individual achieves status as a thief by the level of his or her technical skill. Persons accorded the honorific title of professional thief have little respect for those who have not learned the "correct" methods of stealing.

The profession of theft also includes shared attitudes, or consensus, regarding the criminal activity, its victims, and the law. Out of this consensus develops a common set of codes pertaining to mutual assistance and loyalty. Failure to observe these codes may result in ostracism from the community of thieves. That is why a thief will submit to severe punishment at the hands of the police rather than violate the rule against informing on others.

Thieves associate with those who share in underworld activities and are isolated from the rest of society. An important aspect of such association concerns the notion of membership. "A person who is received in the group and recognized as a professional thief is a professional thief. One who is not so received and recognized is not a professional thief, regardless of his methods of making a living" (Sutherland, 1937: 207).

Since the association among thieves includes rules for membership, codes, status, and consensus, professional theft can be thought of as a highly organized and systematic form of criminality. Sharing information regarding other thieves and locations conducive to successful crimes and helping thieves who are in trouble characterize the group nature of theft as a way of life. Access to this organization implies having the "status of a professional thief in the differential association of professional thieves" (Sutherland, 1937: 211), a status dependent upon selection and tutelage. Only a few selected for training ever reach professional status.

# The Language of Professional Thieves

*Edwin H. Sutherland*

[Isolation of professional thieves from the larger society has resulted in the development of a separate language. This underworld slang is passed by word of mouth from generation to generation.]

Many people believe that these expressions are used in order to conceal the meaning from the public who may be listening in and that they are thus for the purpose of giving secrecy to the conversation. That interpretation is out; there is nothing to it. When thieves are talking in a place where others may overhear, they do not use their slang, for it would immediately attract attention to themselves. They use regular words with inflections or winks which indicate their meaning. For instance, three thieves were riding on a train. One of the mob went into a drawing-room and stole some property. Later the three thieves went into the dining-car and sat at a table for four. The owner of the drawing-room came into the diner and was seated at the table with them. He did not know the thief who had entered his room, and the thief did not know him, though the other two thieves did recognize the owner. So when the owner was sitting down, one thief said, "It is rather warm in here," and glanced at the man from the drawing-room. The other thief immediately knew what was meant.

Sometimes a professional thief is greatly embarrassed when he appears in public with an amateur who does not understand this indirect language of the professional thieves. A professional thief reported the following instance:

> I was eating supper in a cafeteria with an occasional thief and drug addict who was a student in a law school. Two coppers were sitting at another table near by. The occasional thief had selected our table and had not recognized them as coppers. They were not in uniform, but a uniform is not needed to advertise to a professional that a copper is a copper. They could not possibly have been anything else. My friend said loud enough so the coppers could hear, "Did you hear what Jerry Myers got?" I knew alright that Jerry got four years, but I was not going to let the coppers know that we were talking about anyone who had received a bit, and I had to hush the youngster up. I could not say, "Nix!" as a thief might have said if the coppers had not been able to hear, for that word in itself would have informed the coppers that we were worth watching, and besides my friend would not have understood what the word meant in that connection. So I said, "I understand the doctor said he got tonsillitis." A professional thief would have sensed danger at once and would have carried on along that line, but my friend thought I must be hard of hearing or else a fool and he started in again, "No, I mean. . . ." but I kicked him under the table and butted in again with some more information about tonsillitis. The police were watching us carefully, and I could not office (warn) my partner by moving my eyes toward them. As soon as I hesitated for a moment on the tonsillitis, he started in again on what Jerry got, so I had to get up and go to the counter for something more to eat. When I returned I picked up his book on Conveyances and looked at it a moment and then asked, "Have you seen the new book on Abnormal Psychology by Dr. Oglesby?" The policemen, who had finished eating some time before, immediately got up and reached for their hats. I nudged my partner to look at them, and as they stretched up

you could see that each had a revolver in a holster. They doubtless went away thinking, "Just a couple of harmless university students or professors." My partner now understood why I had interrupted him and skinned his shins, and he asked "Why didn't you tell me they were here?" I had told him a half-dozen times in language any professional thief would have understood but which he could not understand, principally because he did not have the attitude of suspicion which is the foundation of the indirect method of conversation, but also because he did not give me credit for good sense.

Source: Edwin H. Sutherland, *The Professional Thief* (Chicago: University of Chicago Press, 1937), pp. 18–20.

## Differential Identification

The application of Sutherland's ideas to more recent forms of professional stealing has not always been successful. The systematic check forgers described by Lemert (1958), for example, bear little resemblance to their counterparts of earlier generations. These check forgers do not think of themselves as professionals, have no associations with other forgers, and display none of the shared norms, codes, or beliefs that characterize Sutherland's thief. The status of this form of theft has changed dramatically since the earlier decades of the twentieth century. With the proliferation of checks among the general population came a corresponding decrease in the skill required to pass fraudulent ones. At the same time, improvements in law-enforcement techniques discourage the check forger's association with other offenders, since such association might lead to easier identification and arrest.

There is also little evidence of group cohesion among contemporary career robbers (Einstadter, 1969). Organization is much more fluid, involving temporary partnerships in the commission of particular crimes. Successful robbery *does* depend on skill and honesty in dealing with other robbers, and robbers appear to have a common view of their victims and of the nature of their crimes. These attributes, however, are brought to the partnership and are not acquired through differential association.

As in the case of check forgery, the difference between the contemporary robber and Sutherland's professional thief appears to be a product of general changes in society. Antitheft security systems have made detection and apprehension easier. Long-term associations, therefore, may prove detrimental to offenders who are trying to protect their identities.

The techniques, motives, drives, and rationalizations required for check forgery and armed robbery may be acquired within the context of what are otherwise legitimate relationships. A person may learn the necessary skills and justifications for these offenses through interaction in the traditional settings of the family, school, and local community. The motivations associated with check forgery, for example, are not unlike those found among "shrewd" businesspeople or people who cheat on their income tax. In like manner, it is possible to learn the techniques of robbery and property theft in such legitimate activities as military training, wild-game hunting, or employment in construction; the familiarity with weapons, tactical planning, and explosives acquired in these areas may eventually be brought to and used profitably in less legitimate activities.

It becomes apparent, then, that criminality need not be learned in *direct* association with criminals. Modern robbers and check forgers have little or no interaction with other offenders. The techniques they bring to their crimes may have been learned in legitimate contexts. Before these techniques can be applied to law-breaking, however, individuals must acquire the motives, drives, and rationalizations for such behavior. Daniel Glaser (1956) has argued that this occurs through a process of *identification* with deviance definitions. These definitions are found in both deviant and nondeviant groups, groups of which an individual may or may not be a member. In general terms,

> a person pursues criminal behavior to the extent that he identifies himself with real or imaginary persons from whose perspective his criminal behavior seems acceptable. Criminal identification may occur, for example, during direct experience in delinquent membership groups, through positive reference to criminal roles portrayed in mass media, or as a negative reaction to forces opposed to crime. [Glaser, 1956: 440]

## Subcultural Learning

Although Glaser's concept of *identification* is more inclusive than the concept of *association*, deviant groups nevertheless can be powerful sources of such identification. Thus, for example, before they enter prostitution, call girls usually establish a relationship with someone already professionally involved (Bryan, 1965). This initial contact assumes responsibility for training the novice. The primary focus of such tutelage has little to do with sexual techniques but is directed toward imparting a value system. All trainees learn certain attitudes and beliefs concerning the exploitability of men, loyalty toward other professionals, and the similarity of their behavior to that of legitimate women who use sex to obtain valued objects from their male friends and husbands. These beliefs serve to create a sense of solidarity and to alienate the novice prostitute from legitimate society.

> The structure of the . . . [initial learning] period seems quite standard. The novice receives her training either from a pimp or from another more experienced call girl, more often the latter. She serves her initial two to eight months of work under the trainer's supervision and often serves this period in the trainer's apartment. The trainer assumes responsibility for arranging contacts and negotiating the type and place of the sexual encounter.
>
>   The content of the training pertains both to a general philosophical stance and to some specifics (usually not sexual) of interpersonal behavior with customers and colleagues. The philosophy is one of exploiting the exploiters (customers) by whatever means necessary and defining the colleagues of the call girl as being intelligent, self-interested and, in certain important respects, basically honest individuals. The interpersonal techniques addressed during the learning period consist primarily of "pitches," telephone conversations, personal and occasionally sexual hygiene, prohibitions against alcohol and dope while with a "john," how and when to obtain the fee, and specifics concerning the sexual habits of particular customers. [Bryan, 1965: 294]

Once call girls have become regularly involved in their profession, the impact of the subcultural beliefs decreases (Bryan, 1966). Although they remain aware of the specific values, they do not, in fact, endorse them. The loosely organized nature of the profession, the limited contact with other call girls after initial training, and the absence of visible stigma relative to other forms of prostitution may account for the progressive decrease in consensus over professional codes.

Drug use may also depend on identification with other drug users through group association. Among college students, for example, the use of marijuana is related to a more general participation in a distinctive student subculture that developed on U.S. campuses during the 1960s (Brown et al., 1974; Thomas et al., 1975). Once college ties are severed through graduation and loss of the student role, drug use generally diminished rapidly. It appears, therefore, that peer group support is required to sustain behavior that is otherwise proscribed by the larger society. Persons who lack this support are more likely to succumb to the societal pressure to conform (Paschke, 1970).

Drug use provides a particularly interesting illustration of the importance of supportive associations, given the nature of the physiological effects produced by the various substances. Ingesting narcotics is not necessarily a pleasurable experience. To the novice, even tobacco and alcohol may produce coughing, dizziness, a burning sensation, or nausea. A taste for these substances most certainly must be cultivated.

This is clear, for example, in the case of marijuana smoking (Becker, 1953). From the inhaled smoke's first assault upon the respiratory system to the subsequent intense thirst, hunger, and sometimes even fear of insanity, the use of marijuana is associated with physiological effects that most people, under different circumstances, would seek to avoid. How, then, does one come to enjoy marijuana?

While curiosity about the drug and about "getting high" may lead an individual to try it, continued use requires the support and instruction of others. First, the novice must learn how to use the drug. Either through imitation or direct tutelage, persons acquire the techniques necessary to ensure that the marijuana will be taken in the manner and dosage required to produce a sensation. "Only when this [is] learned [is] it possible for a conception of the drug as an object which could be used for pleasure to emerge" (Becker, 1953: 237).

In addition to learning the techniques, the user must learn to recognize the state of being high. Being made aware of the specific details of the anticipated experience allows the individual to recognize those sensations produced by the drug. Again, this depends upon the interactive feedback of those more familiar with marijuana use. If the novice cannot recognize the effects of the drug and connect these effects to the fact of having smoked marijuana, marijuana use is not likely to continue. The individual must acquire the "necessary concepts with which to express to himself the fact that he [is] experiencing new sensations caused by the drug" (Becker, 1953: 239).

Finally, the user must learn to enjoy these newly acquired sensations. His or her redefining the physiological effects of the drug as pleasurable depends upon support from veteran users. By downplaying unpleasant effects and expressing envy for the beginner's high, they define the experience as a desirable accomplishment.

In sum:

> No one becomes a user without (1) learning to smoke the drug in a way which will produce real effects; (2) learning to recognize the effects and connect them with drug use (learning, in other words, to get high); and (3) learning to enjoy the sensations he perceives. (Becker, 1953: 242)

The supportive nature of deviant associations may also be seen in the case of male homosexuality (Hooker, 1967). Once an individual has "come out"—that is, has been identified as homosexual both to himself and to others—the process of enculturation into the homosexual world proceeds at a rapid pace. Through association in homosexual groups, the initiate acquires a knowledge of the meeting places, special language, and social types of homosexuals. He also learns the ways of making sexual contacts, the varieties of sexual acts, the methods of concealment, and in some instances, the techniques for evading police.

As these males restrict their associations to homosexual groups, subcultural norms become the dominant force in shaping their reality. Since the central theme of these patterns is the overt expression of homosexuality, individuals will organize their lives accordingly. This reorganization is likely to result in preoccupation with homosexual activity, "cruising for one-night-stands," public solicitation of strangers, narration of sexual experiences, and gossip of sexual exploits (see Leznoff and Westley, 1956; Hooker, 1967; and Farrell and Nelson, 1976, for a discussion of these and other aspects of homosexual subculture). The group also enables an individual to justify a homosexual way of life. This support not only confirms the homosexual in his newly expressed behavioral commitment but shields him from the derision and legal action that may be directed toward him by the larger society.

# Functions of Homosexual Groups

*Maurice Leznoff and William A. Westley*

The primary function of the homosexual group is psychological in that it provides a social context within which the homosexual can find acceptance as a homosexual and collective support for his deviant tendencies. Most homosexuals fear detection and are often insecure and anxious because of this. The following statement illustrates this:

> The thought that you are "gay" is always with you and you know it's there even when other people don't. You also think to yourself that certain of your mannerisms and your ways of expression are liable to give you away. That means that there is always a certain amount of strain. I don't say that it's a relief to get away from normal people, but there isn't the liberty that you feel in a gay crowd. When I associate with normal people I prefer very small groups of them. I don't like large groups and I think I try to avoid them when I can. You know, the only time when I really forget I'm gay is when I'm in a gay crowd.

To relieve this anxiety the deviant seeks collective support and social acceptance. Since the homosexual group provides the only social context in which homosexuality is normal, deviant practices moral, and homosexual responses rewarded, the homosexual develops a deep emotional involvement with his group, tending toward a ready acceptance of its norms and dictates, and subjection to its behavior patterns. The regularity with which he seeks the company of his group is a clear expression of this dependency.

A prohibition against sexual relationships within the group, in a manner suggestive of the incest taboo, indicates the extent to which the group culture is oriented to this function. The quotation which follows is indicative of this taboo:

As far as I know, people who hang around with each other don't have affairs. The people who are friends don't sleep with each other. I can't tell you why that is, but they just don't. Unless you are married you have sex with strangers mostly. I think if you have sex with a friend it will destroy the friendship. I think that in the inner mind we all respect high moral standards, and none of us want to feel low in the eyes of anybody else. It's always easier to get along with your gay friends if there has been no sex. Mind you, you might have sex with somebody you just met and then he might become your friend. But you won't have sex with him any more as soon as he joins the same gang you hang around with.

Within these groups the narration of sexual experiences and gossip about the sexual exploits of others is a major form of recreation. The narration of sexual experiences functions to allocate prestige among the members because of the high evaluation placed upon physical attraction and sexual prowess. Yet it creates hostility and sexual rivalry. The intense involvement of homosexuals in the results of this sexual competition is illustrated in the following statement which was overheard in a restaurant:

Who wouldn't blow up. That bitch is trying to get her clutches into Richard. She can't leave anybody alone. I wouldn't be surprised if she ended up with a knife in her back. I don't mean to say I'm threatening her. But she's not going to get away with that stuff forever . . . playing kneesies under the table all night long. I had to get her away from Richard. That lousy bitch. From now on she better keep away from me.

An additional function is the provision of a social situation in which the members can dramatize their adherence to homosexual values. Thus, the gossip about sex, the adoption and exaggeration of feminine behavior, and the affectation of speech, represent a way of affirming that homosexuality is frankly accepted and has the collective support of the group. The extreme but not uncommon instance of this is the homosexual institution of the "drag" in which the members of the group dress and make themselves up as women. A good description of a drag is contained in the following letter:

Well, doll, last night was one to remember. Raymond of B. (city) gave me a letter of introduction to one of the local belles. He 'phoned yesterday and we arranged to go out in the evening. Met at my room and proceeded to the Frederick Hotel where I was introduced to my new acquaintances. It was decided to hold a party afterwards, Chez Norman, my new acquaintance. He told me they were supposed to be discontinued but we were going ahead in my honor. And in drag. One queen about 45–50 who is a window dresser brought some materials of fine nylon net, 2 yards wide and changing color across the width from yellow to flaming orange. There must have been about 25 yds. Well, he made his entrance wearing nothing but his shorts and this stuff wound around him and proceeded to do an exotic dance. Included in the costume was a blond wig from one of the store mannequins and artificial tropical fruits. It was something to see. It was very ludicrous to begin with and much more so when you realize that he is by no means graceful and has so much hair on him that I am smooth by comparison. Throughout the evening he kept on making variations of the costume—each becoming briefer until he was down to nothing. Really!

Another one, very slim, put on a pair of falsies, a turban hat to hide short hair, and a dress with a wide flair skirt. Other than hair on the chest which showed, the effect of femininity was so convincing (even his heels) that I promptly lost interest. Actually produced a beautiful effect—the kind of woman I would like if I could. Beautiful dancer, and performed all evening. Later borrowed some of the nylon net of the old queen and did a dance with flowing material and wearing *nothing,* but nothing else.

There were only three of us not in drag, including yrs. truly. But when it came time to leave (not alone, I might add) I couldn't resist flinging about my coat a fox fur which happened to be lying around. Really, my dear, it was quite an affair.

These functions reflect the common needs and problems which homosexuals face in hostile society.

Source: Maurice Leznoff and William A. Westley, "The Homosexual Community," *Social Problems* 3 (April 1956): 257–259.

---

Thus far, we have seen that subcultures often provide support for the development of deviant identity. There are also instances, however, where subcultures shield individuals from defining themselves as deviant. The dynamic effect of social and cultural support in this case may be seen among delinquents involved in homosexual prostitution (Reiss, 1961). Boys who engage in this activity define themselves neither as prostitutes nor as homosexuals. Even though they are selling sexual favors to adult males, they view the behavior merely as a means of obtaining money or having fun illegally.

What protects the juveniles from a threat to their masculine self-images are the norms that govern the transaction, norms that are learned from peers in the delinquent group. First, the act is viewed as a way of making money. It is a financial transaction that does not include sexual gratification as a goal. Although gratification may in fact occur, it is incidental. Second, fellation is the only practice allowed, with the boy acting as the insertor. This allows him to engage in the more masculine role during the exchange. Third, affective neutrality is maintained by both interactors. No expressions of endearment or suggestions for a continued relationship are permitted, either from the juvenile or his sexual partner. Finally, should the homosexual violate any of these rules by suggesting alternative sexual techniques or expressing affection, the boy is expected to use violence.

## Rationalization and Commitment to Deviance

We have seen that deviant associations are important sources of nonconformity. They not only provide the skills and incentives for deviance, but an environment of collective support as well. A critical aspect of this support is the provision of *rationalizations* for behavior (Sutherland, 1947).

Conformer and nonconformer alike live in a social system that attaches positive sanction to some activities and negative sanction to others. Since no one can remove himself or herself entirely from these expectations, everyone incorporates, to some degree, attitudes appropriate to conformity. Even individuals who associate almost exclusively with other members of deviant groups must, on occasion, come into contact with the larger society. In some instances, this contact may be limited to encounters with law-enforcement agents; far more frequently it involves participation in the educational, occupational, religious, and economic spheres of social life. In order to neutralize the rejection or demands for conformity that they may experience in these encounters, delinquents develop rationalizations for their behavior. Sykes and Matza (1957: 667–669) have described the major neutralization techniques as follows:[3]

> *Denial of Responsibility* . . . Delinquent acts are . . . [attributed] to forces outside of the individual and beyond his control such as unloving parents, bad companions, or a slum neighborhood. In effect, the delinquent approaches a "billiard ball" conception of himself in which he sees himself as helplessly propelled into new situations. . . .
> *Denial of Injury* . . . The delinquent . . . feels that his behavior does not really cause any great harm despite the fact that it runs counter to law. . . . It may be claimed [that] the persons whose property has been destroyed can well afford it, . . . auto theft may be viewed as "borrowing," and gang fighting may be seen as a private quarrel. . . .
> *Denial of the Victim* . . . [Delinquents display] an insistence that the injury is not wrong in light of the circumstances. . . . Rather, it is a form of rightful retaliation . . . [in that] the victim is transformed into a wrongdoer. . . . [Also,] insofar as the victim is physically absent, unknown, or a

vague abstraction . . . , the awareness of the victim's existence is weakened.

*Condemnation of Condemners* . . . The delinquent shifts the focus of attention from his own deviant acts to the motives and behavior of those who disapprove of his violations. His condemners, he may claim, are hypocrites, deviants in disguise, or impelled by personal spite. . . . By attacking others, the wrongfulness of his own behavior is more easily repressed. . . .

*Appeal to Higher Loyalties* . . . Internal and external social controls may be neutralized by sacrificing the demands of the larger society for the demands of the smaller social groups to which the delinquent belongs such as the sibling pair, the gang, or the friendship clique. . . . Other norms, held to be more pressing or involving a higher loyalty, are accorded precedence.

**Neutralization Techniques in Career Criminality.**   Carl Klockars' (1974) biographical analysis, *The Professional Fence*, provides insight into the nature and role of neutralization techniques in career criminality. For over thirty years, Vincent Swaggi has been in the business of buying and selling stolen goods. Although his behavior constitutes a serious violation of the law, Vincent sees himself as essentially a successful, legitimate businessman.

He denies criminal responsibility by arguing that he has never personally stolen anything and that he does not, therefore, constitute a threat to society. Furthermore, he claims that theft would persist whether he continued to purchase stolen goods or not.

Vincent also denies that his illegal activities involve either victims or injury. The most respectable citizens willingly and knowingly buy stolen merchandise from Vincent, which convinces him that the community not only tolerates but wants his operation. Further, many initial victims of theft do not suffer major economic losses from the crime. Much of the stolen property comes from large department stores or chains that are covered by insurance or can pass the losses on to the consumer through higher prices. Thus, Vincent argues:

> Did you see the paper yesterday? You figure it out. Last year I musta had $25,000 worth of merchandise from Sears. In this city last year they could'a called it Sears, Roebuck, and Swaggi. Just yesterday in the paper I read where Sears just had the biggest year in history, made more money than ever before. Now if I had that much of Sears' stuff can you imagine how much they musta lost all told? Millions, must be millions. And they still had their biggest year ever. . . . You think they end up losing when they get clipped? Don't you believe it. They're no different from anybody else. If they don't get it back by takin' it off their taxes, they get it back from insurance. [Klockars, 1974: 148–149]

The following statement reflects Vincent's condemnation of condemners as he imputes illicit activities to businessmen from whom goods are often stolen:

> Carl, if I told you how many businessmen I know have a robbery every now an' then to cover expenses you wouldn't believe it. What does it take? You get some trusted employee, and you send him out with an empty truck. He parks it somewhere an' calls in an' says he was robbed. That's it. The insurance company's gotta pay up. The driver makes a couple a hundred bucks and it's an open-an'-shut case. You can't do it every year but once in awhile it's a sure thing. Oh, there's millions a ways to do it. You come in the mornin' an' break your window. Call the cops, mess some stuff up. Bang! You got a few thousand from the insurance company. I'm tellin' ya, it happens all the time. [Klockars, 1974: 149]

Planned and deliberate nonconformity such as that discussed above (as opposed to accidental or ascribed deviance) must be *preceded* by the actor's adopting verbalizations that legitimize the behavior in his or her eyes. Another example of this pattern is people who violate trust by embezzling from their employers (Cressey, 1953).

Typically, people who engage in such violations of trust do so because they have a financial problem that they do not believe they can deal with through legitimate means. In order to solve the problem illegally, they must be able to define their activities "(a) as essentially noncriminal, (b) as justified, or (c) as part of a general irresponsibility for which [they are] not completely accountable" (Cressey, 1953: 93). The rationalization, which occurs prior to the misuse of entrusted funds, enables the person to perform the act.

Justifications of people who have had previous experience with trust violations are readily available to the individual. Familiarity with definitions of situations in which crime is "appropriate" comes from such common wisdoms as: "some of our most respectable citizens got their start in life by using other people's money temporarily" and "all people steal when they get in a tight spot" (Cressey, 1953: 96). Individuals who are exposed to these and similar definitions and adopt them are more likely to pursue an illegitimate solution to financial problems. They will rationalize that the money is borrowed, not stolen, and that honesty is impossible under the circumstances. In order to internalize such justifications, the person "necessarily must have come into contact with a culture which defined those roles for him. If the roles were defined differently in his culture, or if he had not come into contact with the group definitions, he would behave differently" (Cressey, 1953: 99).

**Neutralization and Ascribed Deviance.**  For the professional fence and the trust violator, neutralization techniques precede and thus facilitate the criminal behavior. In cases of ascribed or accidental nonconformity, such techniques represent efforts to destigmatize the nonconformist status. Again, these efforts are most often found "in more permanent groupings, especially in social settings where . . . [there is] more or less continuous interaction, where . . . [people] are able to develop their own subculture, norms, and ideology, and where they possess some measure of control over penetrating dissonant and discrediting views from without" (Gussow and Tracy, 1968: 317).

A poignant illustration of learned neutralization *following* the ascription of deviance may be seen in the attempts of leprosy patients to explain the widespread fear of and prejudice toward them. The diagnosis of leprosy is perhaps the most stigmatizing medical label. Patients, when told they have the disease, are likely to suffer a severe identity crisis. This crisis is a product of the realization that, although they are seriously ill, they have not really changed, and yet society now views them in a very different light. Unless they are able to disguise their condition permanently, afflicted persons must learn to adjust to their stigmatized status. One method of adjustment concerns the development of a belief system that effectively counters the more general attitudes with which society defines them. They develop a subcultural solution to the societal response to their condition:

> They formulate a theory of their own to account for their predicament, to de-discredit themselves, to challenge the norms that disadvantage them and supplant these with others that provide a base for reducing or removing self-stigma and other-stigma. [Gussow and Tracy, 1968: 319]

Because diagnosed lepers are required by law to remain in residence or participate in outpatient services at designated hospital-colonies, well-developed patient cultures, including norms and attitudes toward the disease, have evolved. The theory of disease that has emerged from this subcultural interaction focuses on the mythology of leprosy and the improbability of contagion. In general, the theory "is a highly formal explanation of the stigmatic nature of their illness which permits patients to minimize the notion that they are severely afflicted and also provides them with readily available and, to them, provable evidence that society has wrongly labeled them" (Gussow and Tracy, 1968: 318). Through enculturation to subculturally developed explanations of their deviation, persons so defined can maintain positive self-images.

## REFERENCE ASSOCIATION AND
## SOCIAL CONTROL

*Association* with deviant or delinquent groups and *identification* with the norms, standards, and values conducive to deviant behavior are among the processes that lead to nonconformity. Individuals are also members of legitimate groups, however, and may therefore identify with norms that support conformity. A full understanding of social and cultural support theory requires that we also examine these ties to conventional support systems and their impact on the individual's behavior.

Reflecting Durkheim's (1897) discussion of the relationship between social integration and nonconformity (see Chapter 5), Travis Hirschi (1969) has proposed that deviance is a product of the *failure of the social bond.* Elements of this bond include *attachments, commitments, involvements,* and *beliefs* that are consistent with the dominant normative order.

Individual conformity depends on the internalization of societal norms, which is made possible by the *attachment* of the individual to other conforming individuals. When these attachments fail to develop, or when they are disrupted, the internalization process may not occur. Conformity is also encouraged by the systematic distribution of rewards to those who comply with behavioral standards. Over time, individuals accumulate the "goods, reputations, [and] prospects" that increase the importance of continued conformity (Hirschi, 1969: 21). This intensified *commitment* to conventional lines of action will lead persons to avoid the kinds of behavior that would jeopardize not only what they have already acquired but their pursuit of additional rewards as well. *Involvement* in conventional activities promotes conformity by reducing proportionately the time that would be required to engage in deviant behavior. The person who is tied to "appointments, deadlines, working hours, [and] plans" has little opportunity to "think about deviant acts," let alone express these inclinations behaviorally (Hirschi, 1969: 22). Finally, *belief* in a common value system will also impede deviant behavior, for people who strongly agree with societal norms will be compelled to conform to the behavioral expectations of the collectivity.

When the elements of the social bond fail—when individuals do not develop legitimate attachments, commitments, involvements, and beliefs—the motivations and attitudes that ensure conformity are also absent. Persons are then free to establish relationships with groups whose definitions favor deviant behavior.

Ties to conventional and nonconventional associations, therefore, represent alternative, and perhaps mutually exclusive, poles of a single continuum. Individuals will conform, despite their exposure to deviant norms, if their attachments, commitments, involvements, and beliefs are oriented to legitimate society. Children who reside in high delinquency areas, for example, will conform to conventional norms as long as their identifications are with legitimate referents, such as their families or conforming friends. These identifications insulate the individual from prevailing delinquent influences and the adoption of alternative behavior patterns (Reckless et al., 1956, 1957). Conversely, when ties to representatives of conventional society are weak, contact with delinquent peers will more likely result in delinquency (Glaser, 1960; Stanfield, 1966; Hirschi, 1969; Jensen, 1972; Linden and Hackler, 1973; Liska, 1973). This simultaneous consideration of both deviant and nondeviant associations more fully accounts for behavior than does consideration of either alone (Voss, 1969).[4]

## CONCLUSION

Social and cultural support theorists emphasize the instrumentality of reference group association and identification in the development of nonconformity. The acquisition and enactment of this behavior depend on performance as well as on learning structures that provide rewards compatible with deviant group definitions. Very generally, these theorists believe that deviance results from socialization to normative definitions conducive to such behavior. The processes of learning nonconformity are essentially the same as those involved in learning conforming behavior.

The concept of *normative heterogeneity* is an integral part of the theory. Within cultural pluralism are found varying ratios of definitions favorable and unfavorable to the commission of crime. In order to understand more fully the implications of cultural pluralism for the development of deviance and the subsequent societal reactions to it, we may draw upon *theories of social and cultural conflict*, which are the focus of the following chapter.

## NOTES

1. Cloward and Ohlin's (1960) thesis is also complementary to Robert Merton's (1938) theory of the availability of institutionalized means for conformity. They argue that there is a parallel opportunity structure for nonconforming behavior, one composed of both learning and performance structures. The individual whose achievement within legitimate society is frustrated will not turn to deviant adaptations unless he or she has access to illegitimate opportunities for the acquisition and enactment of deviance.

2. Moreover, there is evidence to suggest that violating delinquent statutes in groups increases the likelihood of arrest. Studies of group involvement relying upon official statistics, therefore, may measure not the frequency of group violation but the frequency of arrest of such violators (Erickson, 1971).

3. Sykes and Matza's (1957) discussion of the techniques of neutralization was intended as an argument against the existence of delinquent subcultures. Persons participating in groups that positively evaluated nonconformity would not need to justify their behavior to outsiders. That juveniles do employ neutralization techniques suggested to Sykes and Matza that delinquents are well imbued with the norms and expectations of dominant society.

    The fact that deviants rationalize their behavior, however, does not preclude the existence of deviant subcultures. Sutherland (1947) is clear on this point when he argues that differential association of persons in groups with definitions conducive to criminality involves the learning of the motives, attitudes, drives, and *rationalizations* that facilitate law violation in the face of dominant expectations. Thus, the verbalizations that Sykes and Matza interpret to be individual justifications may in fact be subculturally learned beliefs.

4. Hirschi's (1969) control theory was originally intended as a substitute for the principles of differential association. The integration of the two approaches, however, contributes much to our understanding of deviance. Such a synthesis calls not only for an examination of an individual's involvement with nonconformity but also his or her ties with conventional society. It is reasonable to assume, that is, that an individual is more likely to acquire norms conducive to deviance if his or her participation in legitimate society has been truncated.

## REFERENCES

Akers, Ronald L., Marvin D. Krohn, Lonn Lanza-Kaduce, and Marcia Radosevich
  1979   Social Learning and Deviant Behavior: A Specific Test of a General Theory. American Sociological Review 44 (August): 636–655.
Becker, Howard S.
  1953   Becoming a Marihuana User. American Journal of Sociology 59 (November): 235–242.
Brown, James W., Daniel Glaser, Elaine Waxer, and Gilbert Geis
  1974   Turning Off: Cessation of Marijuana Use After College. Social Problems 21 (Winter): 527–538.
Bryan, James H.
  1965   Apprenticeships in Prostitution. Social Problems 12 (Winter): 287–297.
  1966   Occupational Ideologies and Individual Attitudes of Call Girls. Social Problems 13 (Spring): 441–450.
Burgess, Robert L., and Ronald L. Akers
  1968   A Differential Association–Reinforcement Theory of Criminal Behavior. Social Problems 14 (Fall): 128–147.
Clemmer, Donald
  1958   The Prison Community. New York: Holt, Rinehart and Winston.
Cloward, Richard A., and Lloyd E. Ohlin
  1960   Delinquency and Opportunity: A Theory of Delinquent Gangs. New York: Free Press.

Cressey, Donald
  1953  Other People's Money: A Study of the Social Psychology of Embezzlement. Chicago: Free Press.
Einstadter, Werner J.
  1969  The Social Organization of Armed Robbery. Social Problems 17 (Summer): 64–83.
Erickson, Maynard L.
  1971  The Group Context of Delinquent Behavior. Social Problems 19 (Summer): 114–129.
Farrell, Ronald A., and James F. Nelson
  1976  A Causal Model of Secondary Deviance: The Case of Homosexuality. Sociological Quarterly 17 (Winter): 109–120.
Glaser, Daniel
  1956  Criminality Theories and Behavioral Images. American Journal of Sociology 61 (March): 433–444.
  1960  Differential Association and Criminological Prediction. Social Problems 8 (Summer): 6–14.
Glueck, Sheldon, and Eleanor Glueck
  1950  Unraveling Juvenile Delinquency. New York: Commonwealth Fund.
Gussow, Zachery, and George S. Tracy
  1968  Status, Ideology, and Adaptation to Stigmatized Illness: A Study of Leprosy. Human Organization 27 (Winter): 316–325.
Hindelang, Michael J.
  1971  The Social Versus Solitary Nature of Delinquent Involvements. British Journal of Criminology 11 (August): 127–160.
Hirschi, Travis
  1969  Causes of Delinquency. Los Angeles: University of California Press.
Hooker, Evelyn
  1967  The Homosexual Community. *In* Sexual Deviance. John H. Gagnon and William Simon, eds. Pp. 167–184. New York: Harper and Row.
Jeffrey, C. R.
  1965  Criminal Behavior and Learning Theory. Journal of Criminal Law, Criminology, and Police Science 56 (September): 294–300.
Jensen, Gary F.
  1972  Parents, Peers, and Delinquent Action: A Test of the Differential Association Perspective. American Journal of Sociology 78 (November): 562–575.
Klockars, Carl B.
  1974  The Professional Fence. New York: Free Press.
Lemert, Edwin M.
  1958  The Behavior of the Systematic Check Forger. Social Problems 6 (Fall): 141–149.
Leznoff, Maurice, and William A. Westley
  1956  The Homosexual Community. Social Problems 3 (April): 257–263.
Linden, Eric, and James C. Hackler
  1973  Affective Ties and Delinquency. Pacific Sociological Review 16 (January): 27–46.

Liska, Allen
  1973  Causal Structures Underlying the Relationship Between Delinquent In-
        volvement and Delinquent Peers. Sociology and Social Research 58 (Oc-
        tober): 23–26.
Merton, Robert K.
  1938  Social Structure and Anomie. American Sociological Reivew 3 (October):
        672–682.
Palmore, Erdman B., and Phillip E. Hammond
  1964  Interacting Factors in Juvenile Delinquency. American Sociological
        Review 29 (December): 848–854.
Park, Robert, Robert Burgess, and R. D. McKensie
  1925  The City. Chicago: University of Chicago Press.
Paschke, Walter Richard
  1970  The Addiction Cycle: A Learning Theory–Peer Group Model. Corrective
        Psychiatry and Journal of Social Therapy 16: 1–8.
Phillips, David
  1974  The Influence of Suggestion on Suicide: Substantive and Theoretical
        Implications of the Werther Effect. American Sociological Review 39
        (June): 340–354.
Reckless, W. C., Simon Dinitz, and Ellen Murray
  1956  Self Concept as an Insulator Against Delinquency. American Sociological
        Review 21 (December): 744–746.
  1957  The "Good" Boy in a High Delinquency Area. Journal of Criminal Law,
        Criminology, and Police Science 48 (May–June): 18–26.
Reiss, Albert J., Jr.
  1961  The Social Integration of Queers and Peers. Social Problems 9 (Fall):
        102–120.
Reiss, Albert J., Jr., and A. Lewis Rhodes
  1964  An Empirical Test of Differential Association Theory. Journal of
        Research in Crime and Delinquency 1 (January): 5–18.
Shaw, Clifford, R.
  1929  Delinquency Areas. Chicago: University of Chicago Press.
Shaw, Clifford R., and Henry D. McKay
  1931  Social Factors in Juvenile Delinquency. Report on the Causes of Crime,
        Vol. 2, No. 13, National Commission on Law Observance and Enforce-
        ment. Washington, D.C.: Government Printing Office.
  1942  Juvenile Delinquency in Urban Areas. Chicago: University of Chicago
        Press.
Short, James F., Jr.
  1957  Differential Association and Delinquency. Social Problems 4 (January):
        233–239.
  1958  Differential Association with Delinquent Friends and Delinquent
        Behavior. Pacific Sociological Review 1 (Spring): 20–25.
  1960  Differential Association as a Hypothesis: Problems of Empirical Testing.
        Social Problems 8 (Summer): 14–25.
Stanfield, Robert
  1966  The Interaction of Family Variables and Gang Variables in the
        Aetiology of Delinquency. Social Problems 13 (Spring): 411–417.

Sutherland, Edwin H.
  1937  The Professional Thief. Chicago: University of Chicago Press.
  1947  Principles of Criminology. Philadelphia: J. B. Lippincott.
Swigert, Victoria Lynn, Ronald A. Farrell, and William C. Yoels
  1976  Sexual Homicide: Social, Psychological, and Legal Aspects. Archives of
        Sexual Behavior 5 (September): 391–401.
Sykes, Gresham, and David Matza
  1957  Techniques of Neutralization: A Theory of Delinquency. American
        Sociological Review 22 (December): 664–670.
Tarde, Gabriel
  1912  Penal Philosophy. Boston: Litte, Brown.
Thomas, Charles W., David M. Peterson, and Mathew T. Zingroff
  1975  Student Drug Use: A Re-Examination of the "Hang-Loose Ethic"
        Hypothesis. Journal of Health and Social Behavior 16 (March): 63–73.
Voss, Harwin L.
  1964  Differential Association and Reported Delinquent Behavior: A Replica-
        tion. Social Problems 12 (Summer): 78–85.
  1969  Differential Association and Containment Theory: A Theoretical Con-
        vergence. Social Forces 47 (June): 381–390.
Wertham, Frederick
  1949  The Show of Violence. Garden City, New York: Doubleday.

# 7

## Deviance and Conflict: The Affirmation of Class, Culture, and Power

We have seen that the reference group is central to the development of individual identity and behavior. Since significant others enable the individual to define himself or herself positively, his or her loyalty to them will be high. Individuals show this commitment in their attempts to adhere to the standards and norms that characterize group life. Both deviant and nondeviant behavior are motivated by the desire to maintain the acceptance and support of those people looked to for reward. Deviant groups, however, are in continuous conflict with the larger society. Nonconformity, by definition, opposes dominant behavioral codes. Contact between deviants and members of legitimate society, therefore, creates problems that have consequences for both the deviant and society. The need to defend the self and the position of the group reaffirms the deviant's commitment to subcultural associations, associations that ensure the persistence of the original disvalued behavior. Conflict also legitimates dominant group definitions of deviance; that is, official encounters with deviants and the sanctions imposed on them are visible reminders of the threat of nonconformity to the established order. Group commitment, conflict, and the affirmation of class, culture, and power are the concepts around which *social and cultural conflict theory* is organized.

### NONCONFORMITY AS A CONFLICT OF CULTURE CODES

Complex modern socieites comprise a plurality of groups, each with its own cultural expectations for the behavior of its members. Different cultural norms and values may be found among the various social

194

classes, nationalities, races, age groups, and geographical locations, as well as between the two sexes. These differences appear in the variations of language, dress, and recreational patterns that distinguish the various groups. The play of lower-class children, for example, tends to be less goal-directed than that of middle-class children (Cohen, 1955: 91). The lower-class emphasis on fun for fun's sake differs markedly from the middle-class cultivation of competitiveness, interpersonal skills, and accelerated learning. Similarly, it is obvious that young people's tastes in music and clothing styles bear little resemblance to those of older persons. Even the distinctions in verbal expression by sex, race, class, and region reflect the diversity of cultural forms found within the United States. Some cultural variations will inevitably conflict with those of other groups. This conflict may lead to nonconforming behavior.

According to Thorsten Sellin (1938), when different normative systems come in contact, the person who tries to adhere to one set of standards may unwittingly violate another. If the violation is proscribed by the dominant culture, it may be defined as criminal.

This conflict becomes most visible when, through colonization, conquest, or immigration, the dominant culture's norms are applied to a people who have not been subject to them before. Many ancient tribal codes suddenly became criminal when, in the nineteenth century, the British imposed their laws on parts of Africa. Similarly, immigrants to the United States found that certain behaviors expected of them in the home country were disvalued in U.S. society. Offenders were often surprised when they were sanctioned for activities that may have been demanded in their culture of origin. Thus, Sellin describes the Sicilian father who murdered the seducer of his daughter. This defense of family honor, strongly prescribed in Sicily, was legally condemnable in the adopted culture. The crime, therefore, was an unanticipated consequence of conformity to a set of standards that was at variance with the new normative system.

# Witch Murder in Colonial Africa

*Robert B. Seidman*

> For many Africans, witchcraft belief is an integral part of their *Weltanschauung*, growing out of indigenous theories about the psyche. . . .
> Prior to European overlordship, death, usually in some peculiarly horrible form, was the invariable punishment for proven witches. The colonial governments, having but recently abolished equally barbaric measures

against witches in the metropole, abolished them in the colonies as well. But superstition nevertheless flourished albeit now shorn of institutional protection.

The African who believes in witchcraft is thus faced by a fearful dilemma. He believes in witches to his bones. He knows that they can destroy [him] . . . in sundry mysterious ways, without chance for defence, so that both his physical being and his hope for earthly success are endangered, as much as by threatened blow of panga or spear or matchet. He sees nothing in the societal order to which he can appeal for protection. His tradition approves of capital punishment for witches.

Faced by such dread forces, bereft of societal shield, terrified by the loss of the values at stake, some Africans not surprisingly have struck back in terror and in self-defence. How have the [British] common law judges treated them when they were charged with murder? The response of the courts has been practically unvarying: such defendants are guilty of murder. . . . Whether the claim is nakedly that these defendants lack a guilty mind, or whether an attempt is made to fit them within the conventional categories of self-defence, or defence of others, mistake, insanity, or provocation, it has been rejected by the courts. . . .

In *Erika Galikuwa* (Uganda), the defendant was convicted of killing an unscrupulous witch-doctor. The defendant imagined that he heard the witch-doctor's "spirit voice" repeat a demand for ransom on two occasions, at one point with a threat to kill "by sucking your blood." Terrified, the defendant killed "and saved my life." The court, upholding a conviction for murder, pointed out that a plea of self-defence was not tenable, for "it is difficult to see how an act of witchcraft unaccompanied by some physical attack could be brought within the principles of English Common Law. . . .

In *Konkomba* (Gold Coast), the defendant's first brother died. He consulted a "juju" man who pointed out the [individual who was] . . . the guilty witch. Defendant's second brother became ill, and charged [the same individual] . . . with causing his illness by witchcraft. The defendant slew the supposed witch. He was, of course, found guilty of murder.

The case may fairly be contrasted with the familiar *Bourne*. There the defendant, a socially prominent doctor, was charged with committing abortion upon a fifteen-year-old victim of a brutal rape. His defence in part was that he had relied upon advice of a psychiatrist that, if the pregnancy were permitted to continue, severe psychiatric damage to the child might well ensue. The abortion was held justifiable.

The cases are not dissimilar. In each, the defendant honestly believed that what he did was necessary to save another. Each acted upon the advice of an expert in the relevant field. Yet one man was found guilty, and the other exonerated. The only apparent difference is that the tribunal believed in psychiatry, and not in witchcraft. . . .

[Finally,] in *Gadam* (Nigeria), defendant was convicted of murder. The Crown's case was that he believed that his wife had been bewitched by the deceased, whom he therefore killed. The defendant relied upon a section of the Nigerian Code, affording a defence for a mistake which is both "honest and reasonable." The court conceded that witchcraft belief was common among ordinary members of the community, but held that "it would be a dangerous precedent to recognise that because a superstition, which may lead to such a terrible result as is disclosed by the facts of this case, is generally prevalent among the community, it is therefore reasonable."

The critical question is, of course, the standard to be used in determining what is "reasonable." The measure adopted has invariably been not the average man of the defendant's community, but the reasonable Englishman.

*Att.-Gen. for Nyasaland v. Jackson* (Federation) states the rule with unparalleled bluntness. There the court held squarely that the standard of reasonableness of mistake in the killing of a witch in imagined self-defence "is what would appear reasonable to the ordinary man in the street in England. . . . On this basis, and bearing in mind that the law of England is still the law of England even when it is extended to Nyasaland, I do not see how any court, applying the proper test, could hold that a belief in witchcraft was reasonable so as to form the foundation of a defence that the law could recognize. . . ."

These cases are only examples of a broad spectrum of prosecutions in which what is right and proper in indigenous society is criminal at common law. In all these cases the criminal act is intentional, and the defendants cannot, unless the courts ape Procrustes, be fitted to any recognised defence. It is as though England had been conquered by a nation of Hindus, so that the eating of beef immediately became a high crime. . . .

Source: Robert B. Seidman, "Witch Murder and Mens Rea: A Problem of Society Under Radical Social Change," *Modern Law Review* 28 (January 1965): 46–50, 54.

Competing cultural codes may be found throughout U.S. society. The heterogeneity of the population has resulted in a plurality of definitions for correct performance. In addition, rapid social change has meant that conflicting standards of behavior exist simultaneously. The clash that sometimes occurs between contemporary culture and earlier values that have persisted over time is an example. The survival of frontier mores continues to be reflected in an emphasis on individualism, resistance to political authority, and reliance on vigilante enforcement (Elliott, 1944). The very independence of the new states depended on their active resistance to and violation of British law. Following the Revolution and the passing of the frontier, there came an increased reliance on law to protect individual rights. More and more behaviors were being made illegal, while a cultural tradition that encouraged disrespect and rejection of formal legislative controls still survived. The result is a pattern of selective law violation that typifies U.S. behavior (Elliott, 1944). Thus, many people who otherwise conform believe themselves personally exempt from full compliance with Internal Revenue requirements, drug laws, or traffic regulations.

Although the survival of frontier mores is evident throughout much of the United States, the vitality of these traditions is most apparent in certain isolated regions. When people of these areas come into contact with the dominant culture, a conflict of culture codes may result. This problem has confronted rural Appalachians who have migrated to urban industrialized centers. Differences between these two cultures have led to the application of criminal definitions:

> At the end of the day down home, the workingman and his friend passed a jug around as they sat on the front porch to watch the sunset. There's no porch in Chicago, so they chip in for a six-pack of beer and settle down on the curb in front of a . . . saloon. A squad car goes by and the policemen order the curbstone drinkers to move along. They protest that they aren't doing anything wrong, so the cops give them a routine frisking and come up with a couple of hunting knives. Every able-bodied man carried one down home, but it's against the law in the city and they're hauled off to jail for carrying concealed weapons. [Bruno, 1964: 29]

Conflict-related deviance is not only a problem that accompanies the transplantation of cultures. It will occur wherever there is social differentiation that produces "an infinity of social groupings, each with its own definitions of life situations, its own interpretations of social relationships, its own ignorance or misunderstanding of the social values of other groups" (Sellin, 1938: 66).

## Lower-Class Culture and Deviance

An important source of differentiation is *social class*. Class-specific cultures provide powerful motivations for behavior. If the traditions that guide the activity of a particular class conflict with the values of the larger society, such behavior may be defined as deviant or criminal. It is from this perspective that Walter Miller seeks to explain lower-class gang delinquency. Nonconformity among these youngsters represents an attempt on their part to "adhere to forms of behavior, and to achieve standards of value as they are . . . [prescribed] within . . . [their own] community" (Miller, 1958: 5).

As with any distinctive culture, lower-class life is structured in terms of a number of focal concerns, "areas or issues which command widespread and persistent attention and a high degree of emotional involvement" (Miller, 1958: 6). One of the most salient of these concerns is *trouble*. Avoiding complicated entanglements is the dominant side of this concern. Persons are considered good or bad in relation to their ability to avoid trouble. Getting into trouble, however, especially through law-violating behavior, can also be a source of prestige. A demonstrated ability to flaunt the law is a valued criterion for gang membership among lower-class adolescents. These bipolar dimensions of the cultural emphasis on trouble, then, may be responsible for behavioral commitments to conformity and nonconformity alike. Thus, notes Miller (1958: 8), "not infrequently brothers raised in an identical cultural milieu will become police and criminals respectively."

*Toughness* constitutes a second cultural focus. Physical prowess, masculinity, and bravery are cultivated by both adult and adolescent males. This often takes the form of expressed contempt for characteristics considered feminine. Sentimentality, interest in art and literature, and effeminacy in males are met with scorn and sometimes, in the case of homosexuality, physical attack.

Positive value is also attached to *smartness*, which refers not to familiarity with a particular body of knowledge but to the ability to outsmart, "con," or "take" an unsuspecting target or "mark." Leadership in adolescent street gangs is assumed by members who can demonstrate brains, or smartness. Out of this focal concern develops a cultural admiration for such figures as the card shark, the professional gambler, and the con artist.

The search for *excitement*, or "thrill," is the fourth focal concern discussed by Miller (1958: 11). Flirting with danger through drinking, gambling, sex, and aggression is not only an end in itself but a way of demonstrating trouble potential, toughness, and smartness.

Lower-class culture also emphasizes *fate*, or luck. The belief that an individual's life is essentially a matter of destiny over which he or she has relatively little control manifests itself in the value attached to various forms of gambling. Cards, dice, pool, and the numbers are some of the means by which persons hope to change their lives if only luck will turn their way.

Finally, the question of personal *autonomy* plays a particularly important role in the lives of lower-class individuals. Strong and frequent expressions of resentment at being controlled are reflected in such statements as "No one's gonna push me around," and "I'm gonna tell him he can take his job and shove it."

In relating these focal concerns to the question of delinquency, Miller points to the relative importance accorded the peer group by lower class adolescents. The peer group is the most important referent association for virtually everyone over the age of twelve or thirteen, and the members display a high level of commitment to its norms.

In the adolescent gang, the motivation to conform to group standards is expressed in two additional concerns, *belonging* and *status*. The importance of peer associations for fulfilling the needs of lower-class adolescents is reflected in their concern for remaining in good standing with gang members. An adolescent ensures continued *belonging* by demonstrating an ability to conform to the standards and expectations that operate within the group—trouble, toughness, smartness, and the like. Should the valued aspects of these dimensions include violating the law, members will prefer the resultant censure or sanction from external authority to the risk of exclusion from the peer group.

*Status* in the gang is determined by the degree to which an individual possesses the characteristics associated with lower-class focal concerns. Positions of superiority and subordination within the group are determined by demonstrated ability in these areas. If a member is expected to engage in illegitimate activity to develop a valued reputation, commitment to the group will, again, be far more compelling than the demands of nonmembers in deciding the outcome.

In sum, to the extent that lower-class values conflict with those of the community at large, lower-class culture is a generating milieu for gang delinquency. Adolescent nonconformity is the product of an attempt to achieve status and belonging in a group that provides an important source of identity and mutual support. If the association calls for conformity to standards that run counter to dominant morality and law, the behavior of the group members will be defined as delinquent.

## Interest Group Competition and the Designation of Deviance

It has been argued that deviance, like conformity, develops through interaction with significant others. Since reference associations are important sources of positive self-feelings, individuals persist in their efforts to maintain their membership and the status of their groups by adhering to shared notions of acceptable behavior. If this behavior is condemnable in the eyes of the dominant culture, deviant labels may be applied.

From this perspective, crime and deviance may be viewed as minority group behavior—that is, behavior at odds with standards backed by the threat or use of force by political authority. As the conflict increases, so does loyalty to the group. In the eyes of the juvenile gang, for example, the adult world, as represented by the police, teachers, and parents, stands in opposition to gang members' attempts to achieve valued ends. Although reliance upon illegal means to attain these ends may be objectively reprehensible, protection of group status may require their periodic use. "There are many situations [, therefore,] in which [deviance] is the normal, natural response of normal, natural human beings struggling in understandably normal and natural situations for the maintenance of the way of life to which they stand committed" (Vold, 1958: 218).

There are many groups whose norms are at odds with the dominant expectations. The probability of conflict with authorities, however, depends upon a number of factors in addition to cultural differences. Conflict is most likely to occur if a group's professed norms and its actual behavior patterns are congruous (Turk, 1969: 55–56). When, for example, subordinates have a verbalized commitment to marijuana smoking and use the drug systematically and the authorities' resistance to the practice is both verbal and behavioral, conflict between the two groups will be highest, since there is congruence between the norms and behavior of each collectivity. Conversely, a lack of consistency between professed norms and actual behavior on the part of either group reduces the likelihood of conflict.

The degree of overt conflict is also affected by the level of organization and sophistication of contending parties (Turk, 1969: 58–59). Authorities, by definition, are both highly organized and sophisticated—that is, their positions of domination and power depend upon an integrated network of institutional support as well as knowledge of the behavior patterns of subordinate groups that may be used to manipulate them. Subordinates, on the other hand, vary considerably in extent of organization and sophistication. Highly organized groups are more committed to their behavioral expectations, given the level of support buttressing their codes. Therefore, such groups run a greater risk of coming to the attention of authorities. Groups characterized by a lack of sophistication are also vulnerable; their lack of knowledge of the behavior of authorities and inability to manipulate them lead to direct confrontation.

By combining these two dimensions, we find that the highest probability of conflict between authorities and subordinates will occur when the latter are highly organized but unsophisticated. An example of this pattern is the persistent confrontation of juvenile delinquents with law-enforcement officials. Gang delinquents are organized in that they have a recognized membership and designated leaders. They are also unsophisticated in their ability to manipulate legal authorities to their own advantage. Gang members, therefore, are most likely to conflict with superordinate groups. Unorganized and unsophisticated individuals are next most likely to come to the attention of authorities. Skid row drinkers, for example, have little group support; at the same time, however, their lack of sophistication regarding law-enforcement techniques paves the way for repeated contact with official agents. The third conflict situation occurs when, as in the case of organized crime, subordinates are highly organized and sophisticated. While committed to illegal behavior, this group's ability to manipulate authorities allows it a measure of license. Individuals who are unorganized but highly sophisticated are least likely to experience conflict with superordinates. The professional thief and the con artist escape legal intervention more successfully than other nonconforming groups (Turk, 1969: 59–60; see also Figure 7–1).

**FIGURE 7–1  Expected Relative Probabilities of Normative-Legal Conflict***

| | | | Authorities | | | |
|---|---|---|---|---|---|---|
| | | | HC | | LC | |
| | | | U | S | U | S |
| HC | O | U | 1 | 5 | 17 | 21 |
| | | S | 3 | 7 | 19 | 23 |
| | UO | U | 2 | 6 | 18 | 22 |
| | | S | 4 | 8 | 20 | 24 |
| LC | O | U | 9 | 13 | 25 | 29 |
| | | S | 11 | 15 | 27 | 31 |
| | UO | U | 10 | 14 | 26 | 30 |
| | | S | 12 | 16 | 28 | 32 |

(Subjects)

HC = High congruence of cultural and social norms.
LC = Low congruence of cultural and social norms.
 O = Organized.
UO = Unorganized.
 S = Sophisticated.
 U = Unsophisticated.
 *  1–32 = Highest-lowest probabilities.

From Austin T. Turk, "A Theory of Criminalization," *Criminality and Legal Order*, p. 63. Copyright © 1969 by Rand McNally and Company.

## THE CREATION AND IMPLEMENTATION OF LAW

As groups compete to improve their positions relative to other collectivities, they seek the legislative support of the political state. The victory of one group means the simultaneous derogation of another. "The whole political process of law making, law breaking, and law enforcement becomes a direct reflection of deep seated and fundamental conflicts between interest groups and their more general struggles for the control of the police power of the state" (Vold, 1958: 208–209). The legal system that emerges from this process is the means by which those who come into power ensure the preservation of their position (Quinney, 1970; Chambliss and Seidman, 1971).

Evidence of the political contest that underlies law making is abundant. As we have seen earlier, the religious elite of colonial New England relied on its legistlative power to secure its right to leadership by defining those who threatened its authority as criminal (Erikson, 1966; Chambliss, 1976). Similarly, Prohibition (Gusfield, 1967) and attempts to pass anti-pornography laws (Zurcher et al., 1971) resulted from interest group competition. In each case, influential segments of the U.S. middle class, through their legislative efforts, have sought to validate the morality to which they stood committed. Perhaps the classic illustrations of the relationship between law and socio-political interests have been provided by analyses of English laws concerning theft (Hall, 1952) and vagrancy (Chambliss, 1964).

Before the fifteenth century, English laws pertaining to theft were narrowly conceived. An individual was guilty of unlawful taking only if he also committed trespass in acquiring the victim's property. Since feudalism was the dominant economy, such a definition was appropriate; the law provided sufficient protection for landowners, whose property was generally confined within the boundaries of their land. Should someone gain access to that property and remove some of it, a crime had clearly been perpetrated.

With the advent of commerce and trade, the traditional ties of property to privately owned land were diminished. Property became a commodity to be bought and sold. To assist in the transfer of goods, *carriers*—people entrusted to deliver property to its new owner—were needed. Since the carriers came into possession of the materials legally, without trespass, they did not commit an act of theft by absconding with them. Fault lay with the merchant, who should have been more careful in selecting trustworthy employees. As mercantilism replaced the feudal economy, laws pertaining to theft were modified to protect the interests of merchants. The turning point came in 1473 with the *Carrier's Case.*

The defendant was hired by an Italian merchant to transport bales of cloth to Southampton. Instead of making the delivery, he carried the bales to another place, broke them open, and confiscated the contents. Following indictment by a tribunal of judges, he was eventually found guilty of a felony: a new law of theft was created. The legal, political, and economic conditions surrounding the event made possible this historical departure from tradition.

The most powerful forces of the time were interrelated very intimately and at many points: the New Monarchy and the *nouveau riche*—the mercantile class; the business interests of both and the consequent need for a secure carrying trade; the wool and textile industry, the most valuable, by far, in all the realm; wool and cloth, the most important exports; these exports and the foreign trade; this trade and Southampton, chief trading city with the Latin countries for centuries; the numerous and very influential Italian merchants who bought English wool and cloth inland and shipped them from Southampton. The great forces of an emerging modern world, represented in the above phenomena, necessitated the elimination of a formula which had outgrown its usefulness. A new set of major institutions required a new rule. The law, lagging behind the needs of the times, was brought into more harmonious relationship with the other institutions by the decision rendered in the Carrier's Case. [Hall, 1952]

The creation of vagrancy laws was also the product of attempts to protect dominant interests (Chambliss, 1964). In 1274, a statute forbade homeless travelers from using the Church for food and shelter. The primary goal of this early law was to protect the Church, and the ruling elite it represented, from the impoverished lower classes. This groundwork paved the way for a series of mid–fourteenth century statutes that made giving alms to the able-bodied unemployed a crime and prohibited the unemployed from refusing work when it was offered and from fleeing the employment when they had accepted it.

Vagrancy laws emerged during a decline in feudalism. The Crusades and the many wars against France and Scotland had forced English landowners to sell the serfs their freedom to obtain the funds required to finance such ventures. Cheap labor, therefore, became increasingly unavailable. A crisis was reached when, in 1348, the Black Death struck England and destroyed nearly 50 percent of the labor force. The vagrancy statutes were expressly designed to force persons to accept employment at low wages to ensure feudal landowners an adequate supply of laborers. The legislation, in short, became an effective substitute for serfdom.

As the economy changed, so did the nature of vagrancy laws. By the middle of the sixteenth century, such statutes were less concerned with the control of laborers and more with the criminal activities of the unemployed. Feudalism was dying rapidly. In its place was emerging an economic dependence on commerce and trade. Laws were required to protect persons engaged in such enterprises. A rewording of dormant vagrancy statutes served this purpose well: "Persons who had committed no serious felony but who were suspected of being capable of doing so could be apprehended and incapacitated" (Chambliss, 1964: 72). The new laws sought to open the highways to the merchant and to make the way safe for an increasingly powerful mercantile class.

In sum, the history of vagrancy statutes between the fourteenth and sixteenth centuries reflects the changing legal needs of economic interests:

The vagrancy laws emerged in order to provide the powerful landowners with a ready supply of cheap labor. When this was no longer seen as necessary, and particularly when the landowners were no longer dependent upon cheap labor nor were they a powerful interest group in society, the laws became dormant. Finally a new interest group emerged and was seen as being of great importance to the society and the laws were then altered so as to afford some protection to this group. [Chambliss, 1964: 77]

The ability to influence the creation of law, then, is an important resource in securing positions of power, status, and wealth. Certain behaviors become deviant or criminal to the extent that it is in the interest of the dominant class to define them as such. From this perspective, "crime is not inherent in behavior, but is a judgment made by some about the actions and characteristics of others" (Quinney, 1970: 16).

In class-stratified societies, more powerful groups' greater access to the legal machinery of the State also means that the implementation and enforcement of law will work to their advantage. That is, since "interests cannot be effectively protected by merely formulating criminal law," its enforcement and administration are also required (Quinney, 1970: 18). Through selective application of criminal statutes and differential processing of criminal defendants, people who are seen as a potential threat to the dominant order are effectively controlled.

The legitimacy of the class system of rule would be seriously jeopardized, however, if application of the law were openly discriminatory. Rather, legal processing decisions are guided by an imagery of criminality that operates to the disadvantage of the lower classes. This imagery, shaped by the more powerful segments of society, is based on a stereotype of lower-status groups as prone to lives of criminality (Quinney, 1970: 23; Swigert and Farrell, 1976, 1977).

The stereotype of the lower classes as criminal has a long tradition in U.S. society. Even the "expert" contributes to the perpetuation of this popular conception of crime. " 'Psychopathy,' . . . 'social disorganization,' 'under-socialization,' 'immaturity,' 'weak super-ego,' are all value-laden concepts despite the ongoing pretense of objectivity. It is [interesting] to note how these principles are generally only applied to lower working-class criminals" (Young, 1970: 38)—and therefore, we might add, to a sizable portion of the black population.

The consequences of such stereotypes for the lives of groups whose behavior has been defined as inherently criminal appear in the saturated police patrol of slums and lower-class neighborhoods (Robison, 1936; Swett, 1969), harassment of suspicious persons (Foote, 1956; Chambliss, 1964), and selection for treatment of those whose behavior or demeanor most closely approximates the guiding imagery of the stereotype (Goldman, 1963; Piliavin and Briar, 1964). The self-fulfilling effects of these practices, in the form of inflated arrest rates and criminal records among the black and the poor, serves ultimately to legitimize the original stereotype and to confirm legal authorities in their strategies of differential law enforcement.

The emergence and diffusion of the criminal stereotype are reflective of a more general process of social differentiation. As we have seen, in a culturally plural society such as that of the United States, social distance leads to stereotypical evaluations of out-groups. Since society is also politically organized, the evaluations of some groups will influence official policies toward others. Thus, in order to protect its own interests, the dominant culture defines as criminal some of the behaviors of subordinates. These definitions and the strategies they inspire are shaped by the perceived threat posed to dominant interests by culturally different groups.

For example, among the police—a group trained in the values and standards of the dominant culture—"the culturally different represent a threat to the existing sociocultural order and, by extension, to the person of the officer as well" (Swett, 1969: 88). In the court too, cultural differences frequently work to the disadvantage of the lower-class defendant. The cultural homogeneity of court professionals (Blumberg, 1967; Swett, 1969), cultural bias in jury selection (Robinson, 1950; Strodtbeck et al., 1957; Erlanger, 1970), and the existence of a negative stereotype (Swett, 1969) constitute a built-in bias in courtroom procedure:

> Prosecutors may thus be more willing to prosecute a member of a cultural minority than the actual evidence may warrant, if the offense is one that criminal statistics indicate to be "typical" of that minority. Defense counsel, on the other hand, may be reluctant to take a case in which the client's cultural characteristics constitute a handicap in the cultural environment of the courtroom. If persuaded to take the case, a defense counsel may feel that his client's best interests will be served by an out-of-court deal with the prosecutor to plead guilty to a lesser offense in a non-jury trial, regardless of actual guilt or innocence. [Swett, 1969: 100]

Similarly, the award of bail, jury deliberations or the decisions of judges concerning the guilt or innocence of a defendant, as well as the determination of an appropriate sentence, may, in fact, involve assessment of the degree to which the characteristics of the offender and offense approach the popular conception of criminality. In such a situation, conformity to the stereotype becomes a crucial determinant of final adjudication (Swigert and Farrell, 1976, 1977).

These patterns of decision making point to the importance of distinguishing between overt discrimination and reliance on class-related imageries in the administration of justice. Legal safeguards of the rights of lower-status persons would make authorities who flagrantly violate these rights accountable. If the decision to invoke negative sanction occurs within the rationale of popular beliefs regarding crime and punishment, however, the legal authority is free to act.

## POLITICAL ECONOMY AND SOCIAL CONTROL

We have seen that crime and deviance are intimately related to the social structure in which they occur. The kinds of activities proscribed and the treatment strategies invoked are shaped by dominant political and economic conditions. A thorough understanding of nonconformity, therefore, requires a careful consideration of the political economy that underlies its definition and control. For this we turn to *critical conflict theory*.

According to Karl Marx (1867), the mode of production is the nucleus around which all other aspects of human life are organized. The history of civilization has seen a progressive movement from slavery and feudalism to capitalism. Each of these economies, at one time, formed the infrastructure, or foundation, of society. In modern U.S. society, a capitalist mode of production is the dominant force that determines the nature of social relationships. The underlying economic forces give rise to the *superstructure*, institutions that reflect the needs of the infrastructure and thereby preserve the dominance of those whose interests it represents. These institutions—family, religion, education, government, and law—operate to preserve the hierarchy of status, wealth, and power of the capitalist order. Through these institutions, the attitudes, values, and beliefs appropriate to the class structure are diffused. (See Figure 7–2.)

Central to Marxist theory is the idea that since class societies are based on inequality, the seeds for the dissolution of capitalism are ever present. Accordingly, Steven Spitzer has argued that an important role of the superstructure is to deal with populations that are potentially disruptive of the prevailing economic conditions. The poor who steal from the rich call into question the capitalist use of human labor; people who refuse or are unable to work challenge the conditions that make capitalism possible; people who escape through drugs and alcohol disturb expectations for production and consumption; the rebellious are critics of socialization to acceptable beliefs and behaviors; and revolutionaries propose that an alternative system is desirable (Spitzer, 1975).

**FIGURE 7–2 Marxist Conception of the Structure of Society**

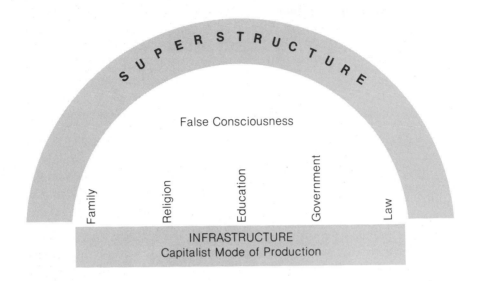

Problem populations such as these are the product either of fundamental contradictions within capitalism itself or of disturbances within the class system of rule.

Spitzer has argued that one of the inherent contradictions that leads to problem populations is the accumulation of surplus labor—a necessary condition for capitalism. This "disposable industrial army" not only ensures the availability of workers but acts as a control on wages by providing for the replaceability of the employed. At the same time, growth in the labor surplus requires the expense of maintaining the unemployed and controlling the revolutionary potential of a disaffected population. The need for a surplus of workers, on the one hand, and the problems that the masses of marginally employed or unemployed pose, on the other hand, constitute a contradiction within the capitalist economy.

Contradictions may also result from the nature of class rule. For example, education, as a superstructural institution, is designed to train essential personnel and diffuse the values that support corporate capitalism. At the same time, however, compulsory education exposes the "oppressiveness and exploitative nature" of capitalist institutions to large numbers of people who occupy lower positions in the economic order (Spitzer, 1975: 644). Education, therefore, serves to "create troublesome populations (i.e., drop outs and student radicals) and [to] contribute to the very problems . . . [it was] designed to solve" (Spitzer, 1975: 644).

## Social Junk and Social Dynamite

The effort to control problem populations includes defining and processing large numbers of people as deviant. Two categories of deviants emerge from this attempt: "social junk and social dynamite" (Spitzer, 1975: 645). *Social junk* is costly but harmless to the social order. The deviation of people in this category is passive and consists of their inability to function in, or their withdrawal from, the competitive market. Here are found the aged, handicapped, mentally ill, and retarded. *Social dynamite*, on the other hand, consists of people whose activities call into question capitalist relations of production and domination. Individuals in this category are "more youthful, alienated, and politically volatile than social junk" (Spitzer, 1975: 646). Included here are juvenile delinquents, criminal offenders, and political radicals.

Institutional containment and welfare maintenance, rather than suppression or elimination, are the official policies for dealing with *social junk.* The development of asylums for the mentally ill is a case in point. According to Andrew Scull (1977), prior to the eighteenth century, the control of deviants was essentially the responsibility of the family and local community. The market relationships ushered in by capitalism, however, destroyed this sense of social obligation. One of the first groups to be affected was the poor (Scull, 1977). At the same time, expansion of industrialism produced growing numbers of people living in poverty. The creation of institutions to deal with this population allowed representatives of the new economy to oversee the distribution of relief while simultaneously filtering out those able bodied but unemployed who, denied financial assistance, were forced into the labor market.

Factory-like workhouses were constructed in order to better distinguish between the unemployed and the employable. The variety of problems represented in workhouses, however, soon created problems of management. The mentally ill, in particular, clearly disrupted the order and routine on which these institutions depended. Special services for the insane included their segregation into asylums and the gradual emergence of professional psychiatry. "Just as the separation of the insane into madhouses and asylums helped to create the conditions for an occupational group [psychiatrists] . . . laying claim to expertise in their care and cure, so too the nature and content of the restorative ideal these doctors espoused," with its emphasis on order, rationality, and self-control through work, "reinforced the commitment to the institutional approach" (Scull, 1977: 345).

One of the most vociferous and controversial critics of the social institution of insanity is Thomas Szasz. Comparing psychiatry to the Inquisition of the Middle Ages, he argues that each provides a system for the ritualized affirmation of the sanctity and power of dominant beliefs. By prosecuting heretics and witches, the Inquisition affirmed the fundamental assumptions of Christianity. In a similar manner, says Szasz, psychiatry validates contemporary behavioral standards. He suggests, in fact, that the "belief in witchcraft gave way to the belief in mental illness" and that the "practices of the inquisitors were superseded by those of institutional psychiatrists; . . . the ritual sacrifice of the heretic . . . was thus . . . [supplanted] by the ritual sacrifice of the madman" (Szasz, 1970: 62).

# The Mind Stealers:
# Psychosurgery and Mind Control

*Samuel Chavkin*

Under the glare of operating room lights, a seven-year-old boy, heavily anesthetized but awake enough to respond to questions, is strapped down on an operating table. Standing directly behind is the surgeon, his eyes riveted on a scalpel that he carefully slides down a penciled line, making an incision of several inches across the boy's shaven head.

While a nurse is sponging away the blood, another hands the surgeon a drill, a conventional type or one that is power-driven, which he applies to different points of the exposed skull. A few brief bursts of the drill, accompanied by the sound of a shrill metallic whine and the smell of burning bone, and the skull openings, or burr holes, are completed.

The surgeon then begins pushing electrodes, thin wires, into the target areas of the brain. Depending on the particular approach, some surgeons will implant twenty or thirty electrodes, others may use several dozen. The electrodes are activated to stimulate different sections of the brain so as to elicit EEG tracings. The cascading, spiraling EEG patterns from a given site of the limbic system are considered to be the indicators of the area in which the trouble lies. And so with a stronger charge of electricity than is used to spark the brain responses, the "pathological" tissues are burned out. The operation takes about three hours. . . .

Quite obviously, the young boy undergoing psychosurgery is no longer going to be obstreperous or drive his teachers up the wall, as he used to when he flailed about in bursts of blind fury to express something he himself could not define in words. Critics contend that with his brain function now altered by electrical destruction of parts of the thalamus or of the amygdala, the boy is likely to begin living an emotionally flat, subdued existence. Much of his intellectual or perception potential may be gone forever. In sum, he was forced to forfeit his original personality and take on a new one that would be of convenience to those about him, rather than being of primary benefit to him. . . .

[Similarly, if] the balky young Chicano, or the rebellious Black Panther prisoner, behind bars because of an altercation with police during a ghetto protest rally, continues to be defiant of authority, the prison psychiatrist may ponder: Is there something uncontrollably impulsive about this man? Is such recalcitrance possibly brought on by the malfunctioning of certain brain cells? Is he then a suitable object for a brain-scanning procedure? If the answer is yes, then electrodes would be implanted to stimulate parts of the inner brain, and if the resulting electroencephalogram squiggles form a pattern that some would consider abnormal, then the prisoner could be regarded as a candidate for psychosurgery.

Source: Samuel Chavkin, *The Mind Stealers: Psychosurgery and Mind Control* (Boston: Houghton-Mifflin, 1978), pp. 39–40, 89–90.

The power of psychiatry, like that of the Inquisition, lies in the fact that it operates in areas not distinctly covered by the law. "Policemen and judges are constrained by the Rule of Law. They can punish only what the law forbids. Mental hygiene laws, like the orders of the Dominican Inquisitors, recognize no such bounds" (Szasz, 1970: 62). In both instances, groups that hold power are allowed to use it to oppress others. In earlier times the justification for such oppression came from the Church; today it is provided by the scientific establishment.

[Psychiatry] furnishes a covert, extralegal system of penalties by means of which the ruling classes can maintain their social dominance. . . . Whistling could never be made illegal; but a Negro who whistled at a Southern white woman (or was said to have whistled at one) could be lynched. Lynch-law was thus an adjunct to Southern law on the books; it helped whites to keep the Negroes "in their place." So too is Institutional Psychiatry an implementation of the unwritten laws of power-maintenance in a society insufficiently committed to honoring the Rule of Law. Feeling sad cannot very well be made illegal; but a poor woman who is depressed (and refuses to play the role assigned her in society) can be committed. Commitment-law is thus an adjunct to American law on the books; it helps the rich and well-educated to keep the poor and ill-educated in their place. [Szasz, 1970: 64]

# The Case of Mr. Louis Perroni

*Thomas S. Szasz*

Until May 5, 1955, Mr. Louis Perroni operated a filling station in Glenview, a Syracuse suburb. On that day his world fell apart. . . . [The dates and the names of persons, places, and institutions (except the Onondaga County Court's and the Matteawan State Hospital's) are fictitious; otherwise, the account is factual.]

Early in 1955, Perroni was informed that the lease on his filling station, which was to expire on July 1, was not going to be renewed. The station he had operated for approximately ten years was in an area that was to be razed in preparation for a new shopping center.

During the winter, Perroni was approached by agents of the real estate developer with a request that he vacate his premises early, preferably no later than May 1. Although offered compensation, Perroni refused. . . .

On May 2, 1955, representatives of the real estate developer erected a sign on what Mr. Perroni considered his gas station. He remonstrated with them and removed the sign. At last, when two men appeared on May 5 and proceeded to erect another sign, Mr. Perroni took a rifle from his station and fired a warning shot into the air. The men departed. Soon Mr. Perroni was arrested by the police. . . .

Mr. Perroni was arraigned but was not indicted. Instead, at the request of the district attorney, the Onondaga County Court judge before whom he appeared ordered him to undergo pretrial psychiatric examination to determine his fitness to stand trial. He was examined by two court-appointed psychiatrists, found incapable of standing trial, and committed to the Matteawan State Hospital.

Aided by his brothers, Perroni tried by every means possible, including an appeal to the United States Supreme Court, to secure his right to be tried. At long last, in June 1961—six years after Perroni was commited to the Matteawan State Hospital—a writ of habeas corpus was heard and sustained by the State Supreme Court judge in Dutchess County (where the hospital is located). Perroni was ordered to be tried or discharged. Nevertheless he was not immediately released. . . . On September 4, however, he was neither indicted nor released. Instead, he was ordered to submit to a fresh pretrial psychiatric examination.

A month later, on October 1, 1961, . . . the court issued a new order for "mental tests" on Perroni. . . . [He] was committed to the Oakville State Hospital near Syracuse to determine once more whether he was competent to stand trial. . . . The hearing was held on April 12, 1962, in Onondaga County Court before a judge and without a jury. It lasted for two full days. The following excerpts from the hearings are taken from the official records of the court stenographer. . . .

James B. Roscoe [psychiatrist], having been called and duly sworn, testified as follows:
*Direct Examination* by Mr. Jordan, Assistant District Attorney
. . .
Q. Now, Doctor, as a result of your examinations of Mr. Perroni were you able to form an opinion whether this patient was in such a state of idiocy, imbecility, or insanity as to be able to understand the nature of the charge against him and to make his defense?
A. Yes.
Q. What is that opinion, Doctor?
A. It is my opinion that Mr. Perroni is in such a state of idiocy, imbecili-

ty, or insanity as to be unable to understand the charges against him, the procedures, or of aiding in his defense.

. . .

*Cross Examination by* Mr. Gross, Defense Counsel

. . .

Q. Have you brought with you in Court, Doctor, the records of Oakville State Hospital pertaining to Louis Perroni?

A. Yes.

Q. And those records go back how far as far as Oakville is concerned?

A. They go back to his first admission in Oakville State Hospital, which I believe was in September of 1961.

Q. Now, taking the very first clinical note that you have, will you tell us the first entry—the date of the first entry?

A. September 3, 1961. 9:30 P.M.

Q. All right. Tell us what that clinical note is.

A. Middle-aged, white male admitted to ward by Mrs. Mason. Quiet and cooperative to admission care. Nutrition good. Cleanliness good. Vermin, none noted. Patient states he has been in the State Prison and does not want to talk about it. Small round scar upper left leg. Pimple on right hip. No skin diseases noted. Vaccination left arm. Temperature 100. Pulse 80. Respiration 20.

Q. Read the date and the next clinical note.

A. The next clinical note is on the same date at 10 P.M. Quiet and cooperative.

Q. Is that all?

A. That's all.

Q. What is the next date and the next note?

A. The next note is the same date. Twelve midnight. Sleeping.

Q. Will you continue on, Doctor, reading the dates and the clinical notes? Give the date and then give the note opposite.

A. September Fourth. Twelve midnight. Asleep all night. Cooperative. Quiet. Urine specimen to lab.

Q. I want you to keep going, Doctor. Read the dates. Give the date on each occasion and give the clinical note.

A. Twelve noon. Temperature 98.6. Pulse 84. Respiration 20. Regular diet. This patient remains quiet and cooperative. Ate well. Offers no complaints. Reads. Watches TV. Patient seems uninterested in ward routine.

. . .

Q. Will you go on with your clinical notes?

A. Five P.M. September 5, 1961. Regular diet. Appetite good. Quiet. Cooperative. Watching TV. Twelve. Sleeping. Another note, the time not given. Patient sleeps well at night. Quiet. Cooperative. Ate good breakfast in the morning. This is on September Sixth.

Q. Keep going.

A. Again September Sixth. Eight A.M. Regular diet. Patient quiet, cooperative. Ate good dinner. Four P.M. Patient reads. Watches TV. Is somewhat seclusive. Offers no complaints.

Q. Doctor, what do you mean by somewhat seclusive? What does that mean?

A. I didn't make that note.

Q. I see. But it is an official record of your hospital?

A. Yes.

Q. You wouldn't know what that meant?

A. I know what the term seclusive means in psychiatry.

Q. What does it mean, Doctor?

A. It means the patient stays by himself and aloof from others.

Q. Is that a significant indication in schizophrenia?

A. It is one of the symptoms that is frequently found in schizophrenia.

. . .

Q. You mean he doesn't socialize with other people?

A. He does not socialize or mingle.

Q. Tell us, how is he supposed to mingle? What is a normal person supposed to do when he is in an institution?

A. *There are no normal people in institutions.* [Emphasis added.]

. . .

Q. Doctor, I want you at this point, please, to go on reading your clinical notes.

[The doctor continues reading the clinical notes indicating that Mr. Perroni has been quiet, cooperative, and in good physical health.]

A. September Tenth. Early in the morning. Nine A.M. Chart closed as of today. This patient seems to have come along quite well on this ward. He is quiet, cooperative. He is friendly. Will do some ward work if asked. He is oriented in all spheres.

Q. What does that mean, that he is oriented in all spheres?

A. That would refer to his orientation as far as time, place, and person.

Q. Go ahead.

A. He eats and sleeps well, offers no complaints, regular diet, no medication. September Seventeenth. Mr. Perroni is oriented in all spheres. His recent and remote memory is good. He is an ambulatory patient who is clean in toilet and personal habits. Eats well and sleeps without complaints. His conversation is rational and coherent. However, he is very suspicious and will tell you that he will talk only to his lawyer as to why he is here. He is quiet and cooperative towards routine. He mingles well with some of the ward cases. Today Mr. Perroni is going to Court at 9:30 A.M. He plays cards, watches TV, and listens to the radio. He does some ward work. He weighs 160 pounds. No medication or treatment.

Q. The next day, Doctor? Go ahead.

A. September Twenty-first. This patient has adjusted well to ward routine. He is quiet and friendly and sociable. He will assist with ward routine willingly. Neat and clean. Showed no abnormal tendencies so far. Mingles well. Plays cards and watches TV. Eats and sleeps regularly. Receives no medication. September Twenty-sixth. This patient discharged into care of Sheriff of Onondaga County. September Twenty-sixth at 9 P.M. Unimproved.

Q. It is marked "Unimproved," isn't it?

A. Yes.

Q. What kind of improvement could there have been, Doctor, when the day before he mingles well, was adjusted well to ward routine, quiet, friendly, sociable, would assist in ward willingly, neat, and clean, shows no abnormal tendencies so far, plays cards, watches TV, eats and sleeps regularly? What do you mean he is unimproved? Unimproved what for?

A. I don't know. I didn't place that note there.

. . .

Q. Now Doctor, none of those things alone that you [have] mentioned would cause you to arrive at the conclusion that Mr. Perroni cannot stand trial, would they?

A. None of them individually.

Q. And taken together, Doctor, could you tell us what the magic ingredient is that cements these things together and leads you to the conclusion that this man cannot stand trial?

A. Any illness, mental or physical, is marked by a combination of symptoms and signs. The things that I have mentioned are symptoms or, rather, signs of an emotional mental illness that would indicate in my opinion that this man is incapable of—suffering—is in such a state of insanity as to be incapable of understanding the charges, or the procedure, or aiding in his defense.

Q. Doctor, did you at any time note any action or any word on the part of this patient or defendant that you could tag as abnormal?

A. Any action?

Q. Yes, any physical action or word or phrase?

A. On occasion he demonstrated a particular mannerism involving his left palpebral fissure.

Q. His what?

A. His left palpebral fissure.

Q. What is that?

A. The left eye.

Q. What do you mean, he twitched his eye?

A. Twitched or looked upwards in a manneristic way.

Q. What does that indicate, Doctor?

A. In itself possibly nothing, but it is an additional thing that added to the other things is frequently, if not commonly, seen in certain mental illnesses.

Q. How many times did you see him twitch his eye?

A. I could not say.

. . .

Q. Let me ask you, Doctor, can Mr. Perroni handle his everyday affairs?

A. I would say no.

Q. All right. Now, as I understand it, you based your answer on the supposition that his judgment is not good?

A. That's correct.

Q. Will you please tell us, Doctor, in what realm his judgment is not good?

A. His judgment in—may I refer to my notes, please?

Q. Yes.

A. I feel that his judgment is affected by his illogical thinking processes.

Q. Doctor, can you give me a single example from the records, from your interview with Mr. Perroni—a single example of any illogical thinking processes?

A. When it was explained to Mr. Perroni the desirability of his cooperating fully for the examinations that we asked him to cooperate in taking, his comment was "What good is that—how is that going to help me?"

Q. Is that the only remark, Doctor, in the entire proceedings?

A. This is one that I clearly recall. There were others.

Q. I see. And can you think of one other, Doctor—just a single one?

A. I cannot recall another one that I am sure of.

Q. Well, Doctor, it is a fact, is it not, that there is such a thing as despair?

A. Yes.

Q. And wouldn't you say, Doctor, that after a man has been incarcerated for seven years, attempting to get out for the purpose of standing trial, that he may feel "What is the use of answering questions"?

A. But it was fully explained to Mr. Perroni that this would add to the objectivity and the completeness of his examination. We very clearly explained to him we had no bias one way or the other. We were trying to determine the state of his mental processes in order to help the Judge in making his decision. We made this very clear to him. . . .

Approximately six weeks after the hearing, Judge Kirby handed down his decision: he found Mr. Louis Perroni incompetent to stand trial. Mr. Perroni was thereupon transferred from the Cedar Street Jail in Syracuse to the Matteawan State Hospital in Beacon, N.Y. Appeals from the Court's ruling have failed. At the time of this writing (February 1965), Mr. Perroni remains confined at Matteawan. He has now been incarcerated for nearly ten years.

Source: Thomas S. Szasz, *Psychiatric Justice* (New York: Macmillan, 1965), pp. 85–88, 90, 95–97, 101–102, 104–107, 132–135, 137–138, 140.

While *social junk* falls largely within the purvue of medicine and social welfare, *social dynamite* is controlled by the legal system (Spitzer, 1975). Through confinement and application of criminal stigma, the potential threat of *social dynamite* is effectively contained. Richard Quinney (1980: 150) points out that the size of this problem population in advanced capitalism is staggering: on any given day in the United

States, 1 in 400 adults is confined in a penal institution. These persons convicted of such conventional crimes as burglary, robbery, homicide, use of illegal drugs, and the like, are typically recruited from the lowest social classes and minority groups. In fact, whereas 1 in 163 adult white males between the ages of 25 and 34 is confined at any given time, the figure for black males in the same age category is 1 in 20. The over-representation of blacks among those considered most threatening to the economic order becomes readily apparent when we consider that one quarter to one third of all black men in their early twenties will spend some time behind bars or on probation (Quinney, 1980: 150).

These confinement figures are in direct proportion to the numbers from the various classes and races who are unemployed. The official unemployment rate among blacks has consistently been twice that of whites, and the rate of unskilled unemployment has been several percentage points higher than that of all other workers (Quinney, 1980: 148). "The prison population increases as the rate of unemployment increases. Unemployment simultaneously makes necessary various actions of survival by the unemployed surplus population and requires the state to control that population in some way" (Quinney, 1980: 149; see also Figure 7–3).

As capitalism progresses through increasing mechanization, the size of the surplus labor population correspondingly increases. That is,

**FIGURE 7–3   Prisons and Unemployment**

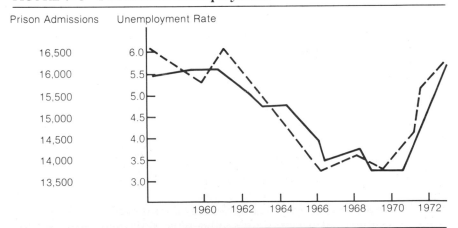

This graph shows how prisoner admissions to the federal prison system rise and fall according to how the national unemployment rate rises and falls. The broken line shows the unemployment rate, while the solid line shows admissions to federal prisons.

Source: NEPA News, February 1976, p. 16. In Richard Quinney, *Class, State, and Crime* (New York: David McKay, 1977), p. 135.

as machines take over the functions of workers, more and more people are relegated to the ranks of the unemployed for longer periods of time. As a consequence, problem populations cause increasing problems both in terms of their size and their insensitivity to the traditional control of promised employment. In addition, as the family and religion lose their effectiveness in producing "obedient and productive" citizens, the state becomes a more important source of problem population control, and the numbers of persons defined as deviant or criminal can be expected to increase.

From a radical conflict perspective, crime and deviance are intimately linked to the economic and political structure of society. Persons engage in nonconformity either (1) to express the alienation they have experienced in a society that does not represent their interests but that exploits their labor or (2) to attempt to achieve control over the means of production (Horton, 1966; Chambliss, 1976). In the first instance we find alcoholism, mental illness, and crimes of passion (Reinhardt, 1969; Staples, 1975; Davis, 1976), while in the second occur political dissent, sabotage, and rebellion.[1] In each case, however, rule violation "is no more than the 'rightful' behavior of persons exploited by the extant economic relations" (Chambliss, 1976; see also Quinney, 1965a, 1965b).

## Class Variations in Crime

Since the inequalities engendered by capitalism affect the lower classes directly, criminality will be most evident among these groups. It must be emphasized, however, that people from all social classes violate the law. A self-report survey conducted by the 1965 President's Commission on Crime, for example, found that 91 percent of all adults in the United States admitted to committing a crime for which they might have been incarcerated. The universal nature of crime in capitalist society is predicated on the competitive and ever-changing nature of the marketplace. Much of human behavior in a capitalist system is motivated by fear of economic insecurity and by the competitive desire to acquire some of the wealth unequally distributed through society. In these efforts, many individuals from all social classes will resort to crime.

The kind of crime committed varies considerably from class to class. Crimes committed by white-collar executives and corporate officials are usually impersonal, discreet, and occur over longer periods of time, largely because of the illegal means available to the higher-status offender. Entrusted with large sums of money and responsible for decisions involving its investment or transfer, white-collar and corporate professionals who decide to break the law can do so fairly easily, in a less offensive and less visible manner (Gordon, 1973). Lower-class offenders, on the other hand, typically must rely on direct confrontation with those who possess the goods desired; they commit burglary, robbery, larceny, and the like—offenses that involve visible actions and victims.

In addition, lower-class crime is more frequently characterized by violence, not only because of the confrontational nature of the offenses but also because of the effects of a history of legal bias. Higher-status offenders run less risk of apprehension and sanction by law-enforcement officials. As long as crimes among the corporate class tend to affect only members of other classes, such as consumers, the state will not act spontaneously to prevent such crime. It is only when the crimes threaten the capitalist class itself that the state will intervene. Lower-class people, then, who run the highest risk of arrest and conviction, may have to rely on the threat or use of force to protect themselves from the disadvantage of their social status. Law-enforcement bias, in the form of differential concentration on lower-class behavior, may be responsible for the qualitative differences in crime found among the classes (Gordon, 1973).

# White Collar Crime

*Edwin H. Sutherland*

[Analyses] of the crimes of corporations have shown that these corporations have committed crimes against one or more of the following classes of victims: consumers, competitors, stockholders and other investors, inventors, and employees, as well as against the State, in the form of tax frauds and bribery of public officials. These crimes are not discreet and inadvertent violations of technical regulations. They are deliberate and have a relatively consistent unity. . . . The principle specifications of white collar crime . . . are elaborated below. . . .

First, the criminality of the corporations, like that of professional thieves, is persistent: a large proportion of the offenders are recidivists. Among the seventy largest industrial and mercantile corporations in the United States, 97.1 percent were found to be recidivists, in the sense of having two or more adverse decisions. None of the official procedures used on businessmen for violations of law has been very effective in rehabilitating them or in deterring other businessmen from similar behavior.

Second, the illegal behavior is much more extensive than the prosecutions and complaints indicate. . . . Many types of violations of law are industry-wide in the sense that practically all firms in the industry violate the law. . . .

Third, the businessman who violates the laws which are designed to regulate business does not customarily lose status among his business associates. Although a few members of the industry may think less of him, others admire him. . . . Important executives of three of the seventy large corporations, according to court decisions, illegally appropriated funds of the corporations to their personal use and continued activities thereafter with no loss of status in the corporation or in the industry; it is reported that one of these executives made his reputation as a shrewd manipulator by this illegal transaction. Such illustrations could be multiplied. They amount to the general principle that a violation of the legal code is not necessarily a violation of the business code. Prestige is lost by violation of the business code but not by violation of the legal code except when the legal code coincides with the business code.

Fourth, businessmen customarily feel and express contempt for law, for government, and for governmental personnel. In this respect, also, they are similar to professional thieves, who feel contempt for law, policemen, prosecutors, and judges. Businessmen customarily regard governmental personnel as politicians and bureaucrats, and the persons authorized to investigate business practices as "snoopers." Businessmen characteristically believe that the least government is the best, at least until they desire special favors from government, and in many cases regard the enactment of a law rather than the violation of the law as the crime. The businessman's contempt for law, like that of the professional thief, grows out of the fact that the law impedes his behavior. . . .

With the . . . objective of protecting their reputations the business organizations have worked for a different implementation of the laws which apply to them. They do not want to be arrested by policemen, hauled before the criminal court, and convicted of crimes. Substitutes for these procedures have been found in orders to appear at a hearing, decisions by administrative commissions, and desist orders. The essential similarity between white collar crimes and other crimes has been partially concealed by this variation in procedures. . . .

The white collar criminal does not conceive of himself as a criminal because he is not dealt with under the same official procedures as other criminals and because, owing to his class status, he does not engage in intimate personal association with those who define themselves as criminals. . . . The public, likewise, does not think of the businessman as a criminal; that is, the businessman does not fit the stereotype of "criminal."

Source: Edwin H. Sutherland, *White Collar Crime* (New York: Holt, Rinehart and Winston, 1949), pp. 217–220, 223–225.

---

Popular concern over crime parallels closely the direction of law enforcement and social control. Although white-collar and corporate crimes involve a much greater economic loss to society, perceptions of the crime problem continue to focus on conventional criminality in the form of murder, robbery, rape, assault, burglary, larceny, and auto theft. Most of these offenses are property crimes, and most are committed by lower-class young adult black males (Gordon, 1973). This perception of crime is not only a product of official commitment to the control of a problem population; as we have seen, it also acts to reinforce original discriminatory policies. Government reports of rising crime rates, media accounts of the vices and inhumanity of inner-city life, and warnings of the infiltration of urban predators into the once-secure suburbs create both an imagery of criminality and a demand for enforcement that focus primarily on lower-class and minority groups (Quinney, 1971; Swigert and Farrell, 1976). Social scientists also have contributed to perpetuating a class-based criminal imagery. Describing lower-class life as conducive to criminality and focusing on the nature and causes of conventional nonconformity serve to legitimize both popular belief and enforcement policies while diverting attention from the power structure (Liazos, 1972; Thio, 1973; Davis, 1976). A widely diffused and scientifically "validated" conception of crime, along with the differential enforcement it supports, may have the self-fulfilling effect of creating the very conditions described (Quinney, 1971; Thio, 1973; Swigert and Farrell, 1976).

A break in this cycle of popular belief, enforcement, and crime would depend upon radical changes in the institutional structure of society—changes, that is, in the competition and inequality upon which capitalism depends. Without such changes, crime patterns will continue to be intimately related to capitalist domination. For crime, especially lower-class crime, (1) perpetuates the belief that the individual rather than the social structure is responsible for human action, (2) protects the job market by eliminating portions of the surplus labor population, (3) neutralizes whatever political threat nonconformers might pose for the state by applying the discrediting stigma of criminality, and (4) masks the need for reform by keeping the criminal both hidden and inhuman (Gordon, 1973).

## CONCLUSION

From a conflict theory perspective, deviants are indistinguishable from nondeviants with regard to personal characteristics. They do differ, however, in the positions they occupy within society. If we are to understand the causes of nonconformity, we must understand the social and cultural conditions associated with these positions and the processes by which deviance definitions emerge to ensure the advantage of certain groups in society at the expense of others. The causes of crime and deviance may be found not within individual offenders but within the social structure that disvalues their behavior.

## NOTES

1. The distinction is one also found in Merton's (1976) treatment of aberrant and nonconforming behavior and Yinger's (1960) discussion of subculture and counter-culture.

## REFERENCES

Blumberg, Abraham S.
  1967  The Practice of Law as a Confidence Game: Organizational Cooptation of a Profession. Law and Society Review 1 (June): 15–39.
Bruno, Hal
  1964  Chicago's Hillbilly Ghetto. Reporter 30 (June): 28–31.
Chambliss, William J.
  1964  A Sociological Analysis of the Law of Vagrancy. Social Problems. 12 (Summer): 67–77.
  1976  Functional and Conflict Theories of Crime: The Heritage of Émile Durkheim and Karl Marx. *In* Whose Law, What Order? William J. Chambliss and Milton Mankoff, eds. Pp. 1–28. New York: John Wiley and Sons, 1976.
Chambliss, William J., and Robert B. Seidman
  1971  Law, Order, and Power. Reading, Massachusetts: Addison-Wesley.
Chavkin, Samuel
  1978  The Mind Stealers: Psychosurgery and Mind Control. Boston: Houghton-Mifflin.
Cohen, Albert K.
  1955  Delinquent Boys. New York: Free Press.
Davis, J. A.
  1976  Blacks, Crime, and American Culture. Annals of the American Academy of Political and Social Science 423 (January): 89–98.
Elliott, Mabel A.
  1944  Crime and Frontier Mores. American Sociological Review 9 (April): 185–192.
Erikson, Kai T.
  1966  Wayward Puritans. New York: John Wiley and Sons.
Erlanger, Howard S.
  1970  Jury Research in America: Its Past and Future. Law and Society Review 4 (February): 345–370.
Foote, Caleb
  1956  Vagrancy-type Law and Its Administration. University of Pennsylvania Law Review 104 (March): 603–650.
Goldman, Nathan
  1963  The Differential Selection of Juvenile Offenders for Court Appearance. New York: National Research and Information Center, National Council on Crime and Delinquency.
Gordon, David M.
  1973  Capitalism, Class, and Crime in America. Crime and Delinquency 19 (April): 163–186.

Gusfield, Joseph
  1967  Moral Passage: The Symbolic Process in Public Designations of Deviance. Social Problems 15 (Fall): 175–188.
Hall, Jerome T.
  1952  Theft, Law and Society. Indianapolis: Bobbs-Merrill.
Horton, John
  1966  Order and Conflict Theories of Social Problems as Conflicting Ideologies. American Journal of Sociology 71 (May): 701–713.
Liazos, Alexander
  1972  The Sociology of Deviants: Nuts, Sluts, and Perverts. Social Problems 20 (Summer): 103–120.
Marx, Karl
  1867  Capital. Moscow: Foreign Languages Publishing House, 1961.
Merton, Robert K.
  1976  The Sociology of Social Problems. *In* Contemporary Social Problems. Robert K. Merton and Robert Nisbet, eds. Pp. 5–43. New York: Harcourt, Brace, Jovanovich, 1976.
Miller, Walter B.
  1958  Lower Class Culture as a Generating Milieu of Gang Delinquency. Journal of Social Issues 14 (November): 5–19.
Piliavin, Irving, and Scott Briar
  1964  Police Encounters with Juveniles. America Journal of Sociology 70 (September): 206–214.
President's Commission on Law Enforcement and Administration of Justice
  1967  The Challenge of Crime in a Free Society. Washington, D.C.: Government Printing Office.
Quinney, Richard A.
  1965a  A Conception of Man and Society for Criminology. Sociological Quarterly 6 (Spring): 119–127.
  1965b  Is Criminal Behavior Deviant Behavior? British Journal of Criminology 5 (April): 132–142.
  1970  The Social Reality of Crime. Boston: Little, Brown.
  1971  Criminology: Analysis and Critique of Crime in America. Boston: Little, Brown.
  1977  Class, State, and Crime. New York: David McKay.
  1980  Class, State, and Crime. New York: Longman.
Reinhardt, James M.
  1969  Alcoholism and Culture Conflict in the U.S.A. International Journal of Offender Therapy 13: 177–180.
Robinson, W. S.
  1950  Bias, Probability, and Trial by Jury. American Sociological Review 15 (February): 73–78.
Robison, Sophia
  1936  Can Delinquency be Measured? New York: Columbia University Press.
Scull, Andrew T.
  1977  Madness and Segregative Control: The Rise of the Insane Asylum. Social Problems 24 (February): 337–351.

Seidman, Robert B.
  1965   Witch Murder and Mens Rea: A Problem of Society Under Radical Social
          Change. Modern Law Review 28 (January): 46–61.
Sellin, Thorsten
  1938   Culture Conflict and Crime. Social Science Research Council Bulletin 41.
Spitzer, Steven
  1975   Toward a Marxian Theory of Deviance. Social Problems 22 (June):
          638–651.
Staples, Robert
  1975   White Racism, Black Crime, and American Justice: An Application of
          the Colonial Model to Explain Crime and Race. Phylon 36 (March): 14–22.
Strodtbeck, Fred L., Rita M. James, and Charles Hawkins
  1957   Social Status in Jury Deliberations. American Sociological Review 22
          (December): 713–719.
Sutherland, Edwin H.
  1949   White Collar Crime. New York: Holt, Rinehhart and Winston.
Swett, Daniel H.
  1969   Cultural Bias in the American Legal System. Law and Society Review 4
          (August): 79–110.
Swigert, Victoria Lynn, and Ronald A. Farrell
  1976   Murder, Inequality, and the Law. Lexington, Massachusetts: D. C. Heath,
          Lexington.
  1977   Normal Homicides and the Law. American Sociological Review 42
          (February): 16–32.
Szasz, Thomas S.
  1965   Psychiatric Justice. New York: Macmillan.
  1970   The Manufacture of Madness. New York: Harper & Row.
Thio, Alex
  1973   Class Bias in the Sociology of Deviance. American Sociologist 8
          (February): 1–12.
Turk, Austin T.
  1969   Criminality and Legal Order. Chicago: Rand McNally.
Vold, George B.
  1958   Theoretical Criminology. New York: Oxford University Press.
Yinger, J. Milton
  1960   Contraculture and Subculture. American Sociological Review 25 (Oc-
          tober): 625–635.
Young, Jock
  1970   The Zookeepers of Deviance. Catalyst 5 (Summer): 38–46.
Zurcher, Louis A., Jr., R. George Kirkpatrick, Robert G. Cushing, and Charles K.
Bowman
  1971   The Anti-Pornography Campaign: A Symbolic Crusade. Social Problems
          19 (Fall): 217–238.

# 8

# The Structure and Process of Deviance

The search for explanations of deviant behavior has given rise to a variety of theoretical paradigms. The most influential are functionalism, definitional theory, the interactionist perspective, anomie theory, social and cultural support theory, and the conflict approach.

As we have seen, the basic tenet of *functionalism* is that deviance is instrumental in confirming the value system of a collectivity. The designation of certain behaviors as falling outside the limits tolerated by the group calls attention to the standards upon which the system is based. In much the same way as the moral leader embodies the cultural ideal, the deviant exemplifies that to which the culture stands opposed. By calling attention to the sins, pathologies, and crimes of the outcase, the group reinforces its cohesiveness and reaffirms its norms. Functionalists have suggested that, since social systems depend upon this process for their very existence, they become organized in such a way as to produce required levels of nonconformity.

*Definitional theory* focuses on the communication of norms and values to group members. Behaviors and events are attributed meaning through the social definition of the situation. Such definitions allow persons to interpret their environment and construct actions based on their interpretatons. Consequently, the definition of the situation is self-fulfilling. By precluding alternative interpretations and lines of action, the assignment of meaning produces outcomes that are consistent with the ascription.

The implications of the definitional process in the case of deviance are clear. Whether through the official activities of agencies of social control or the informal responses of community relationships, persons are defined as deviant and treated accordingly. This attribution and reaction set into motion a socially structured process that amplifies the very traits complained of.

The *interactionist perspective*, or *labeling theory*, posits that nonconformity is the product of the stigmatization and isolation that attend deviance labels. While rule violation is virtually universal, the crystallization of such behavior into deviant careers is a product of societal reaction to initial transgressions. These original, or primary, deviations would remain transient and often subside without the reinforcing effects of the social response. Through the designation of deviance as a master status, application of a negative stereotype, and retrospective and concurrent reinterpretation, however, the individual tends to become engulfed in the deviant role and to organize life and identity around the facts of the deviation.

Deviance as adaptation to stress is the subject of *anomie theory*. Conformity is ensured when group participants are able to comply with the normative expectations that regulate social life. Persons unable to meet these standards experience stress as well as ambivalence regarding the sources of the discomfort. They may adapt by shifting referent identifications to groups wherein they are capable of conformity. To the extent that these groups espouse deviant norms, the new members' commitment to nonconformity will be increased.

*Social and cultural support theory* emphasizes that deviant behavior is learned. Through interaction in groups characterized by a preponderance of normative definitions that encourage and reward nonconformity, persons acquire the motivations, drives, rationalizations, and techniques of deviant behavior. Identification with such groups will most likely occur if the deviant's attachments, commitments, and involvements within the larger society are attenuated. For people who have been excluded from opportunities for the enactment of conforming roles and socialized to and provided with the means for deviant performance, nonconformity is the inevitable outcome.

From the perspective of *conflict theory*, deviance is the result of social and cultural diversity. Modern society is made up of a proliferation of collectivities, each attempting to satisfy its own needs and promote its standards of value. By gaining access to the institutions of social control, successful competitors are able to establish their norms and interests as the dominant ones and derogate groups that would challenge their position of superiority. Nonconformity, therefore, is intimately related to the socio-political organization of society. Whether because of the cultural differences found among groups or because of the privileges and obligations that accompany the various levels of class, status, and power, minority populations are subject to deviance-defining processes that render their situation and behavior condemnable.

Each of these perspectives offers a conceptual scheme that has a distinct orientation. Thus, the several theories have been viewed traditionally as competing and contradictory explanations of deviance. No one of the theories, however, is comprehensive enough to explain the several dimensions of deviance or its many forms. Rather, each approach emphasizes particular aspects of the more general phenomenon. Functionalism and conflict theory focus on the structure of society; requirements for boundary maintenance or the economic imperatives of a political elite determine the parameters of deviant behavior. Definitional, anomie, and social and cultural support theories deal in large part with the group processes that affect behavioral outcomes. Concepts such as self-fulfilling prophecy, reference identification, and associational learning reflect theoretical emphases on the human group as the basic unit of analysis. Finally, the labeling perspective specifies the social-psychological dimensions of deviance designations; self-concept formation and its effects on role performance are a product of interactional processes that are ultimately oriented to the individual deviant.

This is not to argue that these theories focus exclusively on large-scale structural factors, group processes, or social-psychological dimensions. Conflict theory, for example, addresses the implications of structural conditions for individual behavior, and anomie theory very clearly speaks to deviance at each of the levels of analysis. When these perspectives are viewed holistically, however, concepts emerge that characterize the traditions as primarily structural, group oriented, or social psychological.

Yet, the creation of deviance involves the simultaneous interplay of influences operating at all such levels of analysis. Nonconformity is the result of deviant identities that are shaped by group and interactional processes within particular social structures. Moreover, attempts to isolate the single most important antecedents to deviant behavior ignore the mutual causation that occurs among the several components. Deviance is not only the product of structural factors as they operate in interpersonal contexts but it is reciprocally supportive of these interactional and structural processes.

Furthermore, generalizations from each of these traditions are limited. The persistence of competition and conflict among groups challenges functionalist assumptions of normative consensus (Gusfield, 1967; Zurcher et al., 1971; Connor, 1972; Chambliss, 1975; Inverarity, 1976). Definitional theory and the labeling perspective have encountered numerous instances of prophecies that have failed (Gove, 1970; Williams and Weinberg, 1971). Anomie theory does not explain behavior that arises from alternative normative systems (Lemert, 1967), while social and cultural support theory has little application to deviations that occur among individuals who primarily interact with groups that espouse conformist definitions (Lemert, 1958; Einstadter, 1969). Finally, some forms of deviance resist the conflict argument that disvalued behavior and attributes constitute a serious threat to the dominant order. The stigmatization of physical deformity, deviant but consensual sexual practices, and stuttering, for example, are not as readily explained by the conflict approach as are treason, robbery, and industrial sabotage.

Because these theoretical perspectives address different levels of analysis and varying forms of behavior, however, we may utilize elements of each to construct a more comprehensive theory of social deviance. The development of such a theory requires first that certain assumptions be made regarding the nature of society. A theory that distinguishes among levels of analysis and proposes integrating links between them is predicated on a view that society is hierarchically organized—that is, that is consists of interrelated systems which are themselves composed of other subsystems (Simon, 1962; Blau, 1980). Thus, within complex societies we find institutions, which are represented by organizations, within which are groups and, ultimately, individuals. The theory further assumes that the development of higher-order, more inclusive systems follows the completion of lower-order, less inclusive ones (Blau, 1980). At each level, then, relationships among the units of analysis can be characterized by properties unique to that level. Conceptual schemes that are useful at one level, therefore, may be inappropriate at another. Thus, for example, while systemic needs for boundary maintenance may account for the creation of deviant *categories* at the societal level, an interpersonally oriented framework is necessary to explain the creation of deviant *identities*.

The hierarchical nature of subsystems also implies a measure of interdependence among them. Each more inclusive level is the context within which subunits operate (Blau, 1980). By implication, then, once the pattern of relationships becomes established at any one level, it limits the range of alternative patterns available at contiguous levels. Since the process operates in both directions, the structure of relationships at each level will be mutually reinforcing.

Recognition of the hierarchical organization of society and the interdependency of contexts has guided the construction of the theory of deviance that follows. The theory argues that deviance is a socially constructed phenomenon involving structural, group, and social-psychological properties. The theory's central theme is that social systems, in an effort to control behavior, designate certain activities and attributes deviant. Such definitions, by excluding individuals from other opportunities, generate the very populations described. Through role taking and reference identification, people who occupy deviance categories come to adopt the behaviors and identities publically ascribed them. The end product is the legitimation of original definitions and the reaffirmation of deviance careers. In this manner, social structural relationships and the normative standards upon which they depend are maintained.

## DEVIANCE AND SOCIAL STRUCTURE

Systems maintain themselves in part by designating certain behaviors and attributes as deviant. These designations not only control activities that disrupt social organization, but they also lend meaning to the norms, standards, and beliefs required for collective identity. Deviants are visible reminders of the normative limits that define particular social systems. The nonconformist, by standing in marked contrast to prescribed behavior, allows the group to develop a cohesive sense of its own membership (Durkheim, 1904; Mead, 1918; Erikson, 1966).

Empirical explorations of functionalist theory have resulted in a controversy regarding the source of boundary-maintaining designations. Studies of small groups, whether in their natural settings (Dentler and Erikson, 1959; Bensman and Gerver, 1963; Levy, 1971) or under highly controlled experimental conditions (Homans, 1950; Lauderdale, 1976), have suggested that boundaries are established *consensually.* Small groups, however, are characterized by a limited division of labor and minimal stratification. Within such systems, homogeneous experiences and restricted status, wealth, and power differentials give rise to a normative structure that represents the shared sentiments of the community. Behavioral boundaries in complex societies, on the other hand, are more likely to be a result of *value antagonism.* A reanalysis of Erikson's *Wayward Puritans,* for example, suggested to Chambliss (1975) that the crime waves of colonial New England resulted not from the community's rising in angry indignation against a common moral threat but rather from the ruling group's attempting to eliminate "alternative centers of authority" to preserve its own position of power. Studies of the origins of Prohibition (Gusfield, 1967), antipornography campaigns (Zurcher et al., 1971), the Stalinist purge (Connor, 1972), and the lynching of southern blacks during the Populist revolt (Inverarity, 1976) have produced similar findings. In each case, definitions of deviance were not consensually derived but were a product of powerful group efforts.

The challenge to the functionalist assumption of consensus apparent in this research is not surprising. Unlike the small group, larger social systems are characterized by diversity and stratification.

Members of such systems, therefore, do not enjoy the commonality of life experiences and opportunities that gives rise to universal standards. This is particularly true in modern, industrial societies made up of many subgroups that sometimes share, and sometimes differ radically, in values and beliefs. Unlike the structure of small, undifferentiated systems, which emerges from the collective action of group members, that of complex society is determined by groups with sufficient power to institutionalize their positions of superiority. The family, education, religion, law, and economy reflect and transmit values that support dominant interests. Since persons from all status levels participate in the activities of these socializing institutions, such values are diffused throughout the collectivity. The resultant normative structure, including cultural definitions of conformity and deviance, legitimates the relations of dominance and subordination upon which the system is organized. That is, behaviors and situations that contravene activities essential for the maintenance of such relations are designated deviant (Chambliss, 1975; Spitzer, 1975; Quinney, 1977; Scull, 1977).

Social systems, whether consensually or antagonistically organized, exist within the context of other more inclusive systems. Environmental changes, such as shifts in the distribution of competitive advantage or the depletion of resources, will be accompanied by changes in the system's organizational requirements. If a collectivity is to remain viable, it must be capable of adjusting to these new requirements. Among the adjustive mechanisms available is the restructuring of behavioral boundaries. In response to a wide range of conditions, boundaries are redrawn and behaviors realigned relative to the new limits.

Small groups threatened with extinction, for example, have been found to contract their boundaries and to become intolerant of the slightest behavioral deviations; groups in nonthreatening conditions, on the other hand, tend to expand their definitions of acceptable conduct (Lauderdale, 1976). Social change through the modification of behavioral boundaries can also be seen at the societal level. The growth of machine technology in the United States has produced a sizable increase in the number of individuals who are underemployed or unemployed. Since this surplus labor population is both costly to maintain for society and a source of frustration for the unemployed, it constitutes a potential threat to the structure of relations in capitalist society. Efforts must be made, therefore, to adjust to the new conditions (Spitzer, 1975). Reducing the number of hours in the work week, emphasizing leisure activities, and controlling population growth are among the means being used to attempt to solve the problem. Each has had a significant impact on moral boundaries. The increased availability of leisure time has caused a shift in traditional proscriptions regarding hedonistic pursuits, a change reflected, for example, in liberalized drug laws. Similarly, the system's need to limit population growth has produced shifts in social norms regarding birth control, including changing definitions of contraception, abortion, euthanasia, and nonreproductive consensual sex.

In sum, then, deviance is an essential part of social organization. It establishes and legitimates the behaviors, attitudes, and values upon which organization depends. In small groups and societies characterized by minimal levels of diversity and stratification, behavioral boundaries approximate a consensually derived ideal. Within complex societies, on the other hand, a plurality of social and cultural systems impose expectations for conformity on their memberships. Through competition among groups for access to the institutions of social control, the victors acquire the right to impose their standards, which become the norms for which the boundary maintenance functions of deviance are employed. In both cases, boundaries may change in response to alterations in the social contexts within which systems exist. As new conditions are confronted, the normative limits that define deviance are expanded or contracted. Such flexibility is essential if the system is to persist over time.

## THE CREATION OF DISVALUED BEHAVIOR

Whether consensually or politically derived, boundaries are communicated to group members through the group's definition of the situation. The definitional process involves interpersonal mechanisms that range from gossip and the application of epithets to arrest and institutionalization. The assignment of meaning to particular behaviors and attributes illustrates vividly the performance criteria all must conform to. By defining actions that fall outside acceptable limits as illegitimate and by excluding those who commit such actions, the group makes visible the requirements of membership and legitimates the values upon which such requirements are based. That is, once situations have been defined, the collectivity becomes sensitized to the importance of conformity and aware of the means for its expression; in this sense, reactions to deviance effect social control (Tittle, 1969; Gibbs, 1975). A portion of the community must remain undeterred, however, if this control function is to be maintained, since the logic of deterrence depends upon the existence of deviants against whom the community can react.

An important source of deviance definitions in complex societies is the popular stereotype. Stereotypes are a product of the social distance that separates the various groups and strata. These typifications allow individuals to anticipate and predict the behavior of others when restricted interaction provides little objective information. While complex societies foster stereotyping among groups generally, the stereotypic definitions of some collectivities are more pervasive and influential in shaping public conceptions of deviance than are those of others. In particular, groups whose interests are represented in the social order will be most effective in institutionalizing their definitions of deviance. These definitions emphasize attributes and behaviors incompatable with the prevailing hierarchy of power, prestige, and wealth.

Beliefs regarding the kinds of people prone to rule violation, the characteristics and behaviors associated with the deviation, and the most appropriate treatment strategies are widely diffused among the general population and operate within the various agencies of social control (Simmons, 1965; Scheff, 1966; Swett, 1969). These imageries guarantee that informal and formal reactions to deviance will focus consistently on groups viewed as potentially troublesome. At the same time, responses guided by such definitions ensure the selection of precisely those individuals who conform to the stereotype.

Definitions of the situation have both structural and social-psychological consequences that produce the definitions' eventual fulfillment (Thomas, 1923; Merton, 1957; Rosenthal and Jacobson, 1968). Their descriptive, evaluative, and prescriptive components allow persons to interpret the conduct and characteristics of others and to construct actions based on such interpretations. Once meaning has been assigned, alternative definitions and lines of action are precluded, and procedures are invoked that produce outcomes consistent with the ascriptions. Whether through the official activities of agencies of social control or the informal responses in interpersonal relationships, the attribution of deviance sets into motion a process that may result in the fulfillment of original predictions.

Instances of the self-actualization of deviance definitions at the structural level are numerous. Categories are constructed and populations identified that confirm the reality of the deviation. Thus, for example, witchcraft in Renaissance Europe was the artifact of an elaborate legal system, stripped of traditional procedural safeguards, to deal with a population whose existence was proclaimed by the Church (Currie, 1968); the emergence of the institutionalized insane as a deviant population was preceded by the perceived need for separate facilities for the care and cure of the mentally ill (Rothman, 1971; Scull, 1977); debt defaulters are the result of the "deliberately staged application of definitions" by creditors, collection agencies, and legal officials (Rock, 1968); and habitual offenders are the product of the very means used to detect their prior criminality (Farrell and Swigert, 1978). In each case, deviance results from the application of deviance definitions and the exclusion of labeled individuals from the opportunities to demonstrate conformity or the inapplicability of the labels.

The social-psychological consequences of deviance definitions are produced by the interactional responses invoked by such ascriptions. Emanating from the informal context of primary and secondary groups as well as from contact with formal control agencies, these responses are filtered through the nonconformer's *subjective* evaluation of the situation. This evaluation may occur as a self, anticipated, or perceived response. *Self-responses* are based on definitions acquired in early socialization and are reaffirmed in the routine interaction of everyday life. Persons who find themselves involved in deviance may call upon these definitions to interpret their own behavior. *Anticipated responses* emerge from previous experiences with other people's reactions to the deviation. Expecting continuity in the social response, the individual predicts that his or her own behavior will elicit similar treatment. *Perceived responses* are the meanings assigned by an individual to the behavior of others. This attribution involves either an assessment of the actions of others as they conform to cultural symbols that indicate recognition of deviance or the projection onto others of self and anticipated responses. Whatever the context, interactional responses may become structured in such a way that individuals organize life and identity around the public definition. Original, specific, and often transient incidents of rule violation *(primary deviance)* are thereby transformed into a deviant role *(secondary deviance)* (Lemert, 1951, 1967).

The social response that brings about this transition is shaped by the highly salient nature of the deviant status. Although an individual may occupy a variety of positions, that of deviant tends to overshadow them and to become the primary basis of identification (Davis, 1961; Becker, 1963). As a result, the individual becomes increasingly aware of the deviation and develops a paranoid-like sensitivity to the motives and actions of others (Lemert, 1962; Scott and Lyman, 1968). This reaction is not unfounded but is in accordance with the deviant's perception that interaction has become structured around the disvalued status (Lemert, 1962).

Central to this interaction process is the concurrent and retrospective reinterpretation of the deviant's total situation (Garfinkel, 1956; Kitsuse, 1962; Schur, 1971). The search for evidence that the nonconformer has always been and continues to be primarily deviant allows for a uniform response to him or her. Viewing the individual solely in terms of the disvalued status neutralizes whatever uncertainty may exist regarding the applicability of the public definition. This biographical reconstruction also has the effect of further emphasizing the deviation while discrediting any claims to legitimacy. The construction of a consistent and generalized definition of the individual's situation impedes interaction based on statuses other than that assigned. Excluded form conforming positions and consistently responded to as deviant, the individual finds it increasingly difficult to maintain a nondeviant conception of self.

Finally, as we have seen, the position of deviance carries with it a configuration of attributes and behaviors thought to be typical of persons who occupy this category (Nunnally, 1961; Simmons, 1965; Scheff, 1966; Scott, 1969; Reed and Reed, 1973). People assume, that is, that the nonconformer possesses other undesirable traits associated with the deviant one (Becker, 1963; Goffman, 1963). Diffused throughout the collectivity, these stereotypes allow persons to deal with the nonconformer in a routine and unilateral manner (Tannenbaum, 1938; Goffman, 1963). The lack of reciprocal interaction, in its turn, prevents the individual from negotiating a legitimate identity and makes him or her increasingly aware of the stereotypical expectations that prescribe the deviant status. Repeatedly identified in terms of the stereotype by both self and society, the individual will tend to adopt a role consistent with the public definition.

Deviance definitions, then, set into motion an interactive process that fulfills the original ascription. The assignment of deviance as a master status, the reinterpretation of other positions in terms of that designation, and the stereotype that underlies the social response ensure the creation of deviant lives and identities—the visible reminders of the disvalued behaviors and attributes that demarcate society's normative limits.

## DEVIANT IDENTITIES:
## SELECTION AND REINFORCEMENT

Primary deviance is universally distributed. Everyone possesses characteristics or engages in actions at some time or another that may elicit social sanction. Most people have committed crimes for which they could be incarcerated (President's Commission on Law Enforcement and Administration of Justice, 1967), have engaged in deviant sexual practices (Kinsey et al., 1948; Weinberg and Williams, 1980), or have displayed behavior symptomatic of mental illness (Leighton, 1959; Srole et al., 1962; Leighton et al., 1963). To these populations may be added, among others, people who have violated rules of etiquette, behaved inappropriately in public places, or possess impediments of speech or mobility. Yet not all rule violators are identified as such. Rather, the application of deviance definitions is a selective process. Furthermore, not all those who are designated deviant reorganize their lives around that label. Important contingencies affect both the application and the consequences of deviance definitions.

The likelihood of a person's being reacted to as deviant depends upon the status positions he or she occupies within the social system. Sex, race, and social class all play important parts in determining social responses. Those positions most closely identified with the public stereotype of the deviation will elicit the more negative reactions (Simmons, 1965; Farrell and Morrione, 1974; Swigert and Farrell, 1976, 1977; Farrell and Swigert, 1978a, 1978b). For this reason, males, blacks, and members of the lower classes are particularly subject to labeling.

In addition to these structural factors, the nature of the nonconformity and the context within which it occurs also affect the labeling process. Behaviors that are highly visible or disruptive of ongoing social activities will more frequently be designated deviant (Mechanic, 1962; Phillips, 1964; Farrell and Morrione, 1974). Encounters in the public settings of secondary groups will also more likely result in negative responses. Given the impersonality and limited feedback that characterize such interaction, persons tend to rely upon the stereotype to guide their behavior toward the deviant (Farrell and Morrione, 1974).

Interaction within primary groups, on the other hand, is characterized by reciprocity. This mutual exchange allows primary groups to evaluate deviant individuals in light of their total situations. If prolonged interaction with secondary others results in the development of primary ties, initially stereotypic responses will be replaced by more empathic assessments (Farrell and Morrione, 1974). Within this context, persons come to view the actor as specifically rather than generally deviant.

Once the definition of deviance has been applied, it may increase the negative reactions the individual will experience in future social encounters (Phillips, 1964; Caetano, 1974; Weissbach and Zagon, 1975; Loman and Larkin, 1976; Larkin and Loman, 1977). Such a designation may operate as a master status that significantly reduces the possibility of interaction on more legitimate bases. Subsequent responses to the label will vary depending on the nature of the label itself, as well as on the relationship of the audience to the actor and on the socio-cultural context in which the interaction occurs. Labels will be more stigmatizing if they are specific and visible, rather than diffuse and marginally relevant to the ongoing activities of a community (Williams and Weinberg, 1971). Additionally, persons in primary association with the labeled deviant will generally be more accepting than those in secondary associations (Freeman and Simmons, 1961; Ericson, 1977). And finally, significant others who are socially and culturally marginal will less often accept the label as meaningful information in structuring their interaction with the deviant (Freeman and Simmons, 1961; Mercer, 1965; Harris, 1975).

The social response to nonconformity may increase behavioral deviation through the symbolic communication of deviant expectations and the simultaneous isolation of individuals from legitimate roles. A critical dimension of this process is the importance that the individual attaches to other's responses. Labels applied by significant or referent others are much more likely to affect the self and role of the individual than are the reactions of peripheral others. Significant others are most typically found in primary group relationships but are not limited to them. Given the high salience and difficulties associated with the deviant position, deviant persons may become sensitive to the responses of individuals who, under other circumstances, would go unnoticed, particularly if the nonconformer has internalized social definitions of the disvalued behavior or attribute. Prior socialization and earlier experiences regarding negative reactions in similar situations will increase the nonconformer's anticipation of rejection in the present case. In this state of heightened awareness, even interaction in secondary groups and the most subtle responses in public encounters can become important. For the visibly deviant and for deviants highly sensitive to their disvalued status, there is, at least initially, hardly an insignificant other.[1]

Primary groups are generally reluctant to exclude any of their members or to view them solely in terms of the stereotype of nonconformity. Such ties, therefore, shield persons from the amplification of deviance that results from public ascriptions. Thus we find that delinquent boys (Reckless et al., 1956, 1957; Foster et al., 1972) and male homosexuals (Farrell, 1972) who are thought of as essentially nondeviant by their significant others continue to think of themselves as such regardless of their involvement in the deviation. That large numbers of people engage in rule violation and at the same time continue to be thought of—and continue to think of themselves—as essentially conformists may be evidence of the insulating effect of being accepted as nondeviant by the primary group.

Alternatively, reference associations who view the deviant label as legitimate may respond to the individual on the basis of the public definition. Consistently exposed to this response, the individual may become engulfed in the deviation and increasingly organize behavior and identity around its role. Secondary deviance, in this case, is a product of the individual's participation in legitimate groups wherein interaction is based, either explicitly or implicitly, on the mutual acceptance of a deviant label. This pattern can be seen among army units who protect emotionally disturbed members from military authorities (Dentler and Erikson, 1959), wives who resist institutionalization of their psychotic spouses (Schwartz, 1957), and parents of apprehended juveniles who already believe their sons are prone to trouble and continue to accept them in these terms (Foster et al., 1972). In each case, the support of primary others is instrumental in producing secondary deviation. The intensification of deviance that occurs in this context serves to maintain and legitimate behavioral boundaries and moral solidarity for both the immediate group and the larger society of which the nonconformer is also a part.[2]

Nonconformity may constitute such a violation of expectations, however, that the original reference group is compelled to reject the deviator. This sudden loss of membership among persons to whom the individual looks for reward produces stress and presses for some form of adaptation (Parsons, 1951; Cohen, 1955, 1959), especially when the individual strongly identifies with such groups (Elliott, 1966; Rushing, 1971). Having internalized their norms and standards and having identified them as important sources of personal reward, the nonconformer who perceives or merely anticipates rejection will respond intensely. Stress is also related to the stigma that accompanies labeling. The assignment of individuals to disvalued categories constitutes a serious threat to their self-esteem. If the labeled persons' reference associations refuse to validate the label, stress will subside. If, however, those associations are condemnatory, stress will persist.

Attachment to the group, the specter of loosing his or her place in it, and the threat to the self implied by the label may, of course, have a deterrent effect on the behavior of the deviant. The anticipation of negative reaction from referent others may lead the deviant to attempt to demonstrate adherence to group norms and thus preserve the original relationship. The deviant who maintains these attachments, however, without reequilibriating the interaction condemns himself or herself to continued frustration. Persons in this position may attempt to adjust by becoming compulsively conformative or alienative in their behavior. In either instance, the adaptation is likely to compound the stress by eliciting additional negative responses from significant others (Parsons, 1951).

Not all who experience frustration maintain attachments to the sources of that stress. Rather, they may seek equilibrium in new relationships that offer more rewarding interaction (Parsons, 1951; Cohen, 1955, 1959). This search for acceptance is an exploratory process. Through a careful assessment of the situation of the other, the individual seeks to identify people who share his or her problems of adjustment. If this effort to adapt is successful, the individual may transfer reference identification to a group that supports his or her behavior (Cohen, 1955, 1959). By severing ties with the original referents, the individual is freed from the influence of their norms and values (Haskell,

1960; Hirschi, 1969; Linden and Hackler, 1973). Adolescents, for example, who have contact with delinquent peers will more likely engage in delinquency if their ties to conventional society are weak (Glaser, 1960; Stanfield, 1966; Hirschi, 1969; Jensen, 1972; Linden and Hackler, 1973; Liska, 1973).

If the new reference group does not make the deviant label part of its definition of the individual, the initial deviation is likely to remain primary. If, on the other hand, acquired referents accept the nonconformer precisely in terms of that identity and role, the behavior of the individual may progress to the level of secondary deviation.

While the deviant may adopt either deviant or conforming referents, the existence of widespread and generally negative stereotypes may reduce the likelihood of his or her being accepted by legitimate groups. Thus, individuals often adjust by seeking out others who share a similar problem of rejection. This is a subcultural adaptation to a system of roles and definitions that support the deviant behavior.

Reference groups, whether deviant or conforming, are the contexts within which the normative patterns and techniques for behavior are acquired (Sutherland, 1947). Through identification with these groups, individuals learn the role definitions that guide their behavior (Glaser, 1956). Provided with the opportunities (Cloward and Ohlin, 1960; Palmore and Hammond, 1964) and rewards (Jeffrey, 1965; Burgess and Akers, 1968) for the enactment of prescribed roles, persons will engage in behaviors consistent with reference group definitions. For deviance to occur, individuals must identify with the definitions conducive to deviant behavior and be exposed to the opportunities and reinforcements that support its enactment. This may occur through association in deviant groups (Short, 1957, 1958, 1960; Becker, 1963; Reiss and Rhodes, 1964; Bryan, 1965; Stanfield, 1966; Hooker, 1967; Voss, 1969; Paschke, 1970; Jensen, 1972; Liska, 1973; Brown et al., 1974; Thomas et al, 1975) or through a more indirect process of role taking (Cressey, 1953; Lemert, 1958; Eindtadter, 1969).

Deviance stereotypes have important implications for the learning processes involved in reference identifications. To the extent that these definitions are accepted by the deviant and significant others, they will influence social interaction and ultimately the behavior and identity of the nonconformer. Since stereotypes are widely diffused throughout society, they may influence the social relationships of deviants generally, especially in deviant subcultures, which are made up largely of people who have been defined and reacted to in terms of the popular imagery. To the extent that the stereotypes are internalized, they will be reflected in the interaction among members of the deviant community. Through ongoing communication, the stereotypic identities brought to this situation feed into the normative structure of the subculture and ultimately define its role expectations.

In order to neutralize the negative connotations of the deviant role, its stereotypically ascribed characteristics are redefined by the subculture. Thus, for example, the homosexual stereotype includes the attributes of lack of self-control and sexual promiscuity. Within the homosexual subculture, however, the same behavior might be redefined as open expression of affection and freedom from sexual inhibition. While subcultural norms may be based on the public definition of the deviation, then, and may actually reinforce stereotypic behavior, the traits associated with the popular imagery are assigned new meaning. The reinterpretation of the public definition insulates the members' self-concepts from the stigmatizing effects of social rejection.

A related aspect of the learning process is the acquisition of justifications for conduct. These rationalizations enable individuals to enact deviant behavior without questioning its legitimacy and eventual threat to the self (Sykes and Matza, 1957). Whether the deviation is planned and deliberate or ascribed and accidental, the adoption of rationalizations legitimizes the behavior and attributes in the eyes of the actor. The use of rationalizations to justify deviance has been observed in such diverse activities as embezzlement (Cressey, 1953), homosexual prostitution (Reiss, 1961), and professional fencing (Klockars, 1974), as well as among people who have stigmatized physical illness (Gussow and Tracy, 1968). In each instance, individuals have adjusted by adopting a belief system that effectively counters society's more general definitions of them.

We have seen that nonconformists are isolated from full participation in dominant society. Their acceptance as deviant by referent others, therefore, results in their having a high level of commitment to these relationships. Loyalty to the group and behavior that corresponds with its prescriptions take precedence over the counter demands of groups that have excluded them. Since the normative patterns of *deviant groups* are organized almost exclusively around the deviation, commitment to these associations will be particularly influential in amplifying the behavior. Since such supportive associations are not self-sufficient entities, however, the nonconformer must maintain at least minimal relationships with the larger society to secure routine needs. Economic, educational, religious, and recreational services can only be obtained from legitimate sources. Encounters with persons in these contexts result in renewed conflict and rejection. Repeated confrontations between deviants and conformers ensure that deviant categories remain stable over time. Renewed instances of rejection strengthen the deviant's commitment to the supportive and protective environment of the accepting group. The amplification of deviant behavior that results from this increased commitment ultimately affirms society's values and justifies its exclusionary reactions. In this manner, the cycle of definition and deviance amplification maintains conformity within social systems. By assigning certain segments of the population to the margins of society, the system maintains its boundaries and secures its collective identity. Without the deviant to make visible the outer limits of the system, the very survival of society would be threatened. It is a primal process wherein social organization is ensured by the sacrifice of its most expendable members.

## FORMALIZATION OF THE THEORY

The general theory of deviance presented here envisions nonconformity as involving structural, group, and social-psychological dimensions. It addresses the meaning of behavior for the organization of society, the processes by which deviance definitions are communicated through interpersonal relationships, and the impact of such ascriptions on individual actors. The major propositions of the theory follow and are diagramatically illustrated in Figure 8–1.

I. *Deviance functions in social systems to establish and protect boundaries that are consistent with organizational principles.* Deviance is an important source of order and identity within collectivities, especially in modern society, with its heterogeneous assemblage of diverse populations. By demarcating acceptable limits of performance, nonconformity lends meaning and legitimacy to the dominant order and the norms, values, and beliefs upon which it depends. To the extent that the major institutions of social control are effective in diffusing a common culture, deviance also unites group members in a cohesive stand against designated threats to the collectivity. At the same time, the application of stigmatizing labels to certain behaviors and attributes neutralizes potential challenges to established relationships. In this manner, the normative boundaries that legitimate structural relationships and existing hierarchies of status, power, and wealth are secured.

II. *Boundaries are communicated to members of the collectivity through the definition of the situation.* Behavioral boundaries are recognizable only insofar as going beyond them produces censure. This censure is applied through an interpersonal process wherein public condemnation communicates to conformer and deviant alike the nature of the transgression. Whether through informal reproof or formal sanction, definitions of the situation signify concrete instances of the behavioral limits beyond which members cannot go without jeopardizing their continued membership in the group.

**FIGURE 8–1   The Structure and Process of Deviance**

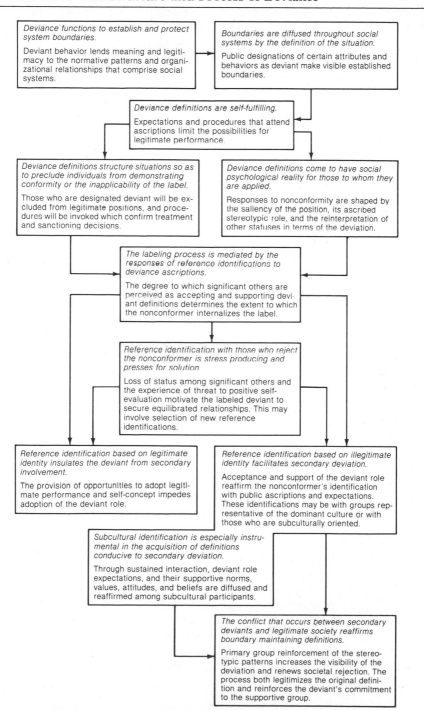

A. *The attribution of deviance definitions depends upon the structural and situational factors that comprise the social context in which labels are applied.* A consistent social response to nonconformity is achieved through the popular imagery that attends deviance definitions. Widely diffused throughout the population, such imageries specify the situations, behaviors, and kinds of actors most likely to manifest deviant characteristics. Along with the nature and visibility of the rule violations, therefore, the conformity of the actor to the popular stereotype also helps determine which persons will be selected for labeling. Since categorical responses characterize situations of limited interaction, stereotypes will most frequently be applied in secondary group settings. Attributions of deviance following initial labeling will, in turn, be related to the specificity and visibility of the label, the level of impersonality of social relationships, and the extent to which relevant actors share in the definition implied by the label.

III. *Once situations have been defined, events are structured and interactional processes set into motion that produce outcomes consistent with the original ascriptions.* Application of a deviance definition carries with it expectations and procedures that are viewed as appropriate to the situation. Based on these ascriptions, the reactions of others have both structural and social-psychological consequences for the nonconformer. Communication of the label and the attendant avoidance, rejection, and withholding of opportunities by members of legitimate society may fix the deviant in the prescribed role.

A. *Social definitions of nonconformity are self-fulfilling insofar as they invoke responses that preclude opportunities for the deviant to conform or to demonstrate the inapplicability of the label.* Once the stereotype is deemed relevant, decisions are made that limit opportunities for the labeled individual to defend a nondeviant status. Since these definitions are institutionalized throughout society, persons designated deviant are excluded from legitimate positions, and procedures are invoked against them that confirm treatment and sanctioning in formal and informal arenas alike. By preventing individuals from demonstrating otherwise, originally ascribed definitions render themselves valid.

B. *Deviance definitions come to have social-psychological reality for persons to whom they are applied because of the interactional dynamics that surround the labeling process.* The creation of deviance as a master status, the reinterpretation of other dimensions of the individual's situation to make them consistent with that status, and the attribution of a role based on the popular stereotype shape identity and behavior. The labeling process, therefore, involves the systematic isolation of persons from sources of legitimate identification. All aspects of life, personality, and behavior are redefined in terms of the attribution. Since the imagery associated with the particular deviation is widely diffused, the perceived, anticipated, and self responses of the nonconformer are likely to be consistent with the objective responses of persons who would exclude him or her. In this manner, deviance definitions come to be shared by actor and audience alike.

IV. *The impact of the labeling process is mediated by reference group definitions and reactions regarding the deviation.* The success of labeling in creating deviant identities depends on the consistency with which the label is used to define the situation of the other. The extent to which reference identifications in particular are perceived to accept and provide support for the label will influence the degree of its internalization by the nonconformer.

   A. *Identification with persons from whom the individual perceives acceptance in terms of a legitimate identity and role will insulate him or her from secondary involvement in the deviation.* Given the disvalued nature of the deviant position, persons will seek to identify themselves with legitimate statuses. Referent others who provide the opportunity for such an identity will impede the labeled individual's engulfment in the deviant role.

   B. *Identification with persons from whom the individual perceives acceptance in terms of the deviant identity and role will facilitate secondary deviation.* Should the individual's reference groups accept the social definition and employ it in their interaction with him or her, the outcome will be a reaffirmation of the deviant role. The acceptance and support found within this context will tend to be guided by the popular stereotype of the deviation, which may be reinterpreted by these referent others in more positive terms and become part of the deviant's identity and performance.

V. *When support is withheld by original reference groups, individuals will shift identification to groups from whom they can obtain acceptance and reward.* This adaptive mechanism is an attempt to ease the stress caused by the labeling process. It represents an attempt to achieve status and maintain positive identity in light of rejection and stigmatization. Through mutual exploration, individuals seek to equilibrate their relationships by introducing more equitable exchange into the interaction.

A.  *A shift of reference identifications to groups from whom the individual perceives acceptance in terms of a legitimate identity will terminate the effects of the labeling process.* Acceptance into a learning environment that rewards and reinforces conformity provides the labeled deviant with the opportunity to assume a more legitimate role. Since the learning includes techniques, motives, rationalizations, and attitudes conducive to conformity, individuals are able to construct both a legitimate definition of self and performance patterns consistent with that new definition.

B.  *A shift of reference identifications to groups from whom the individual perceives acceptance in terms of a deviant identity will produce movement toward secondary deviation.* Adopted referents may be either legitimate or deviant in their dominant normative orientations. In either case, their acceptance and support of the deviant role reaffirms that role's relevance to the nonconformer's self-definition and behavior.

The shift of reference identifications to deviant groups is the subcultural adaptation. While the subculture is based on deviance definitions and is made up largely of other deviants, it provides a structured learning environment that is generically the same as that found in conforming groups. Through ongoing interaction, role expectations and their supportive norms, values, attitudes, and beliefs are diffused among the membership. The process involves both verbal and nonverbal communication, as well as the application of rewards and sanctions. In this manner, the group culture comes to be represented in individuals and reaffirmed through continued interaction.

Individuals who have been rejected by legitimate society show high levels of commitment to deviant as well as nondeviant groups that accept them. Since nonconformity is an important criterion for status and reward within deviant groups, however, this commitment is especially conducive to increased deviation.

VI.  *The interaction that occurs between secondary deviants and conforming others reaffirms boundary-maintaining definitions.* Primary group support for deviance labels reinforces the stereotypic characteristics popularly associated with the behavior. Identification with this imagery becomes manifest in individual actions. The increased visibility of the deviation that ensues validates original definitions and reactions. For critical to the maintenance of deviance categories is the ability to point to observable instances of behavior that conform to stereotypic images. Such evidence enables the system to legitimate its proscriptions of the behavior and persist in its strategies of social control. At the same time, renewed instances of rejection from the larger society further confirm the deviant's commitment to associations that support the nonconformity. Therefore, while the definition mandates that deviant behavior be treated and thus controlled, these same efforts tend to produce and maintain the very outcomes condemned.

## CONCLUSION

The hierarchical structure of society requires that a general theory of deviance address the phenomenon at macro-structural, group, and social-psychological levels. The units of analysis and relationships among them are unique to each level and necessitate independent explanation. Each succeeding level, however, is the context within which the others exist. The mutual influence that this implies requires the construction of integrating links betweeen explanations.

The sociology of deviance consists of theories that have focused on particular analytical levels. In doing so, each theory has limited the range of explanation that it can offer. Through integrating them, we have sought to increase the scope of understanding and to map the conceptual areas that lie between the different approaches. Our attempt has been to provide a framework not only conducive to comprehensive analysis but also capable of identifying and explaining those aspects of deviance unexamined because of traditional commitments to particular paradigms.

By exploring relationships among theories, we have been able to suggest new concepts that both elaborate and link the structures and processes operating at various levels. The political and dynamic nature of behavioral boundaries, the communication of these standards to the collectivity, the manner in which deviance definitions create the positions and roles that ultimately affect individual identity and behavior, the mediating influence of reference identifications, the impact of individual identities on the normative patterns of deviant groups, and, finally, the legitimating effects of behavioral outcomes on original social definitions are the conceptual developments that have emerged from this integration. The scientific study of nonconformity provided the data through which the task of integration could proceed. By treating the contributions not as evidence or refutation of their respective theoretical traditions but as insights into the many stages and dimensions of social behavior, we have proposed a general theory of the structure and process of deviance.

## NOTES

1. In empirical explorations, therefore, it is necessary to establish the individual's designation of significant others rather than rely on *a priori* categories for identifying such groups.

2. The boundary maintenance function of deviance within primary groups does not preclude the operation of other processes. Groups may also deny the nonconformity of one of their members in an effort to (1) avoid sharing the stigma of the disvalued characteristic, (2) avert the guilt associated with the imputed responsibility for having caused the aberration, and (3) protect an individual and a relationship that are intrinsically valued.

## REFERENCES

Akers, Ronald L., Marvin D. Krohn, Lonn Lanza-Kaduce, and Marcia Radosevich
    1979   Social Learning and Deviant Behavior: A Specific Test of a General Theory. American Sociological Review 44 (August): 636–655.

Becker, Howard S.
    1963   Outsiders. New York: Free Press.

Bensman, Joseph, and Israel Gerver
    1963   Crime and Punishment in the Factory: The Function of Deviancy in Maintaining the Social System. American Sociological Review 28 (August): 588–598.

Blau, Peter M.
    1980   Contexts, Units, and Properties in Sociological Analysis. In Hubert M. Blalock, Jr. (Ed.) Sociological Theory and Research. New York: Free Press.

Brown, James W., Daniel Glaser, Elaine Waxer, and Gilbert Geiss
    1974   Turning Off: Cessation of Marijuana Use After College. Social Problems 21 (April): 527–538.

Bryan, James H.
    1965   Apprenticeships in Prostitution. Social Problems 12 (Winter): 287–297.

Burgess, Robert L., and Ronald L. Akers
    1968   A Differential Association-Reinforcement Theory of Criminal Behavior. Social Problems 14 (Fall): 128–147.

Caetano, Donald F.
    1974   Labeling Theory and the Presumption of Mental Illness in Diagnosis: An Experimental Design. Journal of Health and Social Behavior 15 (September): 253–260.

Chambliss, William J.
    1975   Functional and Conflict Theories of Crime: The Heritage of Émile Durkheim and Karl Marx. *In* Whose Law, What Order? William J. Chambliss and Milton Mankoff, eds. Pp. 1–28. New York: John Wiley and Sons.

Cloward, Richard A., and Lloyd E. Ohlin
    1960   Delinquency and Opportunity: A Theory of Delinquent Gangs. New York: Free Press.

Cohen, Albert C.
  1955  Delinquent Boys. New York: Free Press.
  1959  The Study of Social Disorganization and Deviant Behavior. *In* Sociology Today. Robert K. Merton, Leonard Broom, and Leonard S. Cottrell, Jr., eds. Pp. 461–484. New York: Basic Books.

Connor, Walter D.
  1972  Manufacture of Deviance: The Case of the Soviet Purge, 1936–1938. American Sociological Review 37 (August): 403–413.

Cressey, Donald
  1953  Other People's Money: A Study of the Social Psychology of Embezzlement. Chicago: Free Press.

Currie, Elliot P.
  1968  Crimes Without Criminals: Witchcraft and Its Control in Renaissance Europe. Law and Society Review 3 (October): 7–32.

Davis, Fred
  1961  Deviance Disavowal: The Management of Strained Interaction by the Visibly Handicapped. Social Problems 9 (Fall): 120–132.

Dentler, Robert A., and Kai T. Erikson
  1959  The Functions of Deviance in Groups. Social Problems 7 (Fall): 98–107.

Durkheim, Émile
  1904  The Rules of Sociological Method. S. A. Solovay and J. H. Mueller, trans. George E. G. Catlin, ed. New York: Macmillan, 1938.

Einstadter, Warner J.
  1969  The Social Organization of Armed Robbery. Social Problems 17 (Summer): 64–83.

Elliott, Delbert S.
  1966  Delinquency, School Attendance and Dropout. Social Problems 13 (Winter): 307–314.

Ericson, Richard V.
  1977  Social Distance and Reaction to Criminality. British Journal of Criminology 17 (January): 16–29.

Erikson, Kai T.
  1966  Wayward Puritans: A Study in the Sociology of Deviance. New York: John Wiley and Sons.

Farrell, Ronald A.
  1972  Societal Reaction to Homosexuals: Toward a Generalized Theory of Deviance. Ph.D. dissertation, University of Cincinnati.

Farrell, Ronald A., and Thomas J. Morrione
  1974  Social Interaction and Stereotypic Responses to Homosexuals. Archives of Sexual Behavior 3 (September): 425–442.

Farrel, Ronald A., and Victoria Lynn Swigert
  1978a  Prior Offense Record as a Self-Fulfilling Prophecy. Law and Society Review 12 (Spring): 437–453.
  1978b  Legal Disposition of Inter-Group and Intra-Group Homicides. Sociological Quarterly 19 (Autumn): 565–576.

Foster, Jack D., Simon Dinitz, and Walter C. Reckless
  1972  Perceptions of Stigma Following Public Intervention for Delinquent Behavior. Social Problems 20 (Fall): 202–209.

Freeman, Howard E., and Ozzie G. Simmons
1961 Feelings of Stigma Among Relatives of Mental Patients. Social Problems 8 (Spring): 312–321.

Garfinkel, Harold
1956 Conditions of Successful Degradation Ceremonies. American Journal of Sociology 61 (March): 420–424.

Gibbs, Jack P.
1975 Crime, Punishment, and Deterrence. New York: Elsevier.

Glaser, Daniel
1956 Criminality Theories and Behavioral Images. American Journal of Sociology 61 (March): 433–444.
1960 Differential Association and Criminological Prediction. Social Problems 8 (Summer): 6–14.

Goffman, Erving
1963 Stigma: Notes on the Management of Spoiled Identity. Englewood Cliffs, New Jersey: Prentice-Hall.

Gove, Walter R.
1970 Societal Reaction as an Explanation of Mental Illness: An Evaluation. American Sociological Review 35 (October): 873–884.

Gusfield, Joseph
1967 Moral Passage: The Symbolic Process in Public Designations of Deviance. Social Problems 15 (Fall): 175–188.

Gussow, Zachary, and George S. Tracy
1968 Status, Ideology, and Adaptation to Stigmatized Illness: A Study of Leprosy. Human Organization 27 (Winter): 316–325.

Harris, Anthony R.
1975 Imprisonment and the Expected Value of Criminal Choice: A Specification and Test of Aspects of the Labeling Perspective. American Sociological Review 40 (February): 71–87.

Haskell, Martin
1960 Toward a Reference Group Theory of Juvenile Delinquency. Social Problems 8 (Winter): 220–230.

Hirschi, Travis
1969 Causes of Delinquency. Los Angeles: University of California Press.

Homans, George C.
1950 Output Restriction of Norms and Social Structure. In Deviant Behavior and Social Process. William A. Rushing, ed. Pp. 10–15. Chicago: Rand McNally, 1975.

Hooker, Evelyn
1967 The Homosexual Community. In Sexual Deviance. John H. Gagnon and William Simon, eds. Pp. 167–184. New York: Harper & Row.

Inverarity, James
1976 Populism and Lynching in Louisiana, 1889–1896: A Test of Erikson's Theory of the Relationship Between Boundary Crises and Repressive Justice. American Sociological Review 41 (April): 262–280.

Jeffrey, Clarence Ray
1965 Criminal Behavior and Learning Theory. Journal of Criminal Law, Criminology, and Police Science 56 (September): 294–300.

Jensen, Gary F.
  1972  Parents, Peers, and Delinquent Action: A Test of the Differential Association Perspective. American Journal of Sociology 78 (November): 562–575.
Kinsey, Alfred C., Wardell B. Pomeroy, and Clyde E. Martin
  1948  Sexual Behavior in the Human Male. Philadelphia: W. B. Saunders.
Kitsuse, John I.
  1962  Societal Reaction to Deviant Behavior: Problems of Theory and Method. Social Problems 9 (Winter): 247–256.
Klockars, Carl B.
  1974  The Professional Fence. New York: Free Press.
Larkin, William E., and L. Anthony Loman
  1977  Labeling in the Family Context: An Experimental Study. Sociology and Social Research 61 (January): 192–203.
Lauderdale, Pat
  1976  Deviance and Moral Boundaries. American Sociological Review 41 (August): 660–676.
Leighton, Alexander
  1959  My Name is Legion. New York: Basic Books.
Leighton, Dorothea C., John S. Harding, David B. Macklin, Allister M. Macmillan, and Alexander H. Leighton
  1963  The Character of Danger. New York: Basic Books.
Lemert, Edwin M.
  1951  Social Pathology: A Systematic Approach to the Theory of Sociopathic Behavior. New York: McGraw-Hill.
  1958  The Behavior of the Systematic Check Forger. Social Problems 6 (Fall): 141–149.
  1962  Paranoia and the Dynamics of Exclusion. Sociometry 25 (March): 2–20.
  1967  Human Deviance, Social Problems and Social Control. Englewood Cliffs, New Jersey: Prentice–Hall.
Levy, Robert I.
  1971  The Community Function of Tahitian Male Transvestism: A Hypothesis. Anthropological Quarterly 44 (January): 12–21.
Linden, Eric, and James C. Hackler
  1973  Affective Ties and Delinquency. Pacific Sociological Review 16 (January): 27–46.
Liska, Allen
  1973  Causal Structures Underlying the Relationship Between Delinquent Involvement and Delinquent Peers. Sociology and Social Research 58 (October): 23–26.
Loman, L. Anthony, and William E. Larkin
  1976  Rejection of the Mentally Ill: An Experiment in Labeling. Sociological Quarterly 17 (Autumn): 555–560.
Mead, George H.
  1918  The Psychology of Punitive Justice. American Journal of Sociology 23 (March): 577–602.
Mechanic, David
  1962  Some Factors in Identifying and Defining Mental Illness. Mental Hygiene 46 (January): 66–74.

Mercer, Jane
  1965 Social System Perspective and Clinical Perspective Frames of Reference for Understanding Career Patterns of Persons Labeled as Mentally Retarded. Social Problems 13 (Summer): 18–34.
Merton, Robert K.
  1957 Social Theory and Social Structure. New York: Free Press.
Nunnally, J. C., Jr.
  1961 Popular Conceptions of Mental Health. New York: Holt.
Palmore, Erdman B., and Phillip E. Hammond
  1964 Interacting Factors in Juvenile Delinquency. American Sociological Review 29 (December): 848–854.
Parsons, Talcott
  1951 The Social System. New York: Free Press.
Paschke, Walter Richard
  1970 The Addiction Cycle: A Learning Theory-Peer Group Model. Corrective Psychiatry and Journal of Social Therapy 16: 74–81.
Phillips, Derek L.
  1964 Rejection: A Possible Consequence of Seeking Help for Mental Disorders. American Sociological Review 28 (December): 963–972.
President's Commission on Law Enforcement and Administration of Justice
  1967 The Challenge of Crime in a Free Society. Washington, D.C.: Government Printing Office.
Quinney, Richard
  1977 Class, State, and Crime. New York: David McKay.
Reckless, Walter C., Simon Dinitz, and Ellen Murray
  1956 Self Concept as an Insulator Against Delinquency. American Sociological Review 21 (December): 744–746.
  1957 The "Good" Boy in a High Delinquency Area. Journal of Criminal Law, Criminology, and Police Science 48 (May–June): 18–26.
Reed, John P., and Robin S. Reed
  1973 Status, Images, and Consequence: Once a Criminal Always a Criminal. Sociology and Social Research 57 (July): 460–472.
Reiss, Albert J., Jr.
  1961 The Social Integration of Queers and Peers. Social Problems 9 (Fall): 102–120.
Reiss, Albert J., Jr., and A. Lewis Rhodes
  1964 An Empirical Test of Differential Association Theory. Journal of Research in Crime and Delinquency 1 (January): 5–18.
Rock, P. E.
  1968 Observations on Debt Collection. British Journal of Sociology 19 (June): 176–190.
Rosenthal, Robert, and Lenore Jacobson
  1968 Pygmalion in the Classroom: Teacher Expectation and Pupil Intellectual Development. New York: Holt, Rinehart and Winston.
Rothman, David
  1971 The Discovery of Asylum: Social Order and Disorder in the New Republic. Boston: Little, Brown.

Rushing, William A.
  1971  Class, Culture, and "Social Structure and Anomie." American Journal of Sociology 76 (March): 857–872.
Scheff, Thomas J.
  1966  Being Mentally Ill. Chicago: Aldine.
Schur, Edwin M.
  1971  Labeling Deviant Behavior: Its Sociological Implications. New York: Harper & Row.
Schwartz, Charlotte
  1957  Perspectives on Deviance—Wives' Definitions of Their Husbands' Mental Illness. Psychiatry 20 (July–August): 275–291.
Schwartz, Richard D., and Jerome H. Skolnick
  1962  Two Studies of Legal Stigma. Social Problems 10 (Fall): 133–142.
Scott, Marvin B., and Stanford M. Lyman
  1968  Paranoia, Homosexuality, and Game Theory. Journal of Health and Social Behavior 9 (September): 179–187.
Scott, Robert A.
  1969  The Making of Blind Men. New York: Russell Sage.
Scull, Andrew T.
  1977  Madness and Segregative Control: The Rise of the Insane Asylum. Social Problems 24 (February): 337–351.
Short, James F., Jr.
  1957  Differential Association and Delinquency. Social Problems 4 (January): 233–239.
  1958  Differential Association with Delinquent Friends and Delinquent Behavior. Pacific Sociological Review 1 (Spring): 20–25.
  1960  Differential Association as a Hypothesis: Problems of Empirical Testing. Social Problems 8 (Summer): 14–25.
Simmons, J. L.
  1965  Public Stereotypes of Deviants. Social Problems 13 (Fall): 223–232.
Simon, Herbert A.
  1962  The Architecture of Complexity. Proceedings of the American Philosophical Society 106: 467–482.
Spitzer, Steven
  1975  Toward a Marxian Theory of Deviance. Social Problems 22 (June): 638–651.
Srole, Leo, Thomas S. Langner, Stanley T. Michael, Marvin K. Opler, and Thomas A. C. Rennie
  1962  Mental Health in the Metropolis: The Midtown Manhattan Study. New York: McGraw-Hill.
Stanfield, Robert E.
  1966  The Interaction of Family Variables and Gang Variables in the Aetiology of Delinquency. Social Problems 13 (Spring): 411–417.
Sutherland, Edwin H.
  1947  Principles of Criminology. Philadelphia: J. B. Lippincott.
Swett, Daniel H.
  1969  Cultural Bias in the American Legal System. Law and Society Review 4 (August): 79–110.

Swigert, Victoria L., and Ronald A. Farrell
  1976   Murder, Inequality, and the Law. Lexington, Massachusetts: D. C. Heath, Lexington.
  1977   Normal Homicides and the Law. American Sociological Review 42 (February): 16–32.
Sykes, Gresham, and David Matza
  1957   Techniques of Neutralization: A Theory of Delinquency. American Sociological Review 22 (December): 664–670.
Tannenbaum, Frank
  1938   Crime and the Community. New York: Columbia University Press.
Thomas, Charles W., David M. Peterson, and Mathew T. Zingroff
  1975   Student Drug Use: A Re-Examination of the "Hang Loose Ethic" Hypothesis. Journal of Health and Social Behavior 16 (March): 63–73.
Thomas, William I.
  1923   The Unadjusted Girl. Boston: Little, Brown.
Tittle, Charles R.
  1969   Crime Rates and Legal Sanctions. Social Problems 16 (Spring): 409–423.
Voss, Harwin L.
  1969   Differential Association and Containment Theory: A Theoretical Convergence. Social Forces 47 (June): 381–390.
Weinberg, Martin S., and Colin J. Williams
  1980   Sexual Embourgeoisment? Social Class and Sexual Activity: 1938–1970. American Sociological Review 45 (February): 33–48.
Weissbach, Theodore A., and Gary Zagon
  1975   The Effect of Deviant Group Membership upon Impression of Personality. Journal of Social Psychology 95 (April): 263–266.
Williams, Colin, and Martin S. Weinberg
  1971   Homosexuals and the Military. New York: Harper & Row.
Zurcher, Louis A., Jr., R. George Kirkpatrick, Robert G. Cushing, and Charles K. Bowman
  1971   The Anti-Pornography Campaign: A Symbolic Crusade. Social Problems 19 (Fall): 217–238.

# Index